THE FREE ANIMAL

Rousseau on Free Will and Human Nature

The Free Animal

Rousseau on Free Will and Human Nature

LEE MACLEAN

UNIVERSITY OF TORONTO PRESS
Toronto Buffalo London

Toronto Buffalo London
www.utppublishing.com

ISBN 978-1-4426-4495-3

Library and Archives Canada Cataloguing in Publication

MacLean, Lee, 1962–
The free animal : Rousseau on free will and human nature / Lee MacLean.

Includes bibliographical references and index.
ISBN 978-1-4426-4495-3

1. Rousseau, Jean-Jacques, 1712–1778 – Criticism and interpretation.
2. Free will and determinism. 3. Human beings – Philosophy. I. Title.

PQ2053.M32 2013 848′.509 C2012-906818-7

University of Toronto Press acknowledges the financial assistance to its publishing program of the Canada Council for the Arts and the Ontario Arts Council.

Canada Council for the Arts Conseil des Arts du Canada

University of Toronto Press acknowledges the financial support of the Government of Canada through the Canada Book Fund for its publishing activities.

Contents

Acknowledgments

I am grateful to the many people who have aided me during the writing of this book. Clifford Orwin at the University of Toronto was an early champion of this project. His astute responses helped me refine my arguments, and I thank him for his generous help. Ronnie Beiner provided encouragement, perceptive comments, and welcome advice. H.D. Forbes, Arthur Melzer, and the anonymous referees for the University of Toronto Press assisted me in developing my ideas. Diane Lamoureux, Cara Camcastle, and Michael Murphy made helpful comments on previous drafts. Teaching Rousseau at McGill University and Carleton University taught me a great deal, and the book has benefited from the questions of my students. I would particularly like to thank Ruben Levy, Joanna Mullard, Jordon Ross, Kerah Gordon, Troy Riddell, and Ells MacNeil. Daniel Quinlan of the University of Toronto Press provided able guidance and insightful editorial suggestions. I thank Matthew Kudelka for copy editing and Josh Johnson for preparing the index. Special thanks to Alan Patten for thought-provoking lunchtime discussions about Rousseau. I am also indebted to Lisa Alward for insisting that I come to hear the lectures about political philosophy given by Thomas Pangle at the University of Toronto.

I am grateful for the support of the Social Sciences and Humanities Research Council. I would like to thank my family and friends for their faith and support and Christian for his kindness, good cheer, and patience.

THE FREE ANIMAL

Rousseau on Free Will and Human Nature

Introduction

Human beings have an animal nature. But if we are animals, what kind of animals are we? Montaigne remarks that men are dainty animals, Aristotle that men are political animals, and Descartes that men are rational animals. In this book, we suggest that a fundamental dimension of Rousseau's contribution to political philosophy is his suggestion that man is the free animal.[1]

What does it mean to say that, according to Rousseau, man is the free animal? It means that he thinks that man is at once a part of nature and able to be relatively independent of it. As animals, men are clearly a part of nature. But as free, men have spiralled out of the order of nature. As he puts it, 'Man finds himself outside of nature and sets himself in contradiction with himself.' But how does Rousseau understand this partial independence of nature that defines human beings? And what are the implications of his thinking about man's independence of nature for our understanding of him?

Rousseau's earliest and most direct discussion of this freedom from nature that makes us human is in his *Discourse on Inequality*. There he suggests two possible ways of separating men from the animals: free will and perfectibility. Both concepts are ways of expressing man's partial independence of nature.. However, while perfectibility is obviously compatible with the materialist science of Rousseau's day, free will is not.

With this in mind, several recent interpreters have suggested that Rousseau does not truly mean that free will distinguishes man from the animals. According to this view, Rousseau pretends to believe in free will because he thinks that healthy political life depends on this belief and because he wants to avoid persecution by religious authorities. This interpretation further suggests that in basing his explanation of man's development on the quality of perfectibility, he effectively discards the concept of free will.

The argument of this book is that Rousseau believes that men are distinguished by free will. Moreover, he does not discard or abandon this idea. Rather, it plays a significant role in both the *Discourse on Inequality* and *Emile.* In both texts, Rousseau suggests that man's consciousness of free will contributes to the development of morality, convention, and vice. The argument reveals the work that free will does in Rousseau's political psychology: free will helps explain how a naturally good being develops unnatural vice.

In this book, we therefore have two key objectives. Our main objective is to demonstrate that Rousseau's teaching about free will in the *Discourse on Inequality* is proposed in earnest. To meet this objective, we interpret the teachings about free will in the *Discourse on Inequality* and in *Emile*; we consider the counter-arguments and respond to them; we examine Rousseau's accounts of metaphysics and of lying in the *The Reveries of the Solitary Walker,* and, crucially, we reveal how his argument in the *Discourse on Inequality* depends on free will. We argue that in the *Discourse,* Rousseau uses both free will and perfectibility to provide a skilfully multilayered response to the comprehensive materialists of his day and ours. We suggest, then, that our argument that Rousseau believes man has free will has implications for the interpretation of his work as a whole. Our second objective is therefore to consider the implications of our argument for the interpretation of Rousseau's moral and political teaching.

Setting the Problem

In the first part of the *Discourse on Inequality,* Rousseau depicts man in the state of nature as a robust and healthy being, living in independence of political authority and of other men. After describing man in the state of nature from the physical point of view, Rousseau considers him from the moral and metaphysical point of view. It is at that point that he distinguishes man from the animals on the basis of free will and perfectibility. He begins his discussion of free will by observing that animals are governed wholly by instinct, which is to say, by nature's command. Men, on the other hand, have a share in determining their behaviour through willing or choosing. Man feels the call of instinct 'but realizes he is free to acquiesce or resist.'[2] Humans are distinguished from the animals, then, by the power of willing and the consciousness of this power. Moreover, these qualities indicate the 'spirituality' of the human soul; he argues that they cannot be explained by the scientific laws of mechanics.

As Rousseau notes, this understanding of the human species distinction is therefore open to philosophical dispute. The main dimensions of this controversy have not changed all that much from Rousseau's day to our own. The key problem is that a free will appears to be incompatible with the determined causality of the natural realm. Natural science tells us that every effect has a prior cause. If all worldly events are predetermined by their causes, then human action should be, by the same token, determined by prior causes rather than caused by a free act of the will. All events are part of causal chains. Our judgments, attitudes, and characters may determine our actions but they themselves are determined by prior causes. There is no spontaneous dimension to the power of determining our wills, on this view. Nonetheless the moral life as we know it depends upon some version of human free will.[3]

Consider the way Rousseau formulates the problem in his letter to M. de Franquières of 1767. He responds to M. de Franquières, apparently a determinist, as follows:

> How can you not appreciate that this same law of necessity that alone, according to you, rules the working of the world, and all events, also rules all the actions of men, all the thoughts in their heads, all the feelings of their hearts, that nothing is free, that everything is forced, necessary, inevitable, that all the movements of man, directed by blind matter only depend on his will because his will itself depends on necessity; that there are *in consequence* neither virtues, nor vices, nor merit, nor demerit, nor morality in human actions, and that the words 'honorable man' or 'villain' must be, for you, totally devoid of sense. They are not, however, I am very sure. Your honest heart, despite your arguments, declaims against your sad philosophy. The feeling of liberty, the charm of virtue, are felt within you despite yourself. (*OC* 4:1145, emphasis mine)[4]

Rousseau points out that if, according to Franquières, the law of necessity alone rules 'the working of the world,' the law of necessity must also completely determine men's moral actions. Franquières's classic deterministic approach to the universe implies that moral action is determined as well. Rousseau argues, then, that moral action is incompatible with the comprehensive form of materialism that sees everything in the universe as determined.[5]

It is true that Rousseau somewhat overstates the case with regard to the moral consequences of determinism in his response to Franquières, but only somewhat. For example, if determinism were true, the state could nonetheless use deterrence and punishment in dealing with crime. As Spinoza put it, 'Wicked men are not less to be feared, and not less harmful when they are wicked from necessity.'[6] If determinism were true, merit and demerit, virtue and vices would retain an educational or aesthetic sense.[7] But this means the terms would have a narrowed or diminished meaning. If our wills can be free – that is to say, if we determine some of our purposes spontaneously – there is a deeper meaning to moral intention, to praise and to blame, to responsibility and therefore to our ethical and political partnerships.

However, Rousseau is right to present his correspondent with the stark alternative between the existence of free will and the deterministic workings of matter on our wills. The free will problem is intractable because free will requires some basis other than comprehensive determinism. Either one accepts a universe in which everything, including human will, is explained by a deterministic material process of cause and effect or one believes that some causes can be spontaneously started by human decisions through free will. Free will requires that a cause be started of itself, independently of the determinations of material causation.[8]

To clarify the question, let us consider briefly the opposing views of Hobbes, who denied the possibility of free will, and of Kant, who famously argued that the concept of free will is required for morality and could be thought without contradiction. Hobbes bases his denial of the freedom of the will on his material view of the universe. Everything in the universe, he believes, is matter in motion. Even spirits are matter; at one point Hobbes calls them 'thin bodies.'[9] He reasons that there is no separate spiritual substance that could ground free will and therefore that it does not exist.

That, of course, is debatable, but Hobbes accurately sees that what is at stake in the free will problem has to do with how we make decisions through will rather than the distinct question of how free we are to act on our decisions. He suggests that all our decisions are determined by prior causes but that we can be free to act on (or to refrain from acting on) our decisions. For Hobbes, because the will is always determined, the idea of liberty does not apply to the will but only to bodies that move. I can decide to raise my hand, but if someone enchains my wrist, I will not be able to do so and then I will not be free to act in Hobbes's sense. Thus the sovereign can only restrict or enlarge freedom of action. 'A free man,' he writes, 'is he, that ... is not hindered to doe what he has a will to.'[10]

Kant, on the other hand, makes the case that humans do have freedom of will, and he thinks that both moral conduct and criminal law require the independence of human will from the impulsion of natural desires. This freedom in moral conduct he calls practical freedom, and he maintains that the existence of practical freedom implies a causality of human will that can begin a chain of events independently of natural impulsion. He argues that this causality of our will 'independently of those natural causes, and even contrary to their force and influence, can produce something that is determined in the time-order in accordance with empirical laws, and which can therefore begin a series *entirely of itself*'[11] (emphasis in original). This is possible because Kant hypothesizes that in addition to the phenonmenal order – that is, the natural order of appearances – there is a noumenal or intelligible order of things that cannot be grasped through sense.[12] By means of this reasoning, Kant shows that the idea of free will can be thought without contradiction.

Like Kant, Rousseau believes in free will and in the moral need for it, but he recognizes that it is subject to genuine dispute. Therefore, after his argument asserting that free will distinguishes man from the animals, he notes 'the difficulties surrounding this question.' He then suggests another, less controversial quality that may separate us from the animals – perfectibility. Perfectibility is the 'faculty which develops all the others.' Through it, humans are able to progress in their accomplishments. Rousseau argues that after their passage to adulthood, adult humans progress in their development in a way that adult animals do not. Moreover, the human species as a whole shows cumulative progress and development, whereas other animals do not progress in this way. As Buffon, the French naturalist who appears to have influenced Rousseau's understanding of perfectibility, points out, if animals were capable of such progress, 'today's beavers would build their dams with more art and solidity than did the first beavers.'[13] For Rousseau, however, perfectibility is a double-edged sword. This faculty accounts for the emergence of both man's 'enlightenment and his errors.' In the end, it renders him 'the tyrant of himself and of nature' (*OC* 3:142; Masters, 114–15).

Both perfectibility and free will are, we suggest, ways of describing man's relative independence of instinct. Men can appropriate the instincts of the other animals.[14] Possessed of free will and perfectibility, men can set themselves against the order of nature.[15] But, as noted, there is a crucial difference between them: only the faculty of perfectibility is fully compatible with the materialist science of Rousseau's day and with the philosophical determinism that derived from it. It is the faculty 'about which there can be no dispute [*contestation*]' (*OC* 3:142; Masters, 114) He does not want his work to be dismissed by materialist thinkers, as it would be if it were to be based wholly and explicitly on an understanding of free will as a spiritual power. Thus the teaching of the rest of the *Discourse on Inequality* is based on the faculty of perfectibility.[16]

Given this context, it is not surprising that Rousseau's true intentions as regards this presentation of free will have been controversial. What are the main interpretive responses? Some interpreters do assume that Rousseau is completely sincere both about the proposition about free will and about his version of dualism. Two French-speaking Rousseau scholars, Victor Goldschmidt and Jean Starobinski, fall into this category. Starobinski argues that Rousseau asserts that men have free will in order to maintain a metaphysical gap between men and the animals. Goldschmidt draws on a reading of Rousseau's response to Condillac to argue that defining human nature in terms of free will rather than reason is one of Rousseau's original contributions to political thought.[17]

There is, nonetheless, a long history of doubting that Rousseau actually stood behind his more edifying pronouncements; major eighteenth-century figures such as Voltaire and Adam Smith took this view.[18] Leo Strauss also suggested that Rousseau, by defining the human distinction in terms of perfectibility, implies that humanity is so malleable, and so shaped by accident and history, that he casts doubt on his own free will argument. More radically, Strauss suggests that this move also obviates any appeal to the natural as the basis for the defining characteristic of the human species.

A number of interpreters influenced by Strauss have developed these suggestions into new interpretations of Rousseau on free will and perfectibility.[19] The most systematic and complete attempt is contained in Marc Plattner's *Rousseau's State of Nature: An Interpretation of the Discourse on Inequality*. Plattner believes, following Strauss, that Rousseau writes esoterically, which is to say that the surface of the text is written in such a way that it will not corrupt 'the people at large.'[20] He points out that Rousseau himself distinguishes between his common and more thorough readers, and he remarks that only the latter will have the courage to read his notes to the *Second Discourse* (*OC* 4:1139; 936). Plattner therefore suggests that Rousseau may conceal his most radical teachings in these notes. He also implies that Rousseau writes in such a way as to avoid persecution by religious authorities because of the incompatibility of his teaching with orthodox theology. He reminds us of Voltaire's advice to the Encyclopaedists to 'strike and hide your hand' (20). In an era when writers like Diderot and Voltaire were imprisoned for expressing their views, the possibility of persecution did provide a motive for esoteric writing.[21]

Like Strauss, Plattner concludes that Rousseau *pretends* to believe that men are distinguished by free will both to avoid openly contradicting Christian doctrine by endorsing radical materialism and because it is healthier for political life for the people to believe they have free will. He further argues that Rousseau's true view is that there is no natural distinction between men and the beasts. Even perfectibility is a historical distinction rather than a natural one. History alone accounts for the differences between men and the animals. In this respect, he holds, Rousseau is a forerunner of historicism.

A third view suggests that Rousseau actually believes free will to be the species distinction but that he does not endorse the dualistic metaphysics on which it would seem to be based. Judith Shklar articulates one version of this view. Shklar asserts that while Rousseau's argument that free will distinguishes men should be taken at face value, his theory cannot be considered spiritualist. She contends that Rousseau was too disdainful of metaphysics to ground his teaching in this fashion. But Rousseau is obliged to engage to some extent in the metaphysics he often criticizes. He is a metaphysician *malgré lui*. Moreover, the problem of spiritual freedom of the will arises precisely *because* it is unclear that there can be any other kind. If humans have free will, materialist determinism has to be an inadequate explanation in some respect; some factor beyond or outside of materialist determinism must account for it. Rousseau's argument in favour of a 'spiritual' power of willing addresses this need. The middle ground approach, which suggests that Rousseau believes men are defined by free will but that he denies it is spiritual free will, has one other disadvantage: unlike the other two interpretations, it has not, so far, provided a clear motive for Rousseau's statements about the will's 'spirituality,' nor has it done so for his claims that man is a 'mixed being' and 'composed of two substances' (*OC* 4:1139 and 936).[22]

As noted, my own view is that Rousseau truly believes his argument that men are distinguished by free will and by the consciousness of free will. Moreover, free will and consciousness of free will help take men outside of nature and render them unnatural animals. To begin to see how this happens, consider how Rousseau's free will argument emerges in the context of his reflections about what is natural to human beings in the *Discourse on Inequality*.

Rousseau writes the work in response to the question posed by the Academy of Dijon: 'what is the origin of inequality among men and whether it is authorized by natural law.' His response to the Academy's question is that many of the inequalities of his day result from the habits and attitudes of society rather than simply from nature.[23] Because many inequalities are caused by habit, upbringing, and education, the legitimacy of their foundations can be questioned. Even physical inequality, he argues, does not have much significance in the state of nature since in that state men have almost no contact with one another. He concludes the first part of the *Discourse* by saying that inequality in the state of nature is therefore 'barely perceptible' (*OC* 3:162; Masters, 144). The 'spirit of society' he concludes in the second part, engenders much contemporary inequality (*OC* 3:193; Masters, 180).

This striking thesis about inequality continues to stimulate serious political reflection today. Nonetheless, if one focuses solely on the question of the naturalness of *inequality,* one only attains a relatively superficial understanding of Rousseau's accomplishments in the *Discourse on Inequality.* What makes the work so compelling, we would argue, is Rousseau's deep exploration of the distinction between what is natural to humans and what is not. Rousseau himself makes the importance of this theme clear in a passage of the *Confessions.* In it, he describes the writing of the *Discourse on Inequality* and asserts that the work's central purpose is to show how man's nature has been changed and distorted to his detriment:

> Wandering deep into the forest, I sought and I found the vision of those primitive times, the history of which I proudly traced. I demolished the petty lies of mankind; I dared to strip man's nature naked, to follow the progress of time, and trace the things which have distorted it; and by comparing man as he had made himself with man as he is by nature I showed him in his pretended perfection the true source of his misery. Exalted by

> these sublime meditations, my soul soared towards the Divinity; and from that height I looked down on my fellow men pursuing the blind path of their prejudices, of their errors, of their misfortunes and their crimes. Then I cried to them in a feeble voice which they could not hear, 'Mad men who ceaselessly complain of Nature, learn that all your misfortunes arise from yourselves!' (trans. J.M. Cohen, 362; *OC* 1:388–9)

According to the above account, the *Discourse on Inequality* helps show how men move from natural goodness and happiness to societal badness and depravity. Rousseau suggests that the principle that informs all his writing is that '[n]ature made man happy and good but society depraves him and makes him miserable' (*OC* 1:934). But another thing Rousseau is saying in the above passage is that civil man is miserable because he is limited to the path of 'predjudices, errors, misfortunes and crimes.' By contrast, natural man is independent of other men and of their prejudices and errors. Natural man's natural freedom or independence of the wills of other men is a central theme of the *Discourse.* Rousseau tries to uncover the contrast between the independence of natural man and the dependence of civil man in order to accurately diagnose man's dilemma and to contemplate remedies for it.

Concomitantly, in the *Confessions* passage, Rousseau draws our attention to the contrast between man 'as he is by nature' and man as he has 'made himself.' He thus emphasizes the crucial contrast between the natural and the unnatural or preternatural in man. 'It is no light undertaking,' he writes in the Preface, 'to separate what is original from what is artificial in the present nature of man, and to know correctly a state which no longer exists, which perhaps never existed, and about which it is nevertheless necessary to have precise notions in order to judge our present state correctly' (*OC* 3: 123 ; Masters, 92–3). He asks how it will be possible to separate what natural man 'gets from own stock from what circumstances and his progress have added to or changed in his primitive state?' (*OC* 3: 122; Masters, 91).

Rousseau tries, in the *Discourse on Inequality*, to understand the transition from man in the natural state to man in society. He locates two species characteristics, free will and perfectibility, that allow man's independence of nature (*OC* 3:142, Masters, 114–15). We must look to these qualities, then, if we are to understand how man, unlike the other animals, moves beyond nature. Free will and perfectibilty are the powers that might help explain the transition from man as he is by nature to man as he makes himself.

Whereas the role of perfectibilty in Rousseau's account of man's progress is well appreciated, the role of free will in the historical transition that he describes is often neglected. In this book, we argue that Rousseau describes man's capacity for free will as an anti-natural capacity that leads to depravity. Thus free will has a role to play in man's departure from natural goodness. Man makes himself into a self-conscious, free being who through this consciousness of freedom shapes himself in unnatural ways. Aware of our partial freedom of natural causation, we attribute moral responsibility for injuries to other people and thereby contribute to interactions laced with unhealthy forms of the inflated self-love Rousseau calls *amour propre*. The emergence of this dialectic requires not just perfectibility but free will. It involves the consciousness of free will and calls on the unnaturalness of undetermined free will. Perfectibility, we will suggest, is not far enough outside nature to ground man's unnnatural badness and explain human malice and spite.

However, it would be a mistake to think that Rousseau's view of free will is relentlessly gloomy. Rousseau's view of human free will is neither simplistically optimistic nor unremittingly pessimistic. He understands free will as a power or potential that provides human beings with both obstacles and opportunities. Man can choose to be virtuous or vicious, healthy or depraved, happy or unhappy. All of these pairings are important to Rousseau, but the choice between virtue and vice has particular relevance for our study. Because man can choose virtue or vice, justice or injustice, he can be held morally responsible for these choices. He is not fully determined by blind matter.

The plan of the book is as follows. Chapter 1 introduces our interpretation of free will and perfectibilty in the *Second Discourse*. The chapter begins with a careful exegisis of Rousseau's discussion of free will. We pay particular attention to the works of thinkers who may have influenced Rousseau, and we discuss his description of free will as an anti-natural quality. We posit that Rousseau's account of the consciousness of freedom that separates man from nature has a complexity and interest that suggests it is not merely rhetorical. We then investigate Marc Plattner's argument that Rousseau's contention that free will distinguishes the human species is merely rhetorical. The final part of the chapter offers an interpretation of perfectibility; it suggests that Rousseau sees perfectibility as a power that enables man to develop those faculties which are latent in his nature. There we also contest the view that Rousseau's teaching about perfectibility indicates that he thinks man is merely a passive product of his environment and history.

In the first part of chapter 2, we closely examine the implications of Rousseau's statement that the faculties develop contingently, through the action of external causes that 'need never have happened.' Some commentators allege that this claim shows he thinks man's nature is simply shaped and determined by circumstances he cannot control. But since the progress of man's accomplishments also entails his corruption and depravation, Rousseau stresses the accidental or contingent development of the faculties, we suggest, primarily in order to support his teaching that man is by nature good rather than to show that man is simply a passive product of blind chance. Moreover, Rousseau emphasizes the active role that man plays in his own corruption. Man's decline depends upon both accidental factors external to his nature and his own poor decisions rooted in his (free) will.

Free will, we then argue, plays a significant role in what Rousseau calls his genealogy of vice. Man's consciousness of free will contributes to the development of his *amour propre,* morality, and vice. He makes this argument explicitly in *Emile,* but it is implicit in certain passages of the *Discourse on Inequality* itself. We also consider the objection that Rousseau sees free will as a salutary illusion. We concede that some of the most important passages in which he discusses free will are highly rhetorical, but we show that they nonetheless adumbrate stronger arguments about free will that he does endorse.

The third chapter of the book presents arguments for the view that Rousseau actually stood behind the assertions of free will and the critique of materialism contained in the *Profession of Faith of the Savoyard Vicar.* We probe the meaning and significance of the *Profession* and the role of free will within it and consider the question of whether and to what extent Rousseau actually endorses the argument of the *Profession.*

The final chapter examines the evolution and character of Rousseau's intention regarding his belief in free will through a reading of *The Reveries of the Solitary Walker.* Here we concede that in the Third Reverie he acknowledges his growing doubts as to the adequacy of the earlier metaphysical views expressed in the *Profession of Faith,* but we affirm that Rousseau hopes that his earlier views were true, and that he endeavours to ground these hopes upon reason – to turn them into reasonable hopes. In the Fourth Reverie, Rousseau indicates that he was willing to misrepresent the truth for the good of others; but evidence within the *Reveries* suggests that his principles would not have allowed him to lie about his position on freedom of the will.

Rousseau's position, we conclude, is best described as metaphysical ambivalence. To explain this idea, it makes sense to consider how it differs from a few of the most prominent approaches to Rousseau's method. After noting that the argument of the *Discourse on Inequality* is based on perfectibility rather than on free will, Leo Strauss comments that Rousseau's approach in the work is meant to be metaphysically neutral: 'The argument of the *Second Discourse* is meant to be acceptable to materialists as well as to others. It is meant to be neutral with regard to the conflict between materialism and antimaterialism, or to be "scientific" in the present-day sense of the term.'[24] We agree that Rousseau uses the technique of metaphysical neutrality, but we would add that because he stands behind his challenges to comprehensive materialism, his overall position is best characterized as metaphysical ambivalence. His strategy is to use different lines of defence on different fronts. In the *Discourse on Inequality*, he uses materialist perfectibility to insulate himself against attacks on dualism, but he also uses dualism to explain the genealogy of vice. In *Emile*, he replicates this two-track strategy: in the main body of the work, he argues primarily on the grounds of the empiricist materialism of Hobbes, Condillac, and Helvétius, so as not to have his argument dismissed by his contemporaries. At the same time, in the *Profession of Faith of the Savoyard Vicar*, he offers an uncompromising critique of materialism and an anti-materialist theism. In both works, he employs one layer of his argument to throw the adequacy of the materialist understanding of human nature into serious question.

We concede that Rousseau writes esoterically, but it should be remembered that he had to contend not only with the pressures of Christian orthodoxy but also with those of dogmatic materialist *philosophes*. In the *Dialogues*, he suggests that the *philosophes* have made themselves into the leaders of an intolerant party he compares to the Jesuits; he then predicts that defenders of 'theism, tolerance and morality' will face a 'philosophical inquisition' (*OC* 1:968). Writing in the face of this sort of pressure results in a distinctive form of esoteric writing in Rousseau's case; in his texts, the metaphysically neutral layer of the argument is usually the obvious one, while his anti-materialist arguments are often more implicit.

Our reading suggests, then, that the layer of text defending free will supplements the metaphysically neutral layer and reveals its limitations. Nonetheless, the resemblances between our approach and Derrida's deconstructive approach are relatively superficial. Still, given the influence of Derrida's approach and his focus on the work of Rousseau, before turning to our own interpretation it will be worth our while to review some of the relevant differences.

In his interpretation of Rousseau in *Of Grammatology*, Derrida makes a revealing remark about the relation between the critical, post-structuralist way of reading he advocates (a way of reading that, he contends, 'produces' the text), and readings that seek to reproduce the author's intention through an 'effaced and respectful' commentary that 'doubles' the original text:

> Doubtless this moment of doubling commentary [*commentaire redoublant*] should have its place in critical reading. Recognizing and respecting all its classical exigencies is not easy and requires all the instruments of traditional criticism. Without this recognition and respect, critical production would risk developing in no matter what direction and authorize itself to say just about anything. But this indispensible guardrail has always only *protected*, it has never *opened* a reading.[25] (emphasis in original)

Here Derrida rightly emphasizes the need to consider commentary that seeks to reveal a philosopher's intention. But he simultaneously overestimates and underestimates the virtues of such commentaries. He overestimates their virtues because not all such commentaries are equally worthy of respect and, therefore, of recognition (whether this be in view of the skills displayed, the methods used, the knowledge marshalled, or the merits of the conclusions reached). But he underrates them through his term 'doubling commentary,' which obscures the fact that, when they succeed, such commentaries do not double so much as elucidate the text; they set forth its meaning in instructive new ways. Moreover, he underestimates these commentaries focused on elucidating an author's intention when he asserts that they have never 'opened a reading.' For such commentaries can deepen our dialogue with philosophers about important questions, by explicating neglected transitions in the philosopher's thought, for example, or through the precise and deft disclosing of significant distinctions (and this, of course, can be the case whether or not one agrees with the interpreter's conclusions).

This sort of commentary has the power both to uncover new terrain and to challenge our thinking about familiar territory. It acts more, we would suggest, like a compass than as a guardrail. The interpreter of this sort is not unlike a Sherpa. If a commentary that seeks to reveal the author's intention does not open the way to a post-structuralist reading, it nonetheless can liberate a reader.

1 Interpreting Free Will and Perfectibility in the *Discourse on Inequality*

'Nature made man happy and good but society depraves him and makes him miserable' (*OC* 1:934). This is Rousseau's 'great principle.' But although he thinks man is naturally good, he does not think man is naturally virtuous. Rousseau distinguishes between goodness and virtue. Whereas goodness is natural, virtue requires the mastery of natural inclinations. As the tutor says to Emile: 'The word *virtue* comes from *strength*. Strength is the foundation of all virtue. Virtue belongs only to a being that is weak by nature and strong by will' (*OC* 4:817; trans. Bloom, 444; cf. *Lettre à Franquières*, *OC* 3:1143). Man has the strength to resist natural impulse in obedience to a reasoned decision – in obedience, we suggest, to his free will. Humans are naturally good animals who become beings who can be independent of natural imperatives. They have the potential to freely choose to act in accordance with virtue or vice.

This chapter provides the basis for key elements of the above interpretation of Rousseau through a discussion of competing interpretations of free will and perfectibility in the *Discourse on Inequality*. The chapter has three parts. The first part uses a close reading of Rousseau's teaching on free will in the *Discourse on Inequality* to carefully analyse key terms, to probe the question of the influence of other eighteenth-century thinkers on his views, and to examine the role of free will in his critique of arbitrary government. In the second part of the chapter, we analyse an important counter-interpretation – the one contained in Marc Plattner's *Rousseau's State of Nature* – that posits that Rousseau does not truly believe men have free will. As we will see, Plattner makes a compelling argument that Rousseau does not in fact believe his account of free will is true; presenting that argument is crucial for a clear understanding of the controversy. Nonetheless, our objections show that this reading has some notable weaknesses, and that because of these, the way has not been cleared for an understanding of Rousseau as a comprehensive determinist. The third part of the chapter introduces our own interpretation of perfectibility as well as alternative interpretations of it. We consider the argument that Rousseau's view of perfectibility shows he has a lower view of human nature than does Hobbes. Assessing the evidence, we concede that Rousseau has a more minimalist view of men in the state of nature than does Hobbes; but we also argue that, compared to Hobbes's man, Rousseau's man has the potential to choose to follow nobler paths; he can choose to act in accordance with virtue or vice. The second and third sections of the chapter, then, support and develop our overall argument. But before turning to those discussions, we present our exegesis of free will in the *Discourse*.

Part 1: Free Will in the *Discourse on Inequality*

In this exegesis, we interpret Rousseau's description of free will as independence of instinct. We also probe the question of philosophical influences on Rousseau's teaching; we expose the intellectual context in which Rousseau wrote; and we compare his position on how humans differ from animals with those of Buffon, Montaigne, and Condillac. Rousseau's portrayal of free will likely owes a debt to Montaigne's critique of human freedom from instinct. But Rousseau is not a mere disciple of Montaigne. Evidence we present suggests that the originality of his treatment of free will owes something substantial to his confrontations with the views of the great natural historian Buffon as well as those of his underrated friend, Condillac.

We also discuss Rousseau's assertion that consciousness of free will distinguishes humans from the animals. He argues not only that willing or choice is a spiritual power but also that consciousness of free will is a spiritual power. This argument is intriguing – too intriguing, we suggest, to have been merely rhetorical. A more conventional account of free will as the free will to choose between good and evil would have sufficed to satisfy the religious authorities. That Rousseau provides a more elaborate and engaging account of human freedom than is strictly necessary suggests that he does so because he thinks it is plausible and true.

Lastly, we make the case that Rousseau's argument that voluntary slavery can never be legitimate relies on the premise that humans have free will. This is important because his critique of voluntary slavery grounds his critique of despotism and arbitrary government. Thus, here we respond to the argument that free will serves no purpose in the argument of the *Discourse* after Rousseau introduces it by showing his *political* use of the free will premise.

'The Power of Willing and the Consciousness of Freedom': Free Will as the Human Species Distinction

While Rousseau's persistent argument up to the point in the *Discourse* where he discusses free will has been that the state of nature is a relatively peaceful state for man, he introduces free will in terms that signal the distancing of man from the order of nature:

> In every animal I see only an ingenious machine to which nature has given senses in order to revitalize itself and guarantee itself, to a certain point, from all that tends to destroy or upset it. I perceive precisely the same things in the human machine, with the difference that nature alone does everything in the operations of a beast, whereas man contributes to his operations by being a free agent. The former chooses or rejects by instinct and the latter by an act of freedom. (*OC* 3:141; Masters, 113)

This is Rousseau's introduction of the notion of independence of instinct. By referring to animals as ingenious machines, Rousseau employs the language of Descartes and Cartesian dualism. But as Victor Goldschmidt points out, Rousseau's dualism is filtered through that of Buffon:

> With Buffon, Rousseau supports the animal-machine thesis, moderated by the idea of instinct. With Buffon as well, Rousseau adopts a dualism of Cartesian origin, if not obedience: the '"spirituality" of soul' will be opposed to instinct, which according to Buffon is 'an animal principle and purely material.'[1]

Goldschmidt is right that it is a mistake to overestimate the Cartesianism of Rousseau's argument; in the *Second Discourse* Rousseau dissents from Descartes's view that humans escape the mechanistic laws of nature through their ability to reason.[2] While both Descartes and Buffon deny that beasts can think, Rousseau agrees with Condillac, who argues that beasts are able to understand and combine ideas, as we will examine in more detail below.

Notice that, in this introductory paragraph, Rousseau defines free will in relation to and in contradistinction from nature. He depicts nature as the active force that governs animals and that leads them to preserve themselves: 'Nature alone does everything in the operations of the beast.' Nature has a large but not an exclusive role in the operations of man, who contributes to these operations by 'being a free agent.' Therefore nature's overarching government of the beasts provides a foil to man's measure of self-government through choice and free will. Rousseau deepens this contrast between instinctual beasts and willing humans through the use of three striking images:

> A beast cannot deviate from the rule that is prescribed to it even when it would be advantageous for it to do so, and a man deviates from it often to his detriment. Thus a pigeon would die of hunger near a basin filled with the best meats, and a cat upon heaps of fruits or grain, although each could very well nourish itself on the food it disdains if it made up its mind to try some. Thus dissolute men abandon themselves to excesses which cause them fever and death, because the mind depraves the senses and because the will still speaks when nature is silent. (*OC* 3:141; Masters, 113–14)

The standards against which men and beasts, will and nature, are measured here are those of self-preservation and health. These are standards favoured by proponents of modern natural science. Buffon remarked that most animals 'faint and die of hunger rather than take food which is repugnant to them' (*OC* 3:1316n3). For Rousseau and Buffon, a rule prescribed by nature can lead to the death of individual animals; this is why instinct is often called blind. To give another example, lemmings obey their instinct as they jump to their deaths in the sea.

The images of the cat and pigeon controlled by instinct become more meaningful through their juxtaposition with the image of the dissolute men. Together these images present a picture of human free will as a powerful and unnatural force. The juxtaposition is a compelling one in part because the dissolute men are as driven by their wills as the pigeon that starves beside a basin of meats is by its instinct. But while the beasts decline and die because of natural behaviour, the men degenerate and die because of their own *un*natural behaviour. Instinct and free will can both lead to the destruction and death of animate life, but the former does so through an excessive devotion to nature's command and the latter through an abandonment of it. Free will makes its first appearance in the *Discourse* as a strikingly anti-natural quality. It can be more powerful than what is natural within man, and this powerful anti-natural will can be deeply harmful to men.

In his 1909 essay, '*Recherches sur les sources du Discours de l'inégalité*,' Jean Morel explores the possibility that Montaigne influenced Rousseau towards this derogatory portrayal of the will.[3] Morel's analysis is illuminating, but he makes the mistake of taking the passage that includes these metaphors as Rousseau's definitive statement on free will. Following his introduction of free will, Rousseau makes reference to one of Montaigne's reflections in order to support his argument that the difference in reasoning ability of men and animals is simply one of degree. There Rousseau writes that, 'Some philosophers have even suggested that there is more difference between a given man and another than between a given man and a given beast.' Montaigne begins his essay 'Of the inequality that is between us,' as follows:

> Plutarch says somewhere that he does not find so much difference between one animal and another as he does between one man and another. He is talking about the capacity of soul and the inward qualities. In truth, I find Epaminondas, as I imagine him, so remote from some men I know – I mean men capable of common sense – that I would willingly outdo Plutarch and say that there is more distance from a given man to a given man than from a given man to a given animal.[4]

Morel then reminds us that Montaigne is sceptical about high-minded talk about the nobility of human liberty. In the 'Apology for Raymond Sebond,' Montaigne suggests that one should not 'make much, as indeed Socrates does, of this notable prerogative [we have] over the other animals to whom Nature prescribes certain seasons and limits to voluptuousness, whereas she has given us free reign at all hours and occasions.' In the same work, Montaigne asserts that it is 'more honourable, and closer to divinity, to be guided and obliged to act lawfully by a natural and inevitable condition, than to act lawfully by accidental and fortuitous liberty; and safer to leave the reins of our conduct to nature than to ourselves.' He further contends that from this 'freedom of imagination and unruliness of thought springs the principal source of the ills [*les maux*] that oppress [man] – sin, disease, irresolution, confusion, despair.'[5] Morel comments as follows on these reflections of Montaigne's: 'Here is a defence of nature which Rousseau borrows. "Man often deviates to his prejudice from the rule that is prescribed him" [sic]. Montaigne thus inspires his theory of human action.'

Unexpectedly, this is Morel's final word on the question of Rousseau's view of free will. It is true that here and elsewhere Rousseau implies a certain admiration for the rule of natural necessity.[6] By beginning with a criticism of free will, moreover, Rousseau is able to introduce his argument about it in a way that is compatible with his previous argument in the *Discourse* about the beneficence of nature and the agreeableness of life in the state of nature. We could also grant that Montaigne's arguments about the pitfalls of liberty as against nature in the 'Apology for Raymond Sebond' may have influenced Rousseau's argument that men deviate from instinct to their misfortune.[7] But having introduced the example of the dissolute men who deviate from nature's rule, Rousseau does not simply dwell on the implication of the culpability of free will. In fact, his derogatory description of free will is qualified in the following paragraph, where he writes of the spirituality that is attendant upon the power of free choice: 'in the power of willing, or rather of choosing, and in the sentiment of this power are found only purely spiritual acts about which the laws of mechanics explain nothing' (*OC* 3:142; Masters 114).

Morel also ignores the fact that Rousseau's initial criticism of free will appears in a paragraph in which he also describes the obtuseness of nature's prescribed rule, namely, instinct. Free will and nature's command both have their pitfalls; there is a delicate balance underlying Rousseau's prose. The loftiness of human free will is qualified by the sometime depravity of the will (as when dissolute men abandon themselves to excess) and by the general beneficence of nature. The sufficiency of the wisdom of nature is qualified by the obtuseness of its command in some cases (as when a cat starves on a heap of grain) and by the spirituality of soul a man exhibits when he chooses and knows he is free. Interpretations of Rousseau as a romanticist champion of nature, on the one hand, or as a Stoic Republican who advocates freedom as the mastery of natural appetites, on the other, sometimes fail to do justice to this equilibrium.

Rousseau reaches his conclusion that acts of conscious choice are spiritual acts by way of his argument that it is man's free will rather than his understanding that distinguishes him from the beasts:

> Every animal has ideas, since it has senses, it even combines its ideas up to a certain point, and in this regard man differs from beast only in degree. Some philosophers have even suggested that there is more difference between a given man and another than between a given man and a given

> beast. Therefore it is not so much understanding which constitutes the distinction of man among the animals as it is his being a free agent. (*OC* 3:141; Masters, 114)

In this section, Rousseau is less indebted to Montaigne than he is to his friend Condillac (whom he writes about with admiration in the *Discourse* and *Emile*).[8] Victor Goldschmidt makes a compelling case that from the outset Rousseau defines his position about the moral and metaphysical side of man in relation to Buffon's *Discours sur la nature des animaux* and to Condillac's *Traité des animaux*.[9] Condillac's *Traité* is above all a critique of Buffon's argument that beasts do not reason or understand. Buffon, Condillac, and Rousseau all agree that animals are capable of feeling, that they are sensible beings. (Descartes, on the other hand, refers to animals as '*automates insensibles*.') Condillac maintains that if, as Buffon assumes, animals have sensations then they must necessarily have understanding. He writes that an animal has ideas 'because it has sensations which represent to it both exterior objects and its relations with these objects.'[10] He adds that a beast must be able to compare judgments because 'in order to acquire the habit of judging scents and sights with such precision and sureness, it must have been able to compare the judgments it made in one circumstance with those it made in another.'[11] In Condillac's view, animals often learn by experience behaviours that we attribute simply to nature. He gives the example of an animal that learns by experience to avoid a falling stone but not to bother to avoid a falling leaf because the latter will not hurt him.

Rousseau signals his acceptance of Condillac's line of argument when he states that 'Every animal has ideas, since it has senses; it even combines its ideas up to a certain point, and in this regard man differs from beast only in degree.' Rousseau concludes from Condillac's premises that when it comes to understanding, in particular, men generally have not a different quality but a different *quantity* of it than do beasts. On the basis of the same observations, Condillac poses the more radical question of whether there are qualitative differences between men and beasts of any sort. Condillac argues that the needs of animals determine their development; since animals have more limited needs than men do, their development is more limited. He then notes that animals are limited in their ability to communicate with one another, that they do not imitate one another much, and that they do not contribute much to their 'reciprocal perfections.' But since they do think and since some of them understand a bit of our speech, he wonders what the difference between animals and men might be: he asks, 'Is it not one of more or less?'[12] He answers that the difference in their operations likely defines them, but he asserts that it may not be necessary to declare their essence beforehand.

Condillac defines instinct as the habit of direction of animal faculties 'without reflection.'[13] His position is that beasts acquire instinct through reflection, but that since their needs are limited, before long they know all that reflection can teach them. After this initial period of apprenticeship, then, they come to rely on habit and thus they are guided by instinct alone. In the conclusion to the second part of the *Traité*, he sums up his position as follows: 'There is in beasts that degree of intelligence that we call instinct; and in man that superior degree that we call reason.'[14] Condillac assumes the opposition between instinct and reason while also putting it in question. This is important because, if we are to believe Victor Goldschmidt, Rousseau unlike Condillac displaces the opposition between instinct and reason and replaces it with a new one: 'It is liberty which is opposed to instinct and not (as we have seen, for example, in Condillac) reason.'[15] Goldschmidt maintains that because of his focus on liberty, Rousseau is able to offer a new kind of dualism, one that manages to stay on the good side of contemporary science as represented by Condillac's empirical method:

> Rousseau disarms Condillac's critique. In agreeing with him that, when it comes to the formation of ideas 'man differs ... from the beast only more or less,' ... Rousseau puts himself in accord with contemporary science (that of his friend, particularly, and more generally, of the *Encyclopédie*). He abandons this whole question to 'physics' (which is to say to positivist metaphysics), and saves his dualism by taking refuge from the criteria of understanding, in that of liberty.[16]

Although Condillac's major focus is on instinct and reason, he also has something to say about liberty. At the end of the *Traité des Animaux*, Condillac describes the distinctiveness of human liberty in terms of choosing and willing. More than Rousseau does in the *Discourse*, he stresses that reflection is a prerequisite for free will; nonetheless, it is possible that in this section he influenced Rousseau's association of free will with the 'power of choosing.' The passage is therefore worth quoting at length:

> From this reflection, free and voluntary actions are born. Beasts are able to respond like we do without repugnance, and already here is a certain

> condition of the voluntary; but another one is necessary: because *I will* [*je veux*] not only signifies that a thing is agreeable to me, it also signifies that it is the object of my choice: but one only chooses amongst the things one has at one's disposal: one has nothing at one's disposal when one only obeys one's habits, one only follows the impulsion given by circumstances. The right of choice, liberty, then only belongs to reflection. Circumstances command the beasts: man on the contrary judges them, he lends himself to them, or refuses to lend himself to them, he conducts himself, he wills [*il veut*], he is free.[17]

This discussion of choice can only remind the reader of Rousseau's argument about man's power of willing or choosing. But Rousseau takes his reflection on man's ability to choose a step further in his next argument:

> Nature commands every animal, and the beast obeys. Man feels the same impetus, but he realizes that he is free to acquiesce or resist; and it is above all in the consciousness of this freedom that the spirituality of his soul is shown. For physics explains in some way the mechanism of the senses and the formation of ideas; but in the power of willing, or rather of choosing, and in the sentiment of this power are found only purely spiritual acts about which the laws of mechanics explain nothing.[18]

Rousseau's ideas of human powers of choice and sentiment of choice are strikingly similar to Condillac's ideas of human choice and reflection upon the choice; but unlike Condillac, Rousseau presents these powers as 'purely spiritual acts.' What does Rousseau mean when he says that man's power of willing and his consciousness of this power are 'spiritual'? He uses the term 'spiritual' in contradistinction to the 'laws of mechanics.' If man's soul cannot be explained by the laws of mechanics, then it is not simply matter in motion. Rousseau phrases it this way in his *Lettre à Christophe de Beaumont:* 'Man is not a simple being: he is composed of two substances' (*OC* 4:936). Or, as he puts it in his private *Lettre à M. de Franquières*, man is a 'mixed being' (*OC* 4:1139).[19] Rousseau, it is true, sometimes gives voice to doubts about such a dualistic understanding of man, but these expressions of doubt point to the need to understand his true motivation for his assertions about man's 'spiritual' soul.

It is also crucial to note here Rousseau's use of the terms 'consciousness of freedom' and 'sentiment of this power': it is not free will alone but especially the *consciousness* of free will that Rousseau characterizes as 'spiritual.' This is a more interesting – and arguably a path-breaking – formulation of the matter, and as such it poses a challenge for those who argue that Rousseau feigns his belief in free will. A simple nod to the spirituality of willing would have sufficed for encouraging healthy political life or avoiding religious persecution. That Rousseau undertakes a more complex line of argument may suggest the earnestness of his endeavour. Why is consciousness of freedom such a significant idea? Consider the work of Harry Frankfurt and Hans Jonas, two contemporary theorists who have recently defended conceptions closely related to Rousseau's idea that it is the consciousness of freedom that distinguishes humans from the animals.

In an influential essay, Harry Frankfurt has argued that human beings are characterized by a certain kind of self-consciousness about our wills:

> It is my view that one essential difference between persons and other creatures is to be found in the structure of a person's will. Human beings are not alone in having desires and motives, or in making choices. They share these things with members of certain other species, some of whom even appear to engage in deliberation and to make decisions based upon prior thought. It seems to be peculiarly characteristic of humans, however, that they are able to form what I shall call 'second-order desires' or 'desires of the second order.'[20]

Only human beings, Frankfurt suggests, have second-order desires, which is to say, only humans have desires *about* their desires, only men judge and evaluate their desires or volitions:

> Besides wanting and choosing and being moved *to do* this or that, men may also want to have (or not have) certain desires and motives. They are capable of wanting to be different, in their preferences and purposes, from what they are. Many animals appear to have the capacity for what I shall call 'first-order desires' or 'desires of the first order,' which are simply desires to do or not to do one thing or another. No animal other than man, however, appears to have the capacity for reflective self-evaluation that is manifested in the formation of second-order desires.[21]

To will to will is specifically human on this view. Charles Taylor has developed Frankfurt's conception in a somewhat different direction in his essay 'What Is Human Agency?' There he contends that only humans are characterized by the ability to evaluate their desires 'as to worth.' He calls this 'strong evaluation' and suggests it is present, for example, 'when I refrain from acting from a given motive – say spite, or envy – because I consider it base or unworthy.' Taylor suggests that without the capacity for strong evaluation, 'an agent would lack the kind of depth we consider essential to humanity, without which we would find human communication impossible.'[22]

In his fine 'Philosophical Meditation on the Seventh Chapter of Paul's Epistle to the Romans,' Hans Jonas shows that for St Paul the human will is fundamentally reflexive or double and that this reflexive process of the will is a necessary part of human freedom.[23] According to Jonas, St Paul's meditation points to the fact that the will is characterized by an alteration between two different aspects of self-consciousness of the will. One aspect is the self-reflection that he describes by the phrase 'I will that I will thus' or *volo me velle*. This process is self-reflexive because the will posits and affirms itself. (Desire or appetite, on the other hand, is a more direct, 'non-reflective' process.)[24] The other phase of self-conscious will is a process of self-observation, which Jonas describes as *cogito me velle*, and through which freedom looks at a chosen action 'from without as its own observer.'[25] For Jonas, the nobility of freedom can be seen in the dialectic between these two aspects of consciousness of the will. These explorations suggest, I think, that Rousseau's formulation of the free will problem in the *Second Discourse* as one involving a consciousness of freedom that reveals man's spirituality of soul has an interest and complexity that would appear to be gratuitous if his presentation were merely rhetorical.

Most readers of Rousseau would concede that his presentation of consciousness of freedom is thought-provoking. Nonetheless, many interpreters point out that, whatever the interest of Rousseau's descriptions of free will, the anthropology of the *Discourse* is based on perfectibility and not on free will. This is a point we readily grant; but it does not follow that free will therefore has no role to play in the *Dircourse's* argument. In chapter 2 we suggest that Rousseau's concept of the consciousness of freedom forms an aspect of the formation of *amour propre*. In the next section, we suggest that free will has a significant role to play in Rousseau's political teaching in the *Discourse*. For there, as part of an attempt to demonstrate the illegitimacy of the political submission of peoples to their leaders, he argues that the human capacity for free will makes it unjust for individuals to enslave themselves.

Free Will and Political Freedom: Rousseau's Reply to the Defenders of Arbitrary Government

What are the direct political implications of Rousseau's teaching about free will in the *Discourse*? Rousseau is, after all, a radical democrat and a champion of the rights of the people against the abuses of aristocrats and kings. How, precisely, is his belief that we can be undetermined in making decisions related to his teaching about peoples, governments, and power?

The second part of the *Discourse on Inequality* both provides some answers and reinforces our argument that Rousseau truly believes in free will. He tells us that in the second part he will consider the origin and progress of inequality in the 'successive developments of the human Mind' (*OC* 3:162). A key element of this account is his fierce critique of the case for arbitrary government and absolute monarchy. Rousseau understands arbitrary government to be government that is based on arbitrary grounds rather than founded on the consent of the governed.[26] Of the several arguments he makes, we will focus on the last one, that is, on his argument about whether a person can voluntarily become a slave. In this argument, Rousseau examines the contention of Grotius and Pufendorf that because it is legitimate for a person to volunteer for slavery, by analogy, it is legitimate for the people to voluntarily submit themselves to arbitrary government. Rousseau famously responds that the voluntary slave would be responsible for performing crimes commanded by his master. His response suggests it is illegitimate for the slave to transfer his or her freedom to another because the slave has free will; he concludes that, analogously, is it is illegitimate for the people to voluntarily submit themselves to masters.

THE CONTEXT OF THE ARGUMENT

After describing the development of metallurgy and agriculture and the institution of property in the second part of the *Discourse*, Rousseau turns to look at men with all their faculties developed, 'placed in this new order of things' (*OC* 3:162; Masters, 155). He speculates that political association was likely established during a period of great disorder through the influence and deceptive discourses of the rich. He maintains, however, that the exact cause of the origin of societies and laws is 'indifferent to what I want to establish.' What he wants to establish at this point has less to do with the origins of civil association than with the subsequent institution of magistrates to carry out the offices of government.[27] Above all, he seeks to prove that the fundamental maxim of all political right is that 'peoples have given themselves chiefs to defend their freedom and not to enslave themselves' (*OC* 3:181). The people agree to institute government so as to have a body to execute the laws, but this is not an act of submission. The full significance of this argument can better be understood if one considers the arguments against which Rousseau sets himself. Hobbes, Grotius, and Pufendorf see the institution of government as a sign that the people renounce the right to self-government and subject themselves to their leaders.[28] Rousseau emphatically rejects this contention and the arbitrary government that Hobbes and Grotius defend on the basis of it.[29] The four main arguments he makes are as follows: First, he looks at the reasonableness of the terms of the bargain struck by the people with their leaders. Second, he contends that men are not naturally submissive. Third, he maintains that paternal authority does not provide a model for the political authority of governments. Fourth and finally, he insists that just as there can be no valid justification for the individual to enslave himself, so there can be none for a people to renounce its freedom. We focus on the final argument about voluntary slavery because it is this argument that relies on the premise of free will.

VOLUNTARY SLAVERY CONFERS NO RIGHT

Rousseau insists that no voluntary renunciation of freedom from slavery can be legitimate. He argues against the voluntary submission of an individual to slavery in order to show that the voluntary subjection of a people to tyranny cannot be rightful. Rousseau assumes that the two questions are related because that is what his opponents have done. Grotius, for example, argues that the existence of voluntary slavery implies that the people can be subject to absolute monarchy: 'From the Jewish, as well as the Roman law, it appears that anyone might engage himself in private servitude to whom he pleased. Now if an individual may do so, why may not a whole people, for the benefit of better government and more certain protection, completely transfer their sovereign rights to one or more persons without reserving any portion to themselves?'[30]

There is evidence that Rousseau has Grotius in mind as he composes this fourth argument,[31] but his most interesting argument against voluntary slavery in the *Discourse* begins as a response to Pufendorf's view of a part of the question: 'Pufendorf,' he writes, 'says that just as one transfers his goods to another by conventions and contracts, one can also divest himself of his freedom in favour of someone else' (*OC* 3:183; Masters, 167). Rousseau's response to Pufendorf assumes that the voluntary slavery contract is illegitimate because it is morally compromising. He suggests it is morally compromising as he deftly criticizes Pufendorf's analogy between selling one's goods and selling one's freedom. Rousseau puts his point as follows: 'the goods I alienate become something altogether foreign to me, the abuse of which is indifferent to me; but it matters to me that my freedom is not abused, and I cannot, without making myself guilty of the evil I shall be forced to do, risk becoming the instrument of crime.' Notice that Rousseau implies that what the voluntary slave transfers is not freedom of will but freedom of action, that is, the slave transfers the freedom to perform or not perform actions according to the decisions of his will. The slave's free will, that is, the slave's ability to come to a decision without being determined by outside forces, is intact. The master can influence the slave but the slave's thoughts are not completely determined (short of complete brainwashing – not a case Rousseau considers here). However, the slave's freedom of action is, as Rousseau puts it, 'abused.' Although the slave's will is still free, in many cases or habitually he or she has to *act* against that will.[32] But this renunciation of freedom of action is not simply unfortunate but illegitimate because the would-be voluntary slave has free will.

If determinism is true, voluntary slavery may be a very bad decision;it certainly makes the voluntary slave vulnerable to harm and abuse. But if the will is free, voluntary slavery contains another threat; as a voluntary slave I am responsible for crimes commanded by my master. This is either because I (unlike involuntary slaves) made the compromising and even incriminating initial choice through free will to enter a state that I knew could result in the performance of these crimes; or it is simply because I have put myself in the position of disregarding the import of my will's freedom in deciding to obey the free will of another. In either case, because the will is free, I am morally responsible for coerced acts. By contrast, under determinism, it is hard to see how voluntary slaves could be morally responsible for crimes or evil acts commanded by the master. The voluntary slaves Hobbes describes in chapter 20 of *Leviathan*, for example, are not morally compromised. Hobbes assumes that all their decisions and actions are fully determined; he therefore presents their decision to enslave themselves as a matter of prudence rather than as a moral dilemma.

In the next section of his response to Pufendorf, Rousseau develops a contrast between the claim to freedom, which is rooted in nature, and the right of property, which is merely conventional. Freedom and life are 'essential gifts of nature' and 'it would offend both nature and reason to renounce them at whatever the price.'[33] Rousseau then suggests that it is doubtful whether one has the right to divest oneself of freedom because in doing so 'one degrades one's being' (*OC* 3:184; Masters, 168). There is evidence that he assumes that voluntary slavery is degrading because of the connection between freedom of action and freedom of will. Earlier in the passage, he writes that by divesting oneself of freedom, one puts oneself 'on the level of the beasts enslaved by instinct' (*OC* 3:183; Masters, 167). This phrase recalls Rousseau's assertion in the first part of the *Discourse on Inequality* that while beasts choose or reject by instinct, man does so 'by an act of liberty' (*OC* 3: 141–2). It is true that we have suggested that independence of instinct can take the form of perfectibility as well as free will. But the direct textual evidence we just cited points to a reading in terms of free will: man is free from determination by instinct in the sense that he chooses through free will; by divesting himself of freedom of action, he ignores his freedom of will and thus debases himself to the level of the beasts.[34]

Rousseau's argument that voluntary slavery is illegitimate is the final element of his case against arbitrary and despotic government. On the basis of his arguments, he concludes that he has shown that 'government did not begin by arbitrary power.' He then very briefly describes his own view of political legitimacy. He confines himself to a few key observations about the rule of law. The rule of law is based on the people's will: 'the people having, on the subject of social relations, united all their wills into a single one, all the articles on which this will is explicit become so many fundamental laws obligating all members of the State without exception' (*OC* 3:184–5; Masters, 169). But will is not necessarily free will. Although Rousseau's critique of political illegitimacy relies on free will, his conception of political legitimacy in the *Discourse* does not rely explicitly on free will.[35]

However, there is a final aspect of the voluntary slavery argument that deserves our attention. As he does in the *Discourse on Inequality*, in the *Social Contract*, Rousseau again critiques voluntary slavery in order to undermine philosophical arguments that the people can legitimately submit themselves to political masters. But comparing the two accounts, we see that Rousseau's argument against voluntary slavery in the *Social*

Contract implies a markedly different position on the slave's responsibility for crimes. While in the *Discourse* he argues that the voluntary slave has or keeps moral responsibility for crimes the master forces him to commit, in the *Social Contract*, he suggests that a voluntary slave does not have that responsibility. In the *Social Contract* he critiques as follows the idea of a voluntary slave contract: 'To renounce one's freedom is to renounce one's status [*qualité*] as a man, the rights of humanity, even its duties. There is no possible compensation for anyone who renounces everything. Such a renunciation is incompatible with the nature of man and taking away all freedom from his will [*toute liberté à sa volonté*] is taking all morality from his actions' (*OC* 3:356). Rousseau's claim that the slave has renounced the 'duties' of humanity means that the slave has given up responsibility for crimes committed during slavery. My conjecture is that this change is related to fact that in the *Social Contract* Rousseau needs to support his repeated claim in that work that the people's *will* cannot be alienated. The *Discourse* argument is not a good basis for establishing whether a transfer of *will* is legitimate or illegitimate. This is because, according to the *Discourse* description, the slave's *will* is not transferred; rather, the slave is culpable because he *acts* in contravention of the law while remaining a freely willing agent. That is, the argument in the *Discourse* only supports the contention that the slave's freedom of *action* cannot legitimately be transferred. The new *Social Contract* argument about the illegitimate interference with the slave's *will* through enslavement helps support his contention that the people's will should not be alienated – a premise that in turn underlies his critique of the representation of the sovereign power as an illegitimate alienation of the people's will. 'Power can perfectly well be transferred,' he writes in the *Social Contract*, 'but not will' (*OC* 3:368; trans. Masters, 59).

The interesting differences in these arguments, then, have bearing on Rousseau's political teaching. Notably, however, both rely on the free will premise. Free will is not simply cast aside in the *Discourse;* in fact, it grounds his critique of political illegitimacy in that work and in *Social Contract*.

Those who are sceptical that Rousseau believes in free will might respond that even though Rousseau implicitly relies on the idea of free will in his critique of arbitrary government, this does not prove that he thinks men have free will. Such a finding, they might say, does not dislodge the argument that Rousseau has motives (such as encouraging stable politics and avoiding the wrath of the Church) for feigning belief in free will. His reliance on free will to oppose the views of defenders of arbitrary government could also be part of his rhetorical strategy, they might argue. In the next section, we look carefully at the most detailed argument in the literature that Rousseau feigns his belief in free will, and we present our responses to it.

Part 2: The Counter-Case: Marc Plattner's Interpretation of Free Will in the *Discourse on Inequality*

In the first part of this chapter, we examined the passages about free will that engender the controversy. Now let us turn to the controversy itself. In the course of the book, we will consider several versions of the position that Rousseau does not truly believe in his argument that free will characterizes human beings; our overall argument will develop through a dialogue with different variations of the counter-case. But the starting point of my interest in the question was one particularly rigorous and well-argued interpretation. The interpretation in question is by Marc Plattner and is contained in his book *Rousseau's State of Nature: An Interpretation of the Discourse on the Origins of Inequality.*

Plattner's argument that Rousseau does not believe his own proposition that free will is the distinctive species characteristic of man has three main elements. First, he asserts that Rousseau wants to appear to believe that 'liberty proves the spirituality of the soul.'[36] In his view, Rousseau wants to argue for the spirituality of the soul because this creates the impression that he believes in the immortality of the soul, and Rousseau contends that the latter belief is necessary for good politics. Second, Plattner asserts that the argument that human choice is purely spiritual, while human thought is mechanistic, is 'clearly untenable' (44). Third, he observes that the fact that Rousseau points to difficulties surrounding the question of free will that leave his position open to dispute and that Rousseau then goes on to ground the rest of his teaching in the *Second Discourse* on perfectibility indicates that he does not truly believe free will is the faculty distinguishing men from the beasts.

In his first argument, Plattner contends that Rousseau makes the argument he does about free will because it allows him to construct a dualistic metaphysics capable of supporting the possibility of an immortal soul. He makes this argument by way of a contrast between the discussions of free will in the *Discourse* and those in the *Profession of Faith* that Rousseau puts in the mouth of the character of Savoyard vicar in *Emile.*[37] Plattner notes that while Rousseau maintains in the *Discourse* that thought can be explained by the laws of mechanics, the Savoyard vicar denies that thought can be explained in this way. Moreover, the vicar's argument that animals move spontaneously also contradicts the idea upheld in the *Discourse* that all animal behaviour can be explained mechanistically, that is, that animals are simply ingenious machines.

According to Plattner, there are two ways of interpreting these inconsistencies: either Rousseau's opinions changed, or he 'expressed himself differently in accordance with the differing intentions animating these two works' (43). Noting that Rousseau repeatedly insisted on the unity of his system, he decides that the second approach would provide a better account of the inconsistencies between the writings.

He points out that the Savoyard vicar is a fictional character and that after presenting the vicar's principles Rousseau writes in his own name that 'a host of objections' might be made to them (43). He omits to mention that Rousseau adds that he did not make these objections 'because they were less solid than disconcerting and persuasiveness was on the vicar's side.'[38] We can also note Rousseau's comment in the *Lettres écrites de la montagne* about the similarities between Julie's profession on her deathbed and the vicar's profession: 'these two pieces are enough in agreement that one can explain one by the other and from this accord one can presume with some plausibility [*vraisemblance*] that if the author who published the books where they are contained does not adopt the one and the other in their entirety, he favours them a great deal.'[39]

The *Profession of Faith* culminates in an argument for the immortality of the soul. It is true that in *Emile,* Rousseau writes that such a belief is a necessary support for the morality of ordinary minds such as Emile's. Also, Rousseau does not provide an argument for the immortal soul in the *Discourse,* and Plattner suggests that this is because it is meant to be a 'scientific' work wherein Rousseau reveals his principles more explicitly than in his other works: 'It is the *Second Discourse,* then, which should be taken as the most revealing statement of Rousseau's metaphysics' (44). Plattner observes, however, that the *Discourse,* too, has a political aim in the sense that it must not eradicate the foundations of good citizenship. He suggests that Rousseau intends to make the *Discourse* as well as *Emile* consistent with the doctrine of immortality of the soul. In his view, Rousseau has two strong motives for creating the impression that he believes in immortality of the soul: fear of persecution, and his opinion about the requirements for a stable political life: 'It is for these reasons that Rousseau in the *Second Discourse* gives the appearance of upholding a kind of dualist metaphysics by suggesting that human liberty proves the spirituality of the human soul' (44).

This reading implies that Rousseau settled upon liberty as the species characteristic of man in order to appear to resolve another question. But if he had tried to make it appear that he believed in the immortality of the soul through his dualistic metaphysics based on free will in the *Discourse,* does he not undermine this arrangement by altering so substantially his ideas about free will in the *Profession of Faith*? Also, the fact that Rousseau thought the belief in immortality politically essential does not mean he rejected the dualism that can underlie it.[40]

Plattner's next argument is that Rousseau must have had an ulterior motive for his account of free will because 'in itself, the argument that human thought can be explained mechanistically, while human choice is purely spiritual is clearly untenable' (44). As evidence, Plattner cites the opinion of Jean de Castillon, an eighteenth-century critic of Rousseau: 'Liberty [Rousseau] says, shows the spirituality of the soul. Our choice is often ruled by reasons [*motifs*] that certainly are perceived by the principle which wills, since they influence its determinations. Thus the spiritual soul is also capable of thinking. Therefore it is pointless to suppose a thinking being different from the spiritual soul' (cited in Plattner, 45).

We must remember, however, that it is not simply 'liberty' as Castillon contends, nor even 'choice' as Plattner has it, that Rousseau claims shows the spirituality of man's soul. He writes that in 'the power of willing, or rather of choosing and in the *sentiment* of this power are found only purely spiritual acts about which the laws of mechanics explain nothing' (emphasis mine). It does seem difficult to defend the idea that the power of choosing and the consciousness of this power are purely spiritual when they must involve thought, which Rousseau sees as mechanical. Indeed, Kant defends the view that it is the thinking, rational will alone that originates outside the mechanical order of natural phenomena. Nonetheless, it is possible to defend the notion that thinking is a necessary but not sufficient condition for free will and that its other condition(s) might be non-mechanical.

Plattner also points out that, like Castillon, the Savoyard vicar argues that willing is dependent on the judgment provided by the faculty of intelligence. As he notes, the vicar says that in relation to understanding, liberty must be only a 'similar or derivative power.' Two paragraphs later, however, the vicar affirms that 'the principle of every action is in the will of a free being.' In terms recalling the *Second Discourse,* he then declares that man is 'free in his actions and as such is animated by an immaterial substance.'[41] Thus, the context of the vicar's reflections on freedom and reason confirms the overall message of the passage from the *Discourse* under present consideration. And while there is certainly a discrepancy between these two presentations as regards the relation between free will and reason, this does not imply that the first was meant to be rhetorical. While the account in the *Discourse* is the more original, the vicar's account is the more easily defensible of the two. It can therefore be seen as a version that refines and improves upon the earlier one.

It has to be conceded that Rousseau's position that man is distinguished from the animals by free will but not by understanding is ultimately unwieldy. But unwieldy does not mean insincere. Rousseau is forced into this position by the fact that he decides both to accept Condillac's view about the ability of animals to combine ideas and to defend spiritual free will as a species characteristic. Castillon's objections are powerful, but Rousseau could not have read them until after the *Discourse* was published. And it is plausible that Rousseau, who had so much on his plate in this work and who admits that metaphysics is not his *forte*, did not fully anticipate them. As we shall see, in the *Profession of Faith*, Rousseau sensibly avoids putting the vicar in this awkward position.

Plattner refers to the exigencies of Rousseau's system, but his claim to having a system does not, after all, prevent him from ever changing his mind or developing his ideas. He may have altered his view about the relation between freedom and understanding just as he changed his positions about such matters as the naturalness of the family, about *amour propre* and about the causes of the rise of civil society.[42] None of these alterations undermine the central and unifying principle of his system: that men are naturally good but society depraves them and makes them bad. In any case, I think Goldschmidt is right that it is not so much the relation between freedom and reason as the relation between freedom and instinct that is at issue in the *Discourse* passage.[43]

To explain the final element of his case, Plattner cites Rousseau's concluding remark about free will and his introduction of the idea of perfectibility:

> But if the difficulties surrounding all these questions should leave some room for dispute on this difference between man and animal, there is another very specific quality that distinguishes them and about which there

> can be no dispute: the faculty of self-perfection, a faculty which, with the aid of circumstances, successively develops all the others, and resides among us as much in the species as in the individual. (*OC* 3:142; Masters, 114)

Plattner suggests that the fact that Rousseau mentions the difficulties surrounding the question of free will and then proceeds to ground the rest of his teaching in the *Discourse* on perfectibility indicates that Rousseau is not persuaded by his free will argument.[44] But is entirely possible that Rousseau is on the whole persuaded by his account of free will, in spite of the objections that might be made to it. These objections, however, would have substantial weight with Rousseau's Enlightenment contemporaries, many of whom would be highly inclined to dismiss arguments about free will in general and about the spirituality of the soul in particular. La Mettrie, Helvétius, D'Holbach, Diderot, and Voltaire all wrote critiques of the doctrine of free will.[45] Rousseau therefore requires an uncontroversial alternative species distinction, and perfectibility fits the bill very well. As we have seen, perfectibility is the faculty through which humans are able to progress in their accomplishments and in their own development.[46] In part because it is present 'as much in the species as in the individual,' it can serve as a link between the asocial state of nature and civil society. Therefore the flexible concept of perfectibility has an important role in Rousseau's teaching about the transformation of man. It is true that the account of the development of reason, language, and society in the rest of the *Discourse* is based primarily and explicitly upon perfectibility. Nonetheless, we have suggested that Rousseau relies on the premise of free will in his critique of arbitrary government, and in the next chapter, we will make the case that free will is an important, if implicit, feature of his description of the development of *amour propre*.

Plattner's hardest textual evidence occurs in note 10(J) of the *Discourse*. There, he contends, 'Rousseau engages in an extensive discussion of the differences between men and animals without any mention of liberty, and refers unambiguously to the 'faculty of perfecting itself, *which is the specific characteristic of the human species*' (59, Plattner's italics). One would have to consider whether in this reference to 'the specific characteristic of the human species' the 'the' (or, to be more accurate, the '*le*') is intended to be emphasized or whether it is incidental. The context Plattner mentions does give us a clue. Footnote 10(J) is ultimately about how difficult it is to obtain reliable observations about savage men and their close animal relations. It includes an appeal to capable men of science to undertake voyages in foreign lands with a view to composing reliable accounts. Rousseau is particularly concerned that some beings that obtuse explorers took for mere animals really might have been pre-linguistic men. In deciding such a question one would have to look for hard evidence and explicit signs of humanness. Now, the presence of perfectibility in a given species would be easier to observe and verify than would the presence of free will. Kant himself argues that we are ignorant of the degree of real freedom present in our own actions and decisions since the intelligible as opposed to empirical dimension of causality will always be unknown to us. He writes that 'the real morality of actions, their merit or guilt, even that of our own conduct … remains entirely hidden from us. Our imputations can only refer to their empirical character.'[47] If this is the case, we are not in a position to judge with any precision the possible presence of free will in 'anthropomorphic animals,' as Rousseau calls them. We could attempt to understand the empirical evidence, but, partly because we lack the ability to communicate with these animals, any judgments would be highly conjectural. We could, however, judge the presence of perfectibility by the demonstrated achievements of a given species or variety. For example, the context of the quotation that Plattner cites reveals that Rousseau believes that the presence or at least the absence of perfectibility can be tested and verified through experiment. In the midst of a discussion about whether the pongos – possible cousins of the orangutans – are savage men or simply animals, he writes that

> it is well-demonstrated that the monkey is not a variety of man, not only because he is deprived of the faculty of speech, but especially because it is certain that his species does not have the faculty of perfecting itself, which is the specific characteristic of the human species – experiments which do not appear to have been made on the pongo and the orangutan with enough care to allow drawing the same conclusion for them. (*OC* 3:211; Masters, 208)

The possession of perfectibility is thus easier to identify and to test for than the possession of free will. Perhaps this is part of what Rousseau means when he introduces it as a 'very specific' power that separates men from the animals. Given all of this, it is understandable – especially in a note that is largely addressed to men of science capable of making judgments about membership in the human species – that

Rousseau stresses the species characteristic most amenable to practical anthropological observation.[48]

Moreover, in the note, Rousseau responds to the claim by the authors of *Histoire générale des voyages* that the pongos, a group of anthropomorphic animals, are not human with the suggestion that they may exercise *will*. The authors suggest that the fact that the pongos withdraw from the fires that 'Negroes' have lit when they begin to extinguish themselves reveals that they are not intelligent enough to figure out how keep a fire going. In response, Rousseau asks 'how Battel or Purchass or his compliers could have known that the withdrawal was an effect of their stupidity rather than that of their will' (Masters, 207–8). Rousseau implies that if the pongos act on the basis of will, they are more likely to be human. But he can only speculate about whether or not they do act on the basis of will; this cannot be proven one way or the other. This is one more reason why Rousseau is obliged to propose an alternative species characteristic for man – perfectibility.

So far in this chapter, we have interpreted free will and consciousness of free will as forms of independence of instinct. We have also drawn objections to Platter's three arguments and offered counter-interpretations of endnote 10(J). On this basis, we surmise that none of Plattner's arguments allow us to conclude that Rousseau's statements about free will are merely rhetorical. But there are more objections to consider. Having focused thus far on free will in the *Discourse on Inequality*, in the next part of the chapter we direct our attention to the faculty of perfectibility and its role in our argument.

Part 3: The Faculty that Develops all the Others: Rousseau's Teaching about Perfectibility in the *Discourse on Inequality*

Clearly, to fully assess Rousseau's view of free will in the *Discourse* one also has to carefully consider the status of perfectibility, that other species distinction of man. As we noted in the introduction, Rousseau writes that perfectibility is the 'faculty which, with the aid of circumstances, successively develops all the others' (Masters, 114). Of these circumstances, we will have more to say later. As for the other faculties that perfectibility develops, these include reason, language, and the social virtues, as well as foresight and imagination.[49] Perfectibility is the power in man that allows him to develop latent and potential capacities that bring him beyond mere animality. But, for Rousseau, this development is a mixed blessing at best. As he eloquently puts it, perfectibility brings 'to flower [man's] enlightenment and his errors, his vices and his virtue and in the long run makes him the tyrant of himself and nature' (115). Rousseau's portrait of man's distinction from the beasts gives rise to critical reflection on man's estate rather than complacency about it.

How was Rousseau's teaching about perfectibility related to his teaching about free will? Both perfectibility and free will are ways of describing man's relative independence from instinct.[50] But there are some important differences between them. Free will was problematic for Rousseau: as we have seen, since it presumes more than one substance, it is not clear how it could have been compatible with the materialist understanding of the universe that held sway among his Enlightenment contemporaries. The concept of perfectibility need not be encumbered by these metaphysical controversies. It is a newer and above all a more flexible concept than free will,[51] and therefore Rousseau was able to use it to develop an interpretation of man's absence of instinct that would not be dismissed by the materialist men of science among his readers.

Perfectibility is the explicit foundation of Rousseau's anthropology in the rest of the first part of the *Discourse*. Because of this, some interpreters suggest that perfectibility rather than free will accounts in Rousseau for the evolution of man's humanity. According to this view, Rousseau's interpretation of perfectibility assumes a monistic view of human nature. Man's development is characterized by the emergence of the duality of *amour de soi* and *amour propre*. But this duality is not a metaphysical dualism of substances; it does not imply that man is composed of more than one substance. Moreover, this development is, as Rousseau says, provoked by a 'chance combination of external circumstances which need never have happened' (144). Some interpreters therefore maintain that in Rousseau the development of man's humanity does not entail the emergence of a will that is free in the sense of being undetermined by natural causality – instead, they suggest that man's humanity is entirely determined by an environmental and historical process of cause and effect. According to this interpretation, Rousseau's key accomplishment in the *Discourse* is that he has historicized human nature. Man, he suggests, is a malleable animal – the animal whose nature is almost entirely shaped first by the physical environment and then by the history of society itself. But if man's nature is a product of mere cause and effect, how can Rousseau maintain that man is distinguished by an active, spiritual power of free will? In fact, according to this reading, he cannot maintain this, and therefore he 'jettisons' the spiritual free will argument in favour of materialist perfectibility.[52]

But although we concede that perfectibility is the primary explicit foundation of Rousseau's anthropology, this does not mean that free will has been entirely thrust aside, any more than it means that perfectibility simply swallows it up. In keeping with our interpretation of perfectibility as the faculty that allows man to develop his latent natural capacities, we suggest below that free will is a distinctive natural potential within savage man. As we have argued, Rousseau's critique of political illegitimacy in the *Discourse* depends on the concept of free will. Beyond this, as we will show in chapter 2, Rousseau implicitly assumes that the emergence of free will is a crucial moment in the dynamic development of *amour propre*. In his description of how men begin to attribute responsibility for voluntary wrongs to one another, Rousseau implicitly assumes that they attribute free will to one another. Free will and consciousness of free will provide a point outside physical nature that allows men to develop the *amour propre* that sets them against that nature and one another. This dualist understanding of *amour propre*, implicit in the *Discourse*, Rousseau makes explicit elsewhere.[53] However central perfectibility is to Rousseau's anthropology, he does not for all that simply discard the free will argument. Free will is not totally eclipsed by perfectibility. The free will argument stands behind Rousseau's perfectibility-based account of man's development and peeks around the corners. Perfectibility is the scientifically acceptable face of man's freedom from nature's command.

But what of Rousseau's contention that man's road to full humanity is triggered by external circumstances that might never have happened? With this assertion, after all, he is distancing himself from the teleological view that human nature has a goal or end that gradually unfolds. Rousseau's position that the unfolding of human nature is unnecessary and that the development of the faculties is contingent appears more compatible with a modern scientific understanding of nature as governed by necessity and chance and as characterized by the workings of material processes of cause and effect. But, as we argue in the next chapter, if Rousseau stresses the contingency of the faculties' development, it is because this supports his opinion of the natural goodness of man rather than to indicate that he thinks man is merely the product of a history triggered and determined by blind chance, a being explicable wholly in materialist terms. This is not to deny that Rousseau's account of the historicization of human nature is one of the major accomplishments of the *Second Discourse*. But his method of 'stripping man's nature bare,' his very radicalization of the historical approach, reveals its limitations and so points beyond it and back to a view of man as a being possessed of the free will that affords him the potential for moral freedom. But before we examine these arguments we need to further explain our position that free will and perfectibility are both forms of man's relative independence of instinct.

Interpreting Natural Man's Independence from Instinct

First of all, what evidence do we have to support our assertion that free will and perfectibility are different interpretations of man's absence of instinct? There are three key passages in which Rousseau discusses the matter. We have already examined the first passage, in which Rousseau argues that man's freedom to choose whether to resist instinct reveals the spirituality of his soul. Rousseau also describes natural man's independence from instinct in an earlier passage in the *Discourse*. There he explains that natural men may lack instinct and that one way men compensate for this possible lack is by imitating the instinct of all the animals they observe:

> Men, dispersed among the animals, observe and imitate their industry, and thereby develop in themselves the instinct of the beasts; with the advantage that whereas each species has only its own proper instinct, man – perhaps having none that belongs to him – appropriates them all to himself, feeds himself equally well with most of the diverse foods which the other animals share, and consequently finds his subsistence more easily than any of them can. (Masters, 105–6)

Man's relative lack of instinct shows an independence of it and, as it were by default, an ability to choose for himself.[54] At first glance this description of man's mere lack of instinct may not appear to resemble any power to choose through spontaneous acts of will. But when Rousseau writes that natural man 'imitates' and 'appropriates' the instinct of the beasts, he is describing the kind of active initiative that can characterize the power of free will. Moreover, as we have seen, Rousseau in his introduction of the idea of free will makes a similar argument that while a starving pigeon or cat is unable to deviate from instinct and eat whatever is available, man is able to escape the grasp of such instinctual drives.[55] He presents this argument as proof that man can resist instinct through free will. Nonetheless, since at this stage his faculties achieve the same ends as instinct does for the animals, natural man would resemble one animal among others to most observers, as Rousseau argues in footnote 10(J).

The third passage occurs immediately after his introduction of free will and perfectibility. It is one of the most important in the *Discourse:*

> Savage man, by nature committed to instinct alone, or rather compensated for the instinct he perhaps lacks by faculties capable of substituting for it at first, and then of raising him far above nature, will therefore begin with purely animal functions. (J) To perceive and feel will be his first state, which he will have in common with all animals. To will and not will, to desire and fear will be the first and almost the only operations of his soul until new circumstances cause new developments in it. (*OC* 3:142–3; Masters, 115)

This paragraph is subject to widely disparate interpretations. At first sight, it seems to pose some significant obstacles to our main argument. For one thing, it appears to make it more difficult to argue that perfectibility stands in for the more controversial idea of free will in the subsequent argument of the *Discourse*. This is because Rousseau states in the final line of this paragraph that the development of perfectibility is caused by 'new circumstances.' If perfectibility merely responds to the effect of external causes, then it does not appear to resemble the spontaneous, self-determining causality that free will requires. Moreover, Rousseau tells us that savage man begins 'with purely animal functions.'[56] Does this description of savage man's functions as 'purely animal' undermine the significance of the distinctions between man and animal that Rousseau has just established? If man is a 'mixed being,'[57] how can his functions be 'purely animal'? And while Rousseau suggests that at the outset savage man can will and not will, he may be referring simply to animal wants and aversions, which he argues operate mechanistically. Finally, any mention of the consciousness of freedom he extolled a few paragraphs before is entirely absent.[58]

These objections appear daunting until one considers an alternative reading of the paragraph in question. Clearly, it must be conceded that in this passage Rousseau is stressing the distance that savage man has to travel between animality and humanity. But his argument assumes that these dramatic changes are possible only because savage men have latent faculties that replace instinct at the outset and that later raise them above nature. In this sense, through its very emphasis on the simplicity of savage man's operations, the passage underlines the distinctiveness of the latent faculties that will raise him above nature. But how do we know that these faculties are latent? A number of times in the *Discourse* and in *Emile*, Rousseau refers both to men's 'latent faculties' (*facultés virtuelles*) and to the faculties men were given 'in potential.'[59] Moreover, in footnote 10(J), which is appended to this very paragraph – in fact, to his statement that savage man begins with 'purely animal functions' – Rousseau suggests that man's ability to develop his '*facultés virtuelles*' or latent faculties is the indicator of his humanity. There, he writes that some beings whom travellers mistake for beasts might instead 'true savage men whose race, dispersed in the woods in ancient times had not had an opportunity to develop any of its potential faculties [*facultés virtuelles*], had not acquired any degree of perfection and was still found in the primitive state of nature' (204; *OC* 3:208). While to most observers these animals appear to be merely a species of non-human primate, Rousseau wonders whether they are not 'true savage men' because they may be distinguished by their ability to develop their potential faculties. Their faculties are not fully exercised or fully developed,[60] so at this stage to all appearances they act like the other animals. It is in this sense that he suggests that savage man begins 'with purely animal functions.' Savage man's latent powers are not yet fully operative. But his ability to develop them sets him apart.[61] Although he begins with purely animal functions, he does not begin with purely animal faculties. And later on he develops these faculties in such a way that his functions themselves become uniquely human.

This picture of a savage man who begins with purely animal functions follows consistently from Rousseau's initial description of natural man in the *Discourse* as a robust and independent animal who thrives alongside the other animals in the state of nature. This is important because at this stage of the argument, Rousseau needs to reconcile this description of natural man from the physical point of view with his introduction of free will and perfectibility as markers of natural man's moral and metaphysical side.[62] He does so through his doctrine that savage man is an animal but one that is uniquely able to develop his potential faculties. Man's ability to bring his latent faculties to fruition is at the heart of what Rousseau understands by perfectibility.[63]

Given this reading of perfectibility as a natural faculty that develops man's latent faculties, it seems likely that savage man has a rudimentary physical ability to will and not will that later develops into free will.[64] This is a conjecture, but it is supported by evidence in both the *Discourse* and *Emile*. Later in the *Discourse* Rousseau claims that men receive moral freedom as a gift of nature: '*la liberté étant un don qu'ils tiennent de la Nature en qualité d'hommes*' (*OC* 3:184; Masters, 168). The child described in *Emile* appears to develop free will through experience. There Rousseau contends that a newborn's cries are 'purely mechanical effects, devoid of knowledge and will.' A few pages later he suggests that the child should be prepared 'to do his will, as soon as he has one.'[65] In the next chapter we will present evidence that both the savage man of the *Discourse* and the child in *Emile* develop a consciousness of free will through their interactions with other human beings.

But how can savage man have a physical endowment for a spiritual and immaterial capacity? That is, how can free will be physical and *beyond* the physical at the same time? This is a legitimate objection, but it is by no means unexpected. After all, this is the free will problem: the difficulty of reconciling a conception of spontaneous volition with a physical universe based on cause and effect. Rousseau, of course, is aware of this objection: indeed, it is the most important of the difficulties that surround his claim that men have free will.[66] So he steps gingerly around the issue in the text of the *Second Discourse*.[67] Still, when he indicates that man has freedom as a 'gift of nature,' he provides a minimum basis for the free will argument.

A reading of the text yields another objection to be raised against the argument that savage man has the potential for free will – indeed, arguably a more important objection. Rousseau's description of how perfectibility develops the other faculties and brings man's humanity to fruition reveals it to be a reactive faculty – and, some would say, a passive one – that initiates nothing of itself and that merely responds to the impetus of external circumstances. And if he understands the species characteristic of perfectibility as a passive quality, does it not become harder to argue that he understands free will – which requires an active spontaneity, an ability to begin a new series of events – as the other defining characteristic of man? This question, which touches on the character of Rousseau's overall view of human nature, demands our careful attention. In the next section we therefore examine the meaning and force of the objection that perfectibility is passive and we provide our response to it.

The Malleability of Perfectible Man: Hobbes and Rousseau on Human Nature

If humanity is a product of man's capacities as they are shaped by his environment and his history, how is this compatible with an understanding of man as a being possessed of free will? This objection about the passive malleability of Rousseau's perfectible man is one form of a deeper objection – one that takes us to the heart of Rousseau's understanding of human nature and that draws us to the question of his dependence on Hobbes.

To see the force of the objection that Rousseau's perfectible man is passively shaped by circumstances, we need to examine Rousseau's presentation of the way in which the progress of man's reason is driven by his passions. In his account of man's development, Rousseau essentially agrees with Hobbes that a strong fear or desire will often direct the train of our thoughts. As Hobbes puts it: 'From Desire, ariseth the Thought of some means we have seen produce the like of that which we ayme at; and from the thought of that, the thought of means to that mean; and so continually, till we come to some beginning within our power.'[68] Rousseau both develops and radicalizes this notion when he argues that our passions do not just direct the development of our knowledge; they 'derive ... their progress from our knowledge' (*OC* 3:143; Masters, 116). Our passions shape our ideas; but our ideas also shape our passions. Thus, while our passions may have a natural source in the needs of the body, the progress of our enlightenment complicates and often expands those passions, sometimes turning them into obsessions that dwarf our prosaic natural physical needs.

In Rousseau's view, Hobbes mistakenly imports inflated desires that result from society into his description of man in the state of nature. As he states explicitly a little later in the *Discourse*, Hobbes 'improperly included in savage man's care for his preservation, the need to satisfy a multitude of passions that are the product of society' (Masters, 129; Gourevitch, 151). Hobbes underestimated the extent to which man's passions expand through the development of society, reason, and enlightenment.[69] It follows that a clearer understanding of human nature requires a radical and historical excavation of the origins of humanity. Therefore, Rousseau sees it as his task in the *Discourse* to strip away the artificial desires and fears that both hide human nature and weigh it down. As he tells us in the *Confessions*, in writing the *Discourse on Inequality*, he 'dared to strip man's nature bare.'[70]

It is important to grasp that Rousseau's natural man is less passionate than his Hobbesian counterpart because he is less reasonable. 'Nothing,' writes Rousseau of savage man in footnote 11(K), 'must be so calm as his soul and nothing so limited as his mind.'[71] Rousseau's natural man is a simple being indeed. Minimalist, we would say. Jean-Jacques relentlessly and critically disallows every preconception that our habituation to society may bring to cloud our judgment. Taking Hobbes's premise that men are by nature independent seriously leads Rousseau to the radical conclusion that natural man has no innate ideas, no reason, no language, no morality, no fear of death, no virtue, no vice. For these reasons it does not seem exaggerated to call him prehuman.[72] True, he has a desire for self-preservation and a reluctance to see his fellow beings suffer, but his compassion is neither lofty nor noble. It is less a self-abnegating devotion to others than an identification with others based on self-love.[73] And, as others have pointed out, Rousseau's summation of the version of the golden rule that natural pity inspires is starkly unsentimental: 'do what is good for you with the least possible harm to others.' It is easy to understand why some interpreters have suggested that Rousseau has a lower idea of human nature than does Hobbes.[74] But this reading, if accepted as it stands, casts doubt on our assertion that Rousseau thinks man has a consciousness of free choice that reveals the spirituality of his soul. After all, Hobbes denies the possibility of spiritual free will and purports to explain the universe solely through the workings of 'matter in motion.' Like Locke and Condillac after him, Hobbes holds the empiricist view that all human understanding arises through the influence of sensible impressions on the mind.[75] He is also at pains to discredit the lofty ideals of freedom and virtue, which he believes contribute to discord and render men turbulent.[76] If we read Rousseau as having a lower view of human nature than Hobbes, if we concede that he stresses how society, history, and chance shape human nature more than did his empiricist predecessors, we seem to be confronted with a radically historicist thinker – one who in fact debunks the debunkers of human nature. It appears hard to reconcile this Rousseau with the champion of ennobling virtue based on free decisions of spiritual will that our interpretation implies.

But this difficult task of reconciliation is not for that less necessary. For although the suggestion that Rousseau has a lower view of human nature than Hobbes is not wrong, it is incomplete. In fact, Rousseau has both a lower and a *higher* view of human nature than Hobbes. Compared to Hobbes's man in the state of nature, Rousseau's man is unquestionably more primitive; but he also has the (often thwarted) *potential* for virtue and for justice. Rousseau teaches that man's nobler capacities are often unfulfilled: they are undeveloped in the state of nature and they are sidetracked in the civil state. In the state of nature, man does not misuse his faculties; but this is because he does not yet use them. In civil society, man misuses his faculties but this misuse is poignant precisely insofar as the faculties could instead be turned toward excellence. Humankind, as Rousseau puts it in the *Second Discourse*, works 'only to its shame by the abuse of the faculties that do it honour.'[77]

Perhaps the most striking statement of Rousseau's simultaneous perception of the high and low in human nature appears in Book 1, chapter 8 of the *Social Contract*. There he claims that the passage to the civil state gives man the chance to replace physical inclination with the voice of duty. It involves replacing instinct with justice and giving man's actions 'a morality they previously lacked.' Rousseau then writes:

> Although in this state he deprives himself of several advantages given him by nature, he gains such great ones, his faculties are exercised and developed, his ideas broadened, his feelings ennobled, and his whole soul elevated to such a point that if the abuses of this new condition did not often degrade him beneath the condition he left, he ought ceaselessly to bless the happy moment that tore him away from it forever, and that changed him from a stupid, limited animal into an intelligent being and a man. (trans. Masters, 56; *OC* 3:364)

Man in the civil state is frequently debased: he falls below the stupidity of the state of nature. But this is due to the 'abuses of this new condition.' If instead man could bring his faculties to fruition without demeaning himself, he could make good on his potential for justice and morality. As our subsequent argument will illustrate, humankind's abuse of the 'faculties that do it honour' is the touchstone of our interpretation. Because men possess but misuse free will, they lose natural goodness and set themselves against nature without acquiring virtue. Therefore, while our interpretation does suggest that Rousseau is the champion of ennobling virtue, it equally emphasizes that he is a critic of man's unnatural debasement and unhappiness.

In this chapter we have interpreted Rousseau's perfectibility and free will as different faces of man's independence of instinct. Free will is a power that allows man the choice to depart from instinct, with results that are sometimes admirable and sometimes degrading. Man is perilously free in his choice making and conscious of this freedom. Moreover, freedom of will means that freedom of action cannot legitimately be ceded through contractual slavery. This argument helps Rousseau undermine illegitimate conceptions of the basis of political life. Thus, we have contested the view held by Plattner and others that the teaching of the *Discourse* is based only on the idea of perfectibility – its political argument relies on the idea of free will. We have also presented evidence and arguments that raise significant questions about Plattner's assertion that Rousseau merely *pretends* to believe humans have free will in order to *appear* to believe in immortality. As well, our discussion of Condillac's critique of the idea that humans are the only animals who possess understanding provides a needed context for assessing the meaning of Rousseau's assertion in the *Discourse on Inequality* that understanding is not the human species distinction. We have argued that his notion of consciousness of freedom has an interest that the counter-case has yet to explain. All of this throws Plattner's conclusion that Rousseau does not truly think that humans have free will into serious doubt.

However, some crucial pieces of the puzzle are still missing. We have so far only sketched out some of the broadest and most general contours of our interpretation. In what follows, we consider some radically historicist accounts of man's development and provide our own account of Rousseau's views about the emergence of society and morality. How does man develop into such a complex and often unhappy animal? We need a better understanding of this process and of the role of perfectibility and free will within it. We will argue, in particular, that consciousness of free will helps make us into vain and maladjusted animals.

2 Free Will and Human Development: The Genealogy of Vice

Interpreters of Rousseau have rightly focused their attention on his account of how we develop into fully human beings because doing so helps illuminate his views about human nature. This chapter investigates Rousseau's account of human development and assesses its implications for his view of free will. In the *Discourse on Inequality*, Rousseau states that men's faculties of perfectibility, reason, and social virtues only develop through accidental circumstances and that they need never have developed. This position is the wellspring of several different objections to our argument that Rousseau believes men have free will. In the first section of this chapter, starting from the strongest textual evidence for the accidental development of the faculties, we weigh these objections and provide our own alternative interpretation. We argue that Rousseau's insistence that the faculties develop accidentally is due to his concern for vindicating man's natural goodness and original endowment: man's original nature is not to blame for his decline. Moreover, Rousseau emphasizes that man is not just a victim of his corruption: he is also its agent. In fact, reinterpreting the process of man's development enables us to show the role that free will plays in his system, in the emergence of morality, corruption, and vice. As we show in the second section of the chapter, Rousseau describes a process by which humans begin to see other human beings as independent of natural causation in their decision making. This attribution of free will to others contributes to the development of *amour propre*.

Sceptics might argue that Rousseau seeks merely to perpetuate the illusion that men have free will. In the last section of the chapter, we concede that some his exhortations to self-mastery based on free will do have a rhetorical element, but we suggest these are based on a stronger argument that he does endorse – namely, that the workings of the consciousness of freedom provide evidence that people have free will. Moreover, Rousseau often emphasizes that human beings choose corruption and vice through free will. In the chapter's conclusion we analyse his philosophical reflections about our misuse of free will.

Section 1: 'The Chance Combination of Several Foreign Causes Which Might Never Have Arisen': Interpreting the Contingent Development of the Faculties

At the end of the first part of the *Discourse*, Rousseau writes that he has demonstrated that 'perfectibility, social virtues and the other faculties that natural man had received in potentiality could never develop by themselves, that in order to develop they needed the chance combination of several foreign causes which might never have arisen and without which he would have remained eternally in his primitive condition' (*OC* 3:162; Masters, 140; Cf. *OC* 3:140–3, 152, 165).

Rousseau in this way indicates that nothing about man's endowment for the faculties points to an end or goal that would constitute his natural good or fruition. It would seem that there is nothing about man that points toward the development of civilization, reason, or even society. This is clearly not a traditional teleological account of man's development.[1]

How does this non-teleological conception of human progress constitute an obstacle to our contention that Rousseau thinks men have free will? After all, some arguments for free will depend upon teleology, while others do not. Moreover, while most religious thought is teleological, Rousseau's advocacy of free will may be independent of religious teleology and, indeed, of religion in general.[2] Still, thinking through his position on the accidental, unplanned emergence of the faculties leads to two important types of objections to our thesis. The first relates to Rousseau's view of materialism. His claim that man's development is caused by an accidental series of events depends on a modern scientific understanding of nature as material governed by a combination of necessity and chance.[3] Some interpreters suggest that the fact that Rousseau draws on this materialist form of explanation in describing man's development in the *Discourse* indicates that he sees it as a comprehensive explanation of man's nature.[4] Whether this is the case is one of the central questions at issue in this book.

Another set of objections springs from contemplation of the historicist implications of Rousseau's non-teleological approach to the faculties. His position is historicist or proto-historicist in this respect: if man's development is shaped and defined by environmental circumstances, then the historical account of those circumstances is required for understanding that development. At the end of the previous chapter, we probed one possible objection of this sort, namely, the view that if Rousseau believes that man's nature is changed by a dialectic of reason and passion which is itself shaped by accidental circumstances, then Rousseau appears to have an even more minimalist understanding of man's original nature than Hobbes, as well as a more historicist understanding of man's present nature. This is one possible interpretation of Rousseau's position that man's progress is contingent on and provoked by historical circumstances. A related objection stems from his teaching that society shapes man's nature. According to this view, Rousseau thinks that man is steeped in the wrong social habits, and that these – rather than the dualism of spirit and matter in his soul – account for man's corruption and therefore his wickedness. Later in this section, we contest this view and show that Rousseau emphasizes that men actively contribute to their corruption through their wills. First, however, we turn to another, more radical objection to our case, one that arises from the historicist interpretation of Rousseau. This is the argument that, by appealing to the circumstances that form man's nature, he obviates the appeal to the natural as a standard for conduct.[5] Put another way, man's distinctiveness is conferred by history rather than by nature. Along the way, this discussion will bring us face to face with an important and neglected dimension of Rousseau's thought – his use of the term 'faculties.' Few concepts in the history of philosophy have been as batted about as that of the 'faculties.' Proponents of dualism have sometimes tried to anchor their position on the definition of faculty as a spontaneous cause.[6] We will examine what Rousseau means by the faculties of man.

The Objection That Man Is Historical Rather Than Natural

In *Natural Right and History*, Leo Strauss provides a complex and stimulating account of Rousseau's thought. At one point in that account, Strauss suggests that for Rousseau, 'man's humanity is the product of the historical process.' Moreover, in a particularly important passage, Strauss remarks that given that natural man is premoral and prehuman, 'there is no natural constitution of man to speak of: everything specifically human is acquired or ultimately depends on artifice or convention.'[7] Strauss does not elaborate this view into a comprehensive interpretation of Rousseau, but it has gained a hold over many interpreters. Marc Plattner offers a carefully argued elaboration of Strauss's provocative suggestion that man is a product of history and not nature. Considering Plattner's argument will teach us an enormous amount about Rousseau's understanding of nature and the faculties. Moreover, since Plattner combines a number of the objections outlined above and develops them thoroughly and systematically, examining Plattner's argument will help advance our comprehension of Rousseau's overall position on free will. It is important to test and question a view that has, for some, become the axiomatic starting point of thinking about Rousseau.

Plattner suggests that Rousseau's non-teleological account of the development of perfectibility and the faculties leads to the conclusion that history rather than nature is the key source for comprehending 'man's humanity.' And this new historicist understanding renders any conception of a natural species distinction obsolete:

> If man's humanity is the product of a finite succession of events, rather than of his essential and unchanging nature, the record of those events becomes a decisive source for understanding his humanity. In short, man's humanity is the product of his history. To say that man is the being characterized by perfectibility is to say that man as we know him is the *historical* being. Rousseau in the *Second Discourse* is the first philosopher to indicate that the modern scientific view of man's origin and man's nature must lead to this conclusion. (51, emphasis in the original)

Plattner's argument begins from an examination of Rousseau's use of the term 'faculty.' Plattner accepts the traditional, teleological understanding of the term as something 'intended by nature to perform a certain function' (47). With this teleological definition in mind, he reasons that since Rousseau suggests that the faculties of reason, language, and the social virtues developed by accident and, indeed, might never have developed, they 'cannot properly be considered faculties at all' (47). He then suggests that perfectibility itself cannot be a faculty in the traditional sense. Because it too remains inoperative in the primitive state of nature, it cannot have been intended by nature to develop: 'One is forced to conclude, then, that perfectibility also cannot be understood in terms of the traditional notion of a "faculty," for it does not perform a function that is intended by nature' (48).

Plattner then points out that if perfectibility really was a faculty in the teleological sense, then the emergence of society on the basis of this natural quality would have to be a natural development. He notes that this is exactly the objection made by Charles Bonnet, a contemporary of Rousseau, who published his commentary on the *Second Discourse* under the assumed name of Philopolis in 1755 (*OC* 3:1383–6). Philopolis holds that according to Rousseau, the 'state of society results immediately from the faculties of man' (49). If these faculties are themselves natural, Philopolis reasons, then society, as the result of these faculties, would also have to be natural. To blame society, he adds, is to blame God, who gave us the faculties that have led directly to it. Rousseau drafted a letter of response to Philopolis in which he argued that

> the state of society derives [*découle*] from the nature of the human race, not immediately, as you say, but only, as I have proved, with the aid of certain external [*extérieures*] circumstances that could have occurred or not occurred [*qui pouvoient être ou n'être pas*], or at least happened sooner or later and consequently accelerated or slowed down its progress. (quoted in Plattner, 49–50)

Plattner believes that Rousseau's response to Philopolis confirms that he has a mechanistic rather than a teleological understanding of nature. He argues that Rousseau's account of perfectibility's 'dependence on the chance workings of external causes' only serves as further proof that perfectibility is not a natural faculty in the traditional sense (50). In fact, Plattner argues, Rousseau uses the term 'faculties' rhetorically in order to mask the radical character of his teaching about man's development: 'By speaking of perfectibility, reason and the like as "faculties," Rousseau follows his great predecessor Locke in presenting his new understanding of man "clothed in the ordinary fashion and language of the country"' (50). Plattner concludes that although perfectibility may truly distinguish humans from the animals, nature has not ordained that this be so. For the progress that humanity has made, 'man is not beholden to nature. Man's specific distinction can no longer be understood as a natural distinction. It is one that has emerged over time, due to the chance workings of mechanical causation' (50).[8]

In fact, there is strong evidence in *Emile* that Rousseau does view the faculties as natural powers in man's original disposition. He confirms that nature initially gives man faculties that he does not actually use but that he has in reserve: 'It is thus that nature, which does everything for the best, constituted [man] in the beginning. It gives him with immediacy only the desires necessary to his preservation and the faculties sufficient to satisfy them. It put all the others, as it were, in reserve in the depth of his soul, to be developed there when needed' (*OC* 4:304; trans. Bloom, 80). The faculties concerned with self-preservation are active from the start; the others are latent and are activated 'when needed'; but all are given by nature.[9] And as we will see below, Rousseau also tacitly admits the naturalness of the faculties, including the social virtues, in his *Letter to Philopolis*.

Moreover, directly after Rousseau introduces the faculty of perfectibility in the *Discourse*, he comments that savage man is '*by nature* ... compensated for the instinct he perhaps lacks *by faculties* capable of substituting for it at first, and then of raising him far above nature' (Masters, 115; *OC* 3:142–3; emphasis mine). What faculties does Rousseau have in mind here? Rousseau treads gingerly, not even naming the faculties in question, but since perfectibility, language, reason, and sociality do distance man from nature, this description appears to apply to these faculties[10] and perhaps to free will as well.

We would therefore suggest that perfectibility is an original attribute of man's nature. If this is the case, it cannot be totally assimilated to history without obscuring Rousseau's intention. Perfectibility appears to be a natural disposition or openness of disposition that allows humanity to become historical. Chance causation triggers the emergence of perfectibility, but this faculty did have to be there to be triggered in the first place.[11] The capacity for perfectibility pre-exists its manifestations. It is a substantial physical prerequisite. The pre-existing physical capacity for perfectibility is a stumbling block to the reading of man's distinctiveness in purely historical terms.

Also, the fact that the traditional definition of the faculties is too narrow for Rousseau does not prove that he uses the term rhetorically. Rousseau does not define the term 'faculties,' but he appears to use it in the Lockean sense that it is a 'power of operation.'[12] For Rousseau, a human faculty is natural in the sense that it is an original, internal potential in natural man's disposition. The faculties are not teleological in the sense that nature intends for them to develop, but they are natural powers and history could not take place without them.[13] Rousseau, we would argue, has a plausible but modern conception of the faculties, and this indicates that his view of nature is modern in this important respect.

However, one could concede that perfectibility and the other faculties are natural and still argue that the fact that their development is provoked by contingent accidents is problematic for our case. Next, we consider the interpretation that Rousseau's understanding of humanity's distinctiveness is simply a matter of the 'chance workings of mechanical causation,' and the objections that stem from it.

A Counter-Interpretation of the Contingent Development of the Faculties: Rousseau's Letter to Philopolis

The view that humanity is simply the product of the random occurrences that follow natural necessity is certainly at odds with our contention that man is distinguished by his ability to spontaneously oppose that necessity. But our rereading of the evidence suggests an alternative interpretation. What is required is a very careful look at Rousseau's statements about the reasons for the transition to civil society.

Rousseau's position on this matter is actually very subtle. External circumstances – natural accidents such as volcanoes, earthquakes, and the formation of islands – trigger the formation of human societies. To this extent, the acquisition of humanity is a natural process.[14] Now, largely because of his assertion that man is naturally good as well as his consequent opposition to both Hobbes's pessimistic view of man's nature and the doctrine of original sin, Rousseau is at pains to argue that human society and its corruptions do not emerge directly or immediately out of man's natural endowment. For if the emergence of humanity is triggered by a contingent natural process external to man, one cannot blame man's own natural endowment for the emergence of society and the corruption it entails. But if man's endowment is essentially good, one still needs to explain how wickedness and corruption arise. The explanation that man's development is provoked by exterior circumstances allows Rousseau to maintain his teaching about natural goodness. But it still does not give him adequate grounds for explaining how societal corruption emerges from natural goodness.[15] In fact, man contributes to his corruption through the misuse of his endowment, his faculties. We suggest below that man's participation in his own decline is rooted in his ability to act independently of the determinations of physical nature. In his account of man's development, Rousseau implicitly assumes that men have free will, and he uses this assumption to ground the nature/society distinction that underlies his teaching. Free will provides an Archimedean point outside physical nature.

Rousseau's response to Philopolis[16] provides the context for our interpretation. An examination of the quirky, never-published *Letter to Philopolis* suggests that Rousseau's emphasis on society's mediate development derives from his quarrel with Hobbes and with traditional Christian doctrine regarding the natural goodness of man. Moreover, in the *Letter to Philopolis* Rousseau writes that the development of the faculties and the emergence of society do not spring immediately from nature, not only because both depend on accidental external circumstances but also because many such circumstances depend on the 'will of men.' Here Rousseau's argument is that if the 'will of men' plays a role in man's corruption, this helps vindicate man's natural endowment. His assumption is that the will of men is independent of men's natural endowment.

It has to be conceded, I think, that in stressing that society 'might never have arisen,' Rousseau is marking out his distance from Aristotle's assertion that man is a political animal. But at the same time, he emphasizes that the faculties do not develop immediately, because in so doing he is supporting his own defence of the natural goodness of man. Rousseau wants to distance himself from the doctrine of original sin. In his *Lettre à Beaumont*, he complains that 'original sin explains everything except its principle, and it is this principle that it is a question of explaining.'[17] But he also wants to rebut Hobbes's assertion that men are so naturally selfish and warlike that they should relinquish the anarchy of the state of nature for the security provided by an absolute monarch. 'Above all,' he writes in the *Second Discourse*, 'let us not conclude with Hobbes that because [natural] man has no idea of goodness he is naturally evil' (Masters, 128; *OC* 3:153). The motive to contest both the doctrine of original sin and Hobbes's conception of human nature infuses Rousseau's own presentation of the emergence of man's distinctiveness.[18] Rousseau's assertion about the natural goodness of man informs his insistence, in the *Discourse,* that the development of the faculties is contingent.

That Rousseau stresses the extent to which human nature is shaped by history is beyond dispute. What *is* in question is Rousseau's own judgment about this argument for historicization. Rousseau does not insist that the faculties might never have developed in order to show that history *alone* makes up man's humanity or to indicate that he is convinced by a comprehensively materialist understanding of the universe.[19] In stressing that man's humanity *may* have been accidental, he is revealing his distance from traditional teleology, but he is also motivated by the desire to exonerate nature as a standard for judging the health of contemporary societies and to show that the corruption of man's nature is amenable to human control. We can fully grasp his position on the faculties only by keeping in mind his description of his 'great principle' that 'nature made man happy and good but society depraves him and makes him miserable' (*Dialogues*, *OC* 1:934).

A closer reading of the *Letter to Philopolis* will make this clearer. There Rousseau reiterates his argument from the *Discourse* that our decadent societies transgress the proper order of nature. Rousseau begins his response by restating Philopolis' own key objection more cogently than Philopolis was able to do: 'The state of society, you tell me, results immediately from the faculties of man and consequently from his nature. To wish that man had never become sociable would therefore be to wish that he were not man and it is attacking the work of God to protest against human society.' Philopolis' objection raises the important question of how the distinction between nature and convention can be drawn. Rousseau responds by means of an extensive comparison between the senility of the individual in old age and the decadence of enlightened society. Rousseau supposes a hypothetical situation in which scientists have discovered how individuals can accelerate the aging process and the *philosophes* encourage them to do just that. He compares this ability to our own ability to resist or slow down our corruption as a species:

> Since you claim to attack me with my own system, I urge you not to forget that according to me society is natural to the human species just as decrepitude is to the individual, and that arts, Laws, and Governments are as necessary for Peoples as are canes for the elderly. The entire difference is that the state of old age is derived from the nature of man alone, and that of society is derived from the nature of the human race, not immediately as you say but only, as I have proved, with the help of certain external circumstances that may or may not happen, or at least occur sooner or later and consequently speed up or slow down the progress. Since several of these circumstances are dependent on the will of men, to establish a perfect comparison I was obliged to assume that the individual has the power to speed up his old age just as the species has the power to delay its own. The state of society having a terminal point, then, which men are the masters of reaching sooner or later, it is not useless to show them the danger of moving so fast, and the miseries of a condition they take to be the perfection of the species.[20]

Here Rousseau is asserting that society arises not from human nature directly but rather through the action of 'certain external circumstances.' As in the *Second Discourse*, he contends that men's capacities for sociality are triggered or activated by exterior forces. But here Rousseau qualifies his assertion in the *Discourse* that the external causes that push man towards social development 'might never have arisen' (Masters, 140). Here the external circumstances 'may or may not happen, or at least occur sooner or later.' With the qualifier that the circumstances could 'at least have happened sooner or later,' he concedes to Philopolis that society may have been an inevitability rather than a mere possibility.[21]

It is interesting that Rousseau concedes that society *could* be natural in the sense of arising inevitably on the basis of man's nature. It is more important to our case, however, that he says men can use their wills to control several of the external factors that accelerate its progress. 'Several of these circumstances,' he writes, 'are dependent on the will of men.' Men are the masters of slowing down their progress or of forcing themselves more rapidly into decadent society. Man's natural endowment does not lead him directly into society. That route depends both on factors external to his nature and on his own misguided decisions and actions.[22]

In fact, it is Rousseau's emphasis on man's role in his own decline that accounts for the quirkiness of his image of individuals who seek to accelerate their own aging. The aging of individuals normally follows a natural course; but the decadence of society depends not only on the chance workings of nature but also on human intervention. Therefore Rousseau says that in order to set up a precise comparison, he was *obliged* to assume that individuals could speed up their own aging, just as humankind can accelerate or slow down its decline. He strengthens his claim about the extent of human responsibility for man's decline in the sentence directly following this paragraph, where he maintains that the 'list of ills burdening men' are 'their own work.'[23]

While Rousseau admits that society *could* be natural, he describes this as a corrupt form of nature – that is, society is corrupt in the sense of being a *decayed* form of nature. His description of civil society as decrepit assumes a standard of healthy and flourishing nature. When he wrote the *Second Discourse,* Rousseau already had in mind this conception of uncorrupted nature as a standard for judging the health of contemporary societies. In fact, it is in the *Second Discourse* that he first presents this comparison between the aging of the individual and the decline of the species. In introducing the First Part, he describes his attempt to read the history of man 'in nature': 'It is, so to speak, the life of your species that I am going to describe to you according to the qualities you received, which your education and habits have been able to corrupt but have not been able to destroy. There is, I feel, an age at which the individual man would want to stop: you will seek the age at which you would desire your species had stopped.' The species once approximated the the ideal of uncorrupted nature.[24]

Note that Rousseau is suggesting in this passage that 'education and habits' corrupt man's natural capacities. Natural catastrophes such as volcanic eruptions and earthquakes may contribute to the emergence of man's sociality and thus to his misery, but here, human education and habits are identified as agents of man's degeneration. Man's contribution to his own decline is a key theme of the *Second Discourse.* In Note 9(I), Rousseau writes that 'man hardly has any evils other than those he had given himself and nature ... [is] justified.'[25]

So far in this chapter I have argued that Rousseau emphasizes the accidents that provoke man's development not to prove that man is a passive, material being but in order to show that man is not by nature warlike or sinful. Man's corruption is not due to his primitive nature. Instead, accidents provoke a dysfunctional process whereby his primitive nature is made the instrument of his twisted will. In the next section we will make the case that Rousseau sees this will as a free will.

But before we do so, we should consider an objection related to the idea that habit and education corrupt man's nature. This is the argument that Rousseau's teaching about natural goodness implies that men are the victims of society, the playthings of a misguided social order rather than agents who bring their misfortunes on themselves through the free use of their wills. According to this objection, whereas biblical teaching suggested that the prideful abuse of free will leads to men's corruption, Rousseau's teaching on natural goodness suggests that fundamentally innocent men fall prey to social forces and to the emergent contradictions between these social forces and their own nature. This may imply that social habits and institutions not only shape man's nature but also determine their choices. 'They are good,' as one interpreter puts it, 'precisely because they are not free.'[26]

One passage in the *Lettre à Beaumont* could buttress this argument that man's natural goodness implies his determination by social forces. In a description of the development of his ideas, Rousseau writes that once he noticed the extent of men's hypocrisy, he needed to search for the cause:

> I found it in the social order, which, on every point contrary to nature, which nothing destroys, incessantly tyrannizes nature and incessantly makes it reclaim its rights. I followed this contradiction in its consequences, and I saw that it alone explained [*elle expliquoit seule*] all the vices of men and all the evils [*maux*] of society. From which I concluded that it was not necessary to suppose man bad [*méchant*] by nature, when one could trace out the origin and progress of his badness. (*OC* 4:966–7)[27]

Here Rousseau is exculpating man's nature and is placing the blame for men's problems instead on the social order which contradicts nature. Some may interpret this to mean it is the contradiction between society and nature instead of free will that sets man off the track. But as we will see, elsewhere in the *Lettre à Beaumont*, Rousseau gives an account of the 'genealogy of vice' based on a dualistic understanding of *amour propre* and man's emergent self-consciousness.[28] Moreover, while free will is not named in the explanation quoted above, neither is it excluded. (All that is excluded is the supposition that 'man is bad by nature.') Rousseau leaves open the possibility that men contribute through their free will to creating the social order that tyrannizes nature and engenders vice. In the next section, we build the case that man's free will in fact forms a part of his account of the 'origin and progress of his badness.' There we suggest that it is because of Rousseau's teaching about natural goodness – in other words, because of his assertion that man is not 'bad by nature' – that he has recourse to the idea of man's acquisition and misuse of free will, of a will that is free from the determinations of physical nature, to account for the emergence of unnatural vice. Man, in a sense, is bad *because* free.

But Rousseau's teaching differs from the Christian teaching about original sin, and not only in denying that man is bad by nature and in providing an account of the origin of his badness. There is another important difference: according to Rousseau, man does not rebel against God – instead, man attacks nature and, importantly for our purposes, thereby attacks himself. With a sensitivity rivalled only perhaps by Dostoyevsky, Rousseau observes how men are self-destructive, self-abasing, and self-lacerating. Evil and corruption are self-inflicted wounds. Man becomes his own victim.[29]

We by no means want to deny, then, that Rousseau wants to say that men's social habits and structures acquire a rigidity that makes them difficult to resist or oppose.[30] Men's institutions, he suggests, constrain their freedom of thought and in that sense limit their freedom of will.

But there is no need to conclude from this that he thinks their freedom of will is completely determined. If Rousseau stresses that man is a victim of his agency, he is also stresses that he is an agent of his victimization.[31] And it is because man is an agent of his victimization that he has the capacity to resist and avoid some of his miseries.

This is Rousseau's argument in an important passage of his *Lettre à Voltaire* of 18 August 1756. There he responds to Voltaire's characterization of the *Second Discourse* as a 'book against the human race.' Rousseau replies that he 'pleaded the cause of the human race against itself.' He defends his depiction of man's misery in the *Discourse* in this revealing passage:

> My goal was excusable and even praiseworthy, I believe, because I showed men how they made their miseries [*malheurs*] themselves, and as a consequence how they could avoid them.
>
> I do not know how one can look for the source of moral evil [*mal morale*] elsewhere than in free, perfected and thereby corrupted man.[32]

In this description of his purpose in the *Discourse*, making no mention of an accidentally provoked chain of circumstances, Rousseau argues that because men cause their own troubles, they may be able to avert them. He reasons that by showing how men themselves establish and shape the habits, opinions, and institutions that subject them, he can reveal how the energy and effort it takes to make them miserable could be better directed.[33]

Note too that in this passage, Rousseau is arguing that corruption and moral evil are due to both freedom and perfectibility: he presents these qualities as complementary rather than as mutually exclusive components of the explanation. But does he mean to imply by this that man's decline is based on his use of undeterministic free will?[34] I suggest he does. To see why, we need to consider the ways in which he responds to Philopolis' concerns about the dividing line between nature and artifice. This is the starting point of the next section of our argument.

Section 2: The Role of Free Will in the Development of *Amour Propre*: The Genealogy of Vice

Free Will as a Lever of History

As we have seen, Rousseau's argument in the *Letter to Philopolis* vindicates the goodness of man's natural endowment. It would allow him to say with Brecht that 'no man is born a butcher.'[35] But this response provokes the following question: If perfectibility is natural, as Rousseau contends, how can the line between nature and convention be drawn? Philopolis posed the question this way: If our misfortunes arise from something within us – from our faculties, which are rooted in human nature – how much sense does it make to say that their development is artificial or unnatural and to criticize it as such? Rousseau's first-line response is that the development of the faculties is not immediately natural – their development depends on the action of external circumstances. But although these circumstances are external to human nature, they nonetheless appear to be events in the *natural* world, such as the volcanoes and earthquakes Rousseau mentions in the *Discourse* itself. Now, if the potential endowment for humanity is natural and if the external circumstances that trigger the emergence of perfectibility are natural, and if this explanation is seen to be complete and sufficient, then the development of the faculties and the emergence of society must be natural as well. And if society is natural, why decry it as artificial? Rousseau needs a workable distinction between what is natural and what is not natural to man in order to criticize society as unnatural.

Rousseau is well aware of the difficulty of distinguishing the natural from the artificial. As we noted in the introduction, he writes in the Preface to the *Discourse* that 'it is no light undertaking to separate what is original from what is artificial in the present nature of man' (*OC* 3:123; Masters, 92–3).[36] In fact, it is this undertaking that requires the thought experiment of imagining men in their original state. Rousseau's state of nature consists of conjectures about the condition of men before they acquired 'diverse qualities good or bad not inherent in their Nature' (*OC* 3:123, Masters, 92).[37] Rousseau clearly elucidates the obstacles to achieving such knowledge, but at the same time he insists on its fundamental importance. It is not easy, he writes, 'to know correctly a state which no longer exists, which perhaps never existed, which probably will never exist, and about which it is nevertheless necessary to have precise notions in order to judge our present state correctly' (*OC* 3:123; Masters, 93).[38]

Nature and Convention in Emile

Clearly, then, Rousseau needs to be able to distinguish between nature and convention. He addresses the issue in various ways in *Emile*. His first formulation of the problem occurs early in Book 1. There he introduces an intriguing metaphor in order to distinguish between nature and habit:

> Nature, we are told, is only habit. What does that mean? Are there not habits contracted only by force which never do stifle nature? Such, for example, is the habit of the plants whose vertical direction is interfered with. The plant, set free, keeps the inclination it was forced to take. But the sap has not as a result changed its original direction; and if the plant continues to grow, its new growth resumes the vertical direction. The case is the same for men's inclinations. So long as one remains in the same condition, the inclinations which result from habit and are the least natural to us can be kept; but as soon as the situation changes, habit ceases and the natural returns. (*OC* 4:247–8; trans. Bloom, 39)

We can see how nature and habit are distinct by looking at the force involved in the repression of nature. Remove the constraint and the natural inclinations re-emerge.[39] The natural returns.

Rousseau's metaphor is elegant and even moving, but as far as establishing a tenable distinction between nature and society is concerned, it only takes him so far. To see this, one needs to ask: What is habit based upon? Are the forceful habits that distort nature based on something truly distinct from it? If habit emerges from perfectibility – which is to say, if habit emerges from our natural capacities and powers when they are triggered by natural circumstances – then habit itself appears to be entirely natural. And if habit itself is natural, the distinction between nature and habit disappears. If perfectibility is understood as a natural faculty that is wholly explicable in terms of a materialist conception of the natural world, it is not clear how it could take us out of nature. Perfectibility, on this reading, is the direction of our natural inclination, which is provoked by natural accidents. It appears too natural, so to speak, to ground a tenable distinction between nature and convention.

Therefore, Rousseau appears to need recourse to free will in order to respond to Philopolis' objection. Only free will is sufficiently separate from material nature to ground the argument that man's nature is corrupted through artifice. Only free will provides an Archimedean point that is outside physical nature.[40] As we have seen, Rousseau in his reply to Philopolis says that the process of sociality is not immediately natural – it is a natural process *that has been accelerated* by external circumstances, 'many of which depend upon the will of men.' Rousseau is not suggesting that perfectibility and the social virtues are outside nature – and neither are the physical accidents that contribute to this development (unless they are the work of a highly interventionist God). If anything here is outside of nature, it would seem to be the 'will of men.'[41] This interpretation provides us with a role for free will in the argument of the *Discourse*. If Rousseau requires this point outside nature and if only undeterministic free will fits the bill, his teaching on perfectibility does not render superfluous undeterministic free will.

Free Will and the Development of Amour Propre

If perfectibility is too natural – which is to say, too inextricably tied to the material order of nature – to explain how man sets himself against nature, Rousseau must rely on something else to do so. In what follows I suggest that that something is his will outside nature, his undeterministic free will, and his consciousness that human beings as a species are free in this sense. Rousseau's description of man's distancing from nature begins from the premise that the passions develop in an unnatural direction; his psychology in the *Discourse on Inequality* is based on his idea that the natural desire for self-preservation, the primitive self-love he calls *amour de soi*, is transformed into *amour propre*, that self-conscious form of self-love that is the source of vanity, envy, pride, resentment, and ambition. *Amour de soi* is a healthy, natural passion whereas *amour propre* is a factitious sentiment that leads to human corruption and to both morality and immorality.[42] In his account of the emergence of *amour propre*, Rousseau relies on the notion of men's consciousness of free will to explain how man spirals out of nature. In this way, free will allows Rousseau to account for the development of *amour propre*.

By our interpretation, Rousseau is suggesting that the act of attributing a will that is independent of natural causation to other human beings marks an important moment in the development of *amour propre*. This argument is only implicit in the *Second Discourse*, but Rousseau provides a more detailed and explicit account in *Emile*. For that reason, we now turn to *Emile*.

Free Will and the Development of Amour Propre *in* Emile

Rousseau's method in *Emile* is to keep his imagined pupil, Emile, on the 'path of nature' (*OC* 4:290; trans. Bloom, 68). In Books I and II, he sets out his premise that a child should be taught to resign himself to nature's ways, to accept and submit to the rule of natural necessity. He should not, however, see himself as subject to the rule of other people's wills: 'As long as children find resistance only in things and never in wills, they will become neither rebellious nor irascible and will preserve their health better' (*OC* 4:287; trans. Bloom, 66). Rousseau wants his pupil to depend on the forces of natural necessity rather than on the judgments of men: 'Dependence on men, since it is without order, engenders all the vices, and by it, master and slave are mutually corrupted' (*OC* 4:311; trans. Bloom, 85). Rousseau says that by instructing Emile in the 'laws of the possible and impossible alone,' he is using the 'method of well-regulated freedom' (*OC* 4:321; trans. Bloom, 92).

Rousseau makes it clear at the outset that a newborn infant would not have active free will: 'We are born capable of learning, but able to do nothing, knowing nothing. The soul, enchained in imperfect and half-formed organs, does not even have the sentiment of its own existence. The movements and cries of the child who has just been born are purely mechanical effects, devoid of knowledge and will' (*OC* 4:279–80, trans. Bloom, 61).[43]

Soon enough, however, the child begins to develop a form of will.[44] Rousseau suggests that if a child reaches out his arm to try to touch a faraway object, one should carry him around so that he can learn to judge distances. But as soon as he is able to estimate these distances, he must instead be 'carried as you please and not as he pleases, for as soon as he is no longer abused by sense, the cause of his effort changes. This change is remarkable and requires explanation' (*OC* 4:285; trans. Bloom, 64). Rousseau explains that when babies begin to respond to their perceptions about the intentions that adults have towards them, they often begin to act out of caprice rather than out of need. The problem is that the child can develop unhealthy types of will in response to his perceptions about the wills of others towards him.

Rousseau considers two kinds of unhealthy will that can result. If the adults surrounding a child are angry and vindictive in their behaviour towards him, the child becomes angry, unmanageable, rebellious: his will is irascible. But if the adults around him are excessively obliging, overindulgent, and servile, the child becomes imperious: he acquires a will to command.[45]

Let us look at the two cases that produce these unhealthy wills more closely. In response to angry or malicious treatment by adults, the child becomes rebellious. By way of explanation, Rousseau tells the story of the time he saw a nurse hit the baby in her care:

> All the signs of the resentment, fury and despair of his age were in his accents. I feared he would expire in this agitation. If I had doubted that the

> sentiment of the just and the unjust were innate in the heart of man, this example alone would have convinced me. I am sure that a live ember fallen by chance on this child's hand would have made less of an impression than this blow, rather light but given in the manifest intention of offending him. (*OC* 4:286-287; trans. Bloom, 66)

Rousseau's example may appear trivial at first, but it is informative about how he thinks about changes in our perceptions of will. Rousseau notes that the baby is infuriated because he believes that the nurse intended to offend him. The baby thinks the nurse wanted to offend him, and this angers him more than the accidental natural causality of a falling ember would. This is because while the ember's fall is merely a natural random occurrence, the baby thinks that his nurse's will or intention to offend him is not. Without overreading, we can say that the baby has an inkling or impression that the nurse acted on her intention to offend him and might have chosen not to do so; the baby must have some sense that in her attempt to offend him she was forced neither by necessity nor by chance causation. Of course, we are not suggesting that Rousseau is arguing that babies are able to deduce that adults have non-material souls which provoke spontaneous choices or that they work out the existence of two substances. It is not that they engage in metaphysical reasoning. Instead, Rousseau is simply positing that on some level, the baby perceives the phenomenon of an intention enacted free from determination by necessity or chance (a phenomenon that philosophers have used complex and sophisticated ideas inaccessible to babies to try to explain). The baby simply notices the bare phenomena of the nurse's wilful intention to irk him and therefore reacts with feelings of 'resentment, fury and despair.'

Here one might also object that the baby's impression that the nurse acted free from determination by chance is an illusion and that Rousseau intends to show the careful reader that it is. But note that Rousseau is not suggesting that the baby is wrong to think that the nurse's will is free. And he infers that what makes the nurse's action amenable to the charge of injustice is that it emanates from her own free intention rather than the determined order of natural causality.[46] The child's attribution to other human beings of an intention or will that appears free of natural necessity and chance is an important moment in the development of morality, insofar as it begins the attribution of justice and injustice to others.[47] But this knowledge is not ennobling in the first instance. On the contrary, it is problematic: it sets the child on a collision course with others.

Rousseau also considers the child who is surrounded by servile and subservient adults. Here, the child's will becomes imperious; he attempts to bend the adults around him to his power:

> The first tears of childhood are prayers. If one is not careful, they soon become orders. Children begin by getting themselves assisted; they end by getting themselves served. Thus, from their own weakness, which is in the first place the source of the feeling of their dependence, is subsequently born the idea of empire and domination. But since this idea is excited less by their needs than by our services, at this point moral effects whose immediate cause is not in nature begin to make their appearance; and one sees already why it is important from the earliest age to disentangle the secret intention which dictates the gesture or the cry. (*OC* 4:287; trans. Bloom, 66)[48]

The immediate cause of this will to dominate is 'not in nature.' We take this to mean that the underlying cause, the actual need that allows the process, is in nature; but that the immediate cause, provoked by our services, is not natural. How does this happen? What is it about our services that turns a natural need into an unnatural vice?[49] This is partly a question and partly an aporia. But again, it appears that the departure from nature occurs as the child attributes a will independent of natural causation, a free will, to other people.

For a more detailed picture of how we are transformed by our perception that other humans freely will in our favour or disfavour, and how, as a result, we leave the path of nature, we must carefully consider the first pages of Book IV of *Emile*.

Free Will and the Development of Amour Propre *in* Emile, *Book IV*

Rousseau's clearest and most comprehensive description of how there arises an unnatural dimension to the passions is found in his discussion of *amour propre* at the beginning of Book IV of *Emile*. This passage also begins his best and most complete response to the objections of Philopolis. It begins as follows:

> Our passions are the principal instruments of our preservation. It is, therefore, an enterprise as vain as it is ridiculous to want to destroy them – it is to control nature, it is to reform the work of God. If God were to tell men to annihilate the passions which He gives him, God would will and not will;

He would contradict Himself. Never did he give this senseless order. (*OC* 4:490–1; trans. Bloom, 212)

This is a response that turns Philopolis' Christian orthodoxy on its head. (Rouseau wrote of Philopolis in the *Confessions* that 'though a materialist, he is of a most intolerant orthodoxy wherever I am concerned.')[50] Notice, first of all, that the form of the argument recalls and perhaps imitates Philopolis' objection that to condemn society is to complain of the exercise of man's natural endowment from God. Rousseau's own paraphrase of Philopolis' argument against him was that to decry the emergence of society based on the exercise of man's natural faculties would be 'attacking the work of God.' Here in *Emile*, he makes a similar point: he concedes, as it were, that to try to annihilate man's natural endowment is 'to reform the work of God.' But that said, Rousseau shifts the emphasis of his argument away from that of the never-published *Letter to Philopolis*. For here he explicitly defends man's endowment – not of the faculties, though, but of the passions. Man has a disposition for certain natural passions; it is only the unnatural development of these passions, he argues, that is problematic or blameworthy. In this way, Rousseau exculpates man's natural passions as an endowment of God and effectively turns Philopolis' position on its head. By focusing on the passions, he turns the argument for respecting man's natural endowment from God into a deft critique of a misguided Christian asceticism that simply tries to destroy natural desires.

Rousseau's reasoning in *Emile*, while it starts unequivocally from the passions, nevertheless clearly retains the fundamental line of argument he developed in response to Philopolis. He restates, even as he recasts, his basic position that exterior causes alter the endowment of nature:

Would it be reasoning well to conclude, from the fact that it is in man's nature to have passions, that all the passions that we feel in ourselves and see in others are natural? Their source is natural, it is true. But countless alien streams have swollen it. It is a great river which constantly grows and in which one could hardly find a few drops of its first waters. Our natural passions are very limited. They are the instruments of our freedom; they tend to preserve us. All those which subject us and destroy us come from elsewhere. Nature does not give them to us. We appropriate them to the detriment of nature. (*OC* 4:491; trans. Bloom, 212).

Man, then, has a natural disposition for some passions to which are added unnatural elements, alien streams that both cloud and alter his original nature. Rousseau's image here is neither of thwarting nature's growth (as in the image of the plants prevented from growing in a vertical direction) nor of accelerating its decay (as in the image of drugs used to provoke a society's senility) – rather, it is an image of pollution. The term may seem exaggerated; after all, streams are usually part of the physical order of nature. But Rousseau stresses that these alien streams are *not* natural: they 'come from elsewhere. Nature does not give them to us.' He further explains how man acquires these alien dimensions to his natural desires when he describes the transformation of *amour de soi* into *amour propre* in the next section of his argument:

> The source of our passions, the origin and principle of all the others, the only one born with man and which never leaves him so long as he lives is self-love [*amour de soi*] – a primitive, innate passion, which is anterior to every other, and of which all the others are in a sense only modifications. In this sense, if you wish, all passions are natural. But most of these modifications have alien causes without which they would never have come to pass; and these same modifications, far from being advantageous for us, are harmful. They alter the primary goal and are at odds with their own principle. It is then that man finds himself outside of nature and sets himself in contradiction with himself. (*OC* 4:491; trans. Bloom, 213)

The natural, innate impulsion of *amour de soi* inclines men to watch over their own self-preservation. But it is altered by inflated desires that set men against nature and even against their own natural impulsion or instinct for self-preservation. This conception helps explain the actions of the dissolute men Rousseau describes in the *Second Discourse*. Unlike the other beasts, men can resist the impulsion of nature and choose their course of behaviour by an act of freedom. The dissolute men illustrate this independence of instinct. They bring fever and death upon themselves because 'the mind depraves the senses and the will still speaks when nature is silent.'

Note too that here Rousseau is reiterating his position, set out in the *Second Discourse* and the *Letter to Philopolis*, that both external circumstances and man's bad decisions contribute to this development: 'man finds himself outside of nature and sets himself in contradiction with himself.' But how precisely does man go off the track? A few lines later, Rousseau indicates that man departs from the rule of instinct when he attributes free will to others:

> We have to love ourselves to preserve ourselves; and it follows immediately from the same sentiment that we love what preserves us. Every child is attached to his nurse. Romulus must have been attached to the wolf that suckled him. At first this attachment is purely mechanical. What fosters the well-being of an individual attracts him; what harms him repels him. This is merely a blind instinct. What transforms this instinct into sentiment, attachment into love, aversion into hate, is the intention manifested [*manifesté*] to harm us or to be useful to us. One is never passionate about insensible beings which merely follow the impulsion given to them. But those from whom one expects good or ill by their inner disposition, by their will – those we see acting freely for us or against us – inspire in us sentiments similar to those they manifest toward us. We seek what serves us, but we love what wants to serve us. We flee what harms us, but we hate what wants to harm us. (*OC* 4:492; trans. Bloom, 213)

Here Rousseau is describing how the instinctual passion of *amour de soi* – a 'blind instinct' that is 'purely mechanical' – is transformed into a different kind of sentiment, into *amour propre*, which is no longer simply instinctual or purely mechanical. What accounts for this transformation? It is the recognition or perception that others manifest an intention to act freely in our favour or disfavour. Once we come to believe that other people's actions and attitudes are not based on a mere 'impulsion given to them' but on their free will,[51] our own self-love undergoes a radical transformation. *Amour de soi*, the simple desire for bodily self-preservation, changes into a passion that is focused on our perceptions about the character of other people's intentions towards us. Our self-love is refracted, or 'doubled,' as Allan Bloom has put it.[52]

The attribution of free intention to others is the catalyst for this process. When we become conscious that others freely will our good or our harm, we begin to desire that they have certain kinds of intentions towards us. This new self-love, this *amour propre*, is animated by desires about desires. But in the first instance, it is not animated by the desires about one's own desires of which Harry Frankfurt writes.[53] Instead, it is animated by desires about the desires of others. Rousseau's account reveals the way in which *amour propre* often issues in the desire to shape the character of the intentions of others towards us, for example, in the wish that they would respect us, or that they would freely love us.

In terms that recall his treatment in Book I, here again Rousseau describes this development of *amour propre* and the attribution of will to others through the image of the growing child. He tells us that since the child seeks to preserve himself, he becomes attached to those who foster his preservation. But it takes him time to realize that others around him actually *want* to help him. Rousseau next describes how his knowledge will inspire in him new desires for their goodwill towards him or admiration of him. These desires for respect and supportive intentions presuppose and feed off his ability to compare himself to others and to assess their comparative merit. Comparisons are the very currency of *amour propre*.[54] Once the child is able to make these comparisons and once he believes that people freely determine their intentions towards him, he begins to judge whether they esteem and love him or whether they hate, dislike, or despise him. And this dynamic produces a kind of dysfunction. The child becomes 'imperious, jealous, deceitful and vindictive.' *Amour propre* first comes to sight as a harmful and irrational passion: 'Self-love, which regards only ourselves, is contented when our true needs are satisfied. But *amour-propre*, which makes comparisons, is never content and never could be, because this sentiment, preferring ourselves to others, also demands others to prefer us to themselves, which is impossible. This is how the gentle and affectionate passions are born of self-love and the hateful and irascible passions are born of *amour-propre*' (*OC* 4:493; trans. Bloom, 213–14). Man, we might say, is the vain animal. But in addition to vanity, *amour propre* leads to the development of resentment, malice, envy, vengefulness, and ambition, as well as to the desire for honour and the wish to be loved by those one loves. 'A multitude of bad things as against a small number of good ones,' as Rousseau puts it in the *Second Discourse* (*OC* 3:189; Masters, 175). Man, it seems, is the only malicious animal, the only resentful animal. And all this is because he lives outside of himself. Paradoxically, it is because man is the free animal that he is the only authoritarian one. Man is the only animal who seeks to direct not just the bodies and movements of others but their hearts, minds, and wills. It is not clear that all of this is explained just as well through determinism. Some thinkers have seen the doing of evil as a proof of free will.[55]

We are now in a better position to interpret Rousseau's explanation of how unnatural passions or unnatural dimensions to our passions transform our self-love at the outset of Book IV of *Emile*. Returning to this passage, we can take an overview of the whole and consider more precisely how his discussion about recognizing the free wills of others fits into this description of the emergence of *amour propre*. *Amour de soi* is an innate, natural passion – the natural source of other passions. Like a mountain spring, it provides the first waters that come from nature

(*OC* 4:490; trans. Bloom, 212). But the passions that subject us are alien streams (*ruisseaux étrangers*) that do not come from nature: 'All those which subject us and destroy us come from elsewhere. Nature does not give them to us.' Rousseau concedes that these passions may be natural in the specific and limited sense that they have their original source in our innate and primitive self-love. But he calls these new and alien passions 'modifications' of *amour de soi*. And he suggests that most of these modified passions have themselves been produced by 'alien causes [*des causes étrangéres*] without which they would never have come to pass.' Due to the action of these alien causes, the modified passions begin to work against the natural principle of self-preservation.

Rousseau then makes a remark about this process that deserves our attention: he writes that 'it is then that man finds himself outside of nature and puts himself in contradiction with himself' (*OC*, 4:491; trans. Bloom, 213). Again, he reiterates his position that both external circumstances and man's own decisions or actions lead to his corruption. Man is moulded by circumstances ('he finds himself outside of nature') and he moulds himself (he 'sets himself against himself.')

Now, one might object that the formulation that he 'finds himself outside of nature' draws our attention to the way that man is passively shaped by external circumstances. But here it is particularly clear that if Rousseau had instead argued simply that man wilfully relinquished his natural condition and took on passions that 'far from being advantageous are harmful' (trans. Bloom, 213), his critique of original sin and argument for natural goodness would have fallen to the ground. Furthermore, as Alexis Philonenko has suggested, Rousseau's argument may assume that the deployment of free will requires a nudge or a shock to get it going: a random catalyst may be free will's condition. Philonenko comments that in the *Second Discourse*, an '*Antoss*,' a nudge or push, is required 'if the essence of man is not and must not be a fatality. If the essence of man implied a totally internal development, then human liberty would be that of a rotisserie. Therefore it is and will be necessary to have a shock starting from which liberty unfurls itself [*se déploie*], for better or worse – that is not the question here – and constitutes itself as responsibility towards itself – which is the only modality of an auto-affection understood in the practical sense.'[56] According to this view, an external push allows human free will and the consciousness of free will to emerge.[57]

This understanding offers a reasonable interpretation of Rousseau's thinking about the causality of corruption in this passage. The circumstances in which man finds himself outside of nature, on the one hand, and his will, which sets him against himself, on the other, are not mutually exclusive explanations of this process – instead they are complementary. Rousseau endorses both explanations. When he writes that 'what transforms this instinct into sentiment' is our opinion that others have an intention to act freely for us or against us, he is indicating that we think we *discover* that others are outside of nature. There is an element of contingency in this process.[58] It is like the unearthing of a mosaic.

Nevertheless, once we believe that other humans are freely willing rather than 'insensible beings which merely follow the impulsion given to them' (*OC* 4:492; trans. Bloom, 213), we see them as outside of nature, and it is in part our captivation with their gaze that generates new passions in us and so takes us outside of nature. This, it seems to me, is what Rousseau really means by the 'consciousness of freedom.' He describes the process whereby we become conscious of our own free will *qua* human, conscious of our free will as a species.

This recognition of the power to will independently of natural necessity was, of course, a key feature of Rousseau's original account of free will as the species distinction in the *Second Discourse*. There he concedes that humans feel the pull of instinct just as the other beasts do. Unlike the other animals, however, man knows he is free to obey instinct or resist that instinct, and 'it is above all in the consciousness of this freedom that the spirituality of his soul is shown' (*OC* 3:142; Masters, 114). It is man's perception that he is relatively free of instinct in his power to determine his actions, we contend, that marks him as specifically human.

Free Will and Amour Propre *in the* Second Discourse

In the second part of the *Second Discourse*, in his description of the 'successive developments of the human mind,' Rousseau further describes men's consciousness that they act voluntarily and indicates how that consciousness fosters the growth of *amour propre*.

Rousseau describes how savage men begin to hold other human beings responsible for voluntary wrongs, and he implies that this marks an important moment in the historical anthropology of the *Discourse*. Gradually, he suggests, these savage men began to build huts and to form into families and bands. They develop languages and begin to sing and dance. People begin to make comparisons and to conceive esteem for one another, and the idea of love emerges: 'Each one began to look at the others and to want to be looked at himself, and public esteem had a value' (*OC* 3:169; Masters, 149). In this account, as in Book IV of *Emile*, men's captivation with the gaze of others contributes to the formation of *amour propre:*

> As soon as men had begun to appreciate one another and the idea of consideration formed in their minds, each one claimed a right to it, and it was no longer possible to deprive anyone of it with impunity. From this came the first duties of civility, even among Savages; and from this any voluntary wrong [*tort volontaire*] became an affront, because along with the harm that resulted from the injury, the offended man saw in it contempt for his person which was often more unbearable than the harm itself. (*OC* 3:170)[59]

When these men discover 'the idea of consideration,' they become conscious that other human beings can commit voluntary wrongs against them. And if they attribute voluntary wrongs to one another, they understand one another to have volition or will. Attributing will to others, an individual would presumably at some point notice it within himself. The passage also implies that these men recognize themselves and other men as being free to show signs of respect or disrespect. It suggests that it is men's perception that as human, they are able to act on decisions of their wills, that gives value to the consideration and esteem of others and that makes offence and contempt so difficult to bear. Men's perception that their actions towards one another are voluntary leads to a sea change in their behaviour. The passage continues as follows: 'Thus, everyone punishing the contempt shown him by another in a manner proportionate to the importance he accorded himself, vengeances became terrible, and men bloodthirsty and cruel' (Masters, 149–50). If these men perceived that other men's wills were merely determined by natural necessity, why would there be such a sudden and marked change in their behaviour from natural goodness to bloodthirsty vengeance? Rousseau is implying that the emergence of this consciousness of men's ability to act based on free decisions of their wills contributes to the development of *amour propre*.

In Note O(15), Rousseau also implies that man's attribution to other men of this freedom to act independently of natural necessity contributes to the emergence of *amour propre*. It is in this note that he introduces *amour propre* for the first time. He contrasts *amour propre* with natural *amour de soi* as follows:

> *L'Amour de soi-même* is a natural sentiment which inclines every animal to attend to its self-preservation, and which, guided in man by reason and modified by pity, produces humanity and virtue. *L'Amour propre* is only a relative sentiment, factitious, and born in society, which inclines each individual to set a greater store by himself than by anyone else, inspires men with all the evils they do one another and is the genuine source of honour.[60]

Rousseau then suggests that in the genuine state of nature, man could not have *amour propre,* because there he is absolutely self-centred and self-absorbed and is unable to make the comparisons with other humans that it requires. In the genuine state of nature, natural man is immune, so to speak, to the opinions others have about him:

> I say that in our primitive state, in the genuine [*véritable*] state of nature, *l'Amour propre* does not exist; for each particular man regarding himself as the sole spectator to observe him, as the sole being in the universe to take an interest in him, and as the sole judge of his own merit, it is not possible that a sentiment having its source in comparisons he is not capable of making could spring up in his soul. For the same reason this man could have neither hate nor desire for revenge, passions that can arise only from the opinion that some offense has been received; and as it is scorn or intention to hurt, and not the harm that constitutes the offense, men who know neither how to appreciate one another or to compare themselves with one another can do each other a great deal of mutual violence when they derive some advantage from it, without ever offending one another. In a word, every man, seeing his fellow-men hardly otherwise than he would see Animals of another species, can carry off the prey of the weaker or relinquish his own to the stronger, without considering these plunderings as anything but natural events, without the slightest emotion of insolence or spite, and with no other passion than the sadness or joy of a good or bad outcome. (*OC* 3:218)[61]

Several significant points emerge from a close reading of this paragraph. Again, Rousseau's first premise is clear: man in the first state of nature harbours no *amour propre* because he does not have the degree of enlightenment required to compare himself to others. (He writes decisively that it is impossible that *amour propre,* a sentiment that has 'its source in comparisons he is not capable of making, could spring up in his soul.') Rousseau also describes how men in this state 'have neither hate nor the desire for revenge,' for these are the kinds of passions that stem from *amour propre. Amour propre* requires the ability to 'form an opinion of some offense received.' And in order to form such an opinion, men require the degree of enlightenment that allows them to make comparisons. To this point, the argument is compatible with an understanding of man solely in terms of materialist perfectibility. *Amour propre* requires specific forms of enlightenment, and man's perfectibility allows him to obtain them. But in the final lines of this paragraph, Rousseau explains the inability of men in the genuine state of nature to 'appreciate one another or to compare themselves' through the fact that they see one another's plunderings as merely natural events, rather than as events based on the intention to hurt. The idea that other men's actions are based on intentions that are not merely natural occurrences is constitutive of men's opinion that others have slighted them. And this ability to 'form an opinion that some offense has been received' is central to the working of *amour propre.*

It is true that Rousseau in this note does not present consciousness of freedom explicitly as a necessary condition of the development of *amour propre*. (He does not say, as he does in *Emile*, that the thing that changes blind instinct into the sentiment of love or hate is our perception that others act freely and on the basis of their wills.)[62] But it appears to us that his discussion of men's perception of other men's scornful intentions as events that are not natural is more than a simple illustration of how *amour propre* happened to arise. When he writes that 'every man, seeing his fellow-men hardly otherwise than he would Animals of another species, can carry off the prey of the weaker or relinquish his own to the stronger, without considering these plunderings as anything but natural events,' he is explicating his idea of the make-up of men's ability to form an 'opinion of some offense received.' Because we attribute freedom from natural determination to others, harmful actions become understood as insults or affronts.

Our interpretation, then, would run as follows: in the first state of nature, men do not recognize one another as possessed of voluntary intentions, and they see one another's actions as 'natural events.' After a conflict, they are agitated by negative results but they are not moved by the hostile intentions of other humans. But once men begin to see one another as able to make decisions independently of natural necessity, they hold one another (but not animals of other species) responsible for their decisions. They do so, we surmise, because they believe that human causality falls outside the determinism of natural causality. They are no longer indifferent to the wills of other humans; their passions are aroused not merely by outcomes but by intentions. They become sensitive to malice or contempt, to real or imagined slights. They begin to read the glances of others. The consciousness of freedom contributes to the development of *amour propre.*

To summarize, men in the first state of nature are self-absorbed and animated by *amour de soi.* But men who have developed *amour propre* are self-conscious beings; they are conscious of the ways other humans perceive them. Rousseau is implying that the consciousness of the gaze of freely willing beings contributes to making men self-conscious in this way.[63] The consciousness of the human power to will independently of natural determination underlies the self-consciousness that *amour propre* entails.

Amour Propre, *Consciousness of Freedom, and the Stages of Human Development*

In the next section we examine the significance of the *consciousness* of free will in particular, and we show that it is a necessary element of the full and complete emergence of convention. We make this argument by examining Rousseau's teaching about the different stages of man's development. Rousseau suggests that *amour propre,* conditioned by the consciousness of freedom,[64] marks the dividing line between a primitive stage of the state of nature and the savage state of nascent society. This question is complex and controversial; it is best to begin by reviewing the textual evidence.

As we have seen, in Note 15(O), Rousseau states clearly that 'in our primitive state, in the genuine [*véritable*] state of nature, *amour propre* does not exist.' And in the main text of the *Discourse,* Rousseau writes that once men are able to appreciate one another, to make comparisons, to perceive voluntary wrongs and punish them with revenges, they are already 'far from the first state of nature.' He explains that the failure to see this has led many to conclude that man is by nature cruel, but in this they are mistaken:

> On the contrary, nothing is so gentle as man in his primitive state when, placed by nature at equal distances from the stupidity of the brutes and the fatal enlightenment of civil man, and limited equally by instinct and reason to protecting himself from the harm that threatens him, he is restrained by natural pity from harming anyone himself, and nothing leads

> him to do so even after he has received harm. (*Discourse, OC* 3:170; Masters, 150)

In their primitive state, then, men had no *amour propre:* they were naturally self-interested but naturally moderate. Next, he explains that men who are 'far from the first state of nature' punish voluntary wrongs with such violence in order to compensate for the absence of laws. He also remarks that these men have left what he calls the pure state of nature:

> It must be noted that the beginnings of society and the relations already established among men required in them qualities different from those they derived from their primitive constitution; that, morality beginning to be introduced into human actions, and each man, prior to laws, being sole judge and avenger of the offenses he had received, the goodness suitable for the pure state of nature was no longer that which suited nascent society. (*Discourse, OC* 3:170; Masters, 150)

Morality is introduced once men acquire the idea of consideration and perceive the hurt of voluntary wrongs. *Amour propre* informed by the attribution of voluntary intentions to others divides the state of nascent society among savages from a previous, more primitive stage. But what does Rousseau mean by the term 'pure state of nature'?

From the way he uses the term, it is clear that by 'pure state of nature,' he means a state without artifice or convention.[65] Now, in light of what he says about the absence of *amour propre* before the savage state of nascent society, can we say that *amour propre,* conditioned by the consciousness of undeterministic free will, divides the pure state of nature – a state without convention – from civil society that *does* have convention and morality? The answer is, in fact, more complicated than such a formulation allows. It is true that the pure state of nature is a state without either convention or *amour propre.* But according to Rousseau's anthropological narrative, some forms of convention predate men's attribution of freedom to one another. Language is a case in point: language itself is or depends on a form of convention. Rousseau contends that men's substitution of articulated signs for gestures 'cannot be made except by a common consent' (*OC* 3:148; Masters, 123)[66] Moreover, he assumes the existence of an early state of nature during which men developed languages, and he assumes as well that this state was distinct from the pure state of nature: he speaks of the 'immense distance there must have been between the pure state of nature and the need for languages' (*OC* 3:147; Masters, 121).[67] Therefore, *amour propre* and the consciousness of freedom of will are not the sole wellsprings of all convention. And perfectibility, which allows the development of languages, contributes to the emergence of convention in this way. Nonetheless, the explicit evidence in *Emile* and the implicit evidence in the *Discourse* indicate that consciousness of human free will is the beginning of morality and that morality is part of the full development of convention and artifice.[68] Morality requires that humans perceive that the actions of other humans are not merely natural occurrences; it requires what we might call undeterministic *amour propre*. To see why, consider the following.

Amour propre is the catalyst for morality and therefore for the fully conventional world of humans. But given the implicit nature of the evidence in the *Discourse*, how can we be sure that Rousseau understands this *amour propre* that ignites morality in terms that are not just material? Even if we accept that *amour propre* is based on men's consciousness of their independence of nature, what makes us think this independence of nature is not explained by material causation? Hobbes's conception of vain-glory is, of course, not given a dualistic interpretation, and it may be the inspiration for Rousseau's idea of *amour propre*. In V.V. of *De Cive*, the work of Hobbes with which Rousseau was familiar, Hobbes writes that one of the things that distinguishes men from the beasts is their ability to feel offended: 'Animals do not distinguish wrong from harm. This is why they do not criticize their companions when they are doing well themselves. But the men who are the greatest nuisance to their country are those who are allowed the greatest leisure; for men do not usually compete for public office, until they have won the battle against hunger and cold.'[69] But there is a crucial difference between Hobbes and Rousseau on these matters. Hobbes assumes that men by nature have a will to dominate others. He writes that 'men from their very birth, and naturally, scramble for everything they covet, and would have all the world, if they could, to fear and obey them.'[70] Rousseau uses a great deal of energy to refute this idea. But to do so, he needs to find an origin of evil that is other than man's natural endowment. Does free will provide Rousseau with an unnatural origin for evil?

It is clear that what has up to this point appeared as a disadvantage and weakness of the free will argument, here appears as an advantage. The difficulty with free will is that it presumes men can act outside of natural causality. Precisely how this anti-natural spontaneity is possible is not easy to explain, but assuming the possibility of a free will that opposes natural causation has this advantage: it helps explain how men leave the path of nature. The events that men produce by free will are not caused by material necessity, and in this sense they are not 'natural events.'[71]

Nonetheless, I would argue that it is not simply free will but the *consciousness* of free will that provides Rousseau with an unnatural origin for evil. Free will does not by itself ground morality and vice. Perhaps one reason why is that it is still too natural, as it were. The capacity for free will, as we suggested earlier, is part of man's natural endowment. Kant, for his part, argues that free will is part of man's 'supersensible nature.' If men have a natural endowment that allows them to mislead themselves, why (as Philopolis asked) should we decry evil and blame them for behaving badly? So it is not clear that the endowment for free will or even the unselfconscious exercise of free will (which natural men exhibit when they imitate the instincts of other animals) can in itself provide a satisfactory origin for evil. Perhaps only the consciousness of freedom is sufficiently outside of man's natural endowment to be the cause of evil.[72]

Men's consciousness of free will entails something more than their ability to self-legislate. Men who have consciousness of free will do not merely prescribe law to themselves; they also obey it (or disobey it), and this decision about obedience requires reflection on the prior departure from natural causation, on the prior self-legislation. Men's consciousness of their independence from natural causation, then, takes men a step farther from nature than would the unreflective exercise of free will. In order to be outside nature, it appears, men have to take *two* steps away from it.

Moreover, the mere unreflective exercise of free will does not of itself provide a sufficient explanation for the origin of morality and evil because both of the latter require a dialectical and social interaction of wills in which (as Hegel would have it) one freely willing self-consciousness meets and recognizes another. In the *Discourse* and in *Emile,* the subject's recognition that other humans act independently of natural causation leads the subject beyond *amour de soi* and off the path of nature. In Book I of *Emile,* the child's interaction with servile or tyrannical adults is what produces a will to dominate, a will that is characterized by 'effects whose immediate cause is not in nature.' This is why Rousseau contends that the *'conscience de la liberté'* is what, above all, reveals the spirituality of man's soul.

Men capable of morality, virtue, and vice, moreover, are characterized by their consciousness of free will rather than simply by their consciousness of perfectibility. If men believed that other men's actions were made possible solely by materialist perfectibility, determined by natural causation, their intentions would not inspire violent revenges: we are 'never passionate about insensible beings who merely follow the impulsion given to them' (*Emile*, trans. Bloom, 213). Our captivation with the gaze of others contributes to the formation of *amour propre*, but it is captivation with the gaze of humans who are capable of judging others based on voluntary decisions of the mind.[73]

The Three Stages of Human Development

We can see the implications of this reading better if we return to the *Discourse* and to the account of human development that Rousseau presents in it. For our purposes there are three key stages of man's anthropological development: the primitive or first state of nature; the savage state of nascent society (which is the state of 'the Savage peoples known to us'); and the corrupt state of civilized society.[74] In the first or primitive state of nature, men may sometimes act independently of instinct (as when they imitate the instincts of other animals), but they are conscious neither of this freedom nor of its distinctiveness. In the second stage, the savage state of nacsent society, men recognize their independence from nature but they nonetheless approximate nature's command in much of their behaviour. They continue to base their lives primarily on meeting natural needs. If their *amour propre* leads them to violence, it does not lead them to depravity, delusion, or pettiness. Rousseau describes this savage state of nascent society this way:

> This period of the development of human faculties, maintaining a golden mean between the indolence of the primitive state and the petulant activity of our vanity, must have been the happiest and most durable epoch. The more one thinks about it, the more one finds that this state was the least subject to revolutions, the best for man, and that he must have come out of it only by some fatal accident, which for the common good ought never to have happened. The example of savages, who have almost all been found at this point, seems to confirm that the human race was made to remain in it always; that this state is the veritable prime of the world; and that all subsequent progress has been in appearance so many steps toward the perfection of the individual, and in fact toward the decrepitude of the species. (*OC* 3:171; Masters, 150–1)

In contrasting the relatively happy second stage of savage society with the third stage, the stage of civilized society, Rousseau unflinchingly debunks the pretensions of civilized man. Civilized man is depraved and lives by vanity.[75] Conversely, his praise of the 'savage state of nascent society' articulates the model or image of a fully human but less depraved way of life.[76] His image of savages during the 'veritable prime of the world' provides a model for a way of life in society that approximates nature, a way of life that may attenuate but does not stifle the natural goodness in our hearts. Once we are conscious that we are independent of nature in formulating our intentions, once we perceive human intentions as voluntary, we are liable to develop the inflated and obsessive *amour propre* that impedes us from living a life based on natural need. Liable, that is, but not necessarily destined.

In the foregoing we have presented reasons for thinking that Rousseau's description of the rise of vengeful acts in response to voluntary wrongs – a description found in the *Discourse* and in his introduction of *amour propre* in Note 15(O) – implicitly relies on a conception of free will. We have suggested that the dualism of free will versus material nature underpins his argument in the *Discourse*. He was reluctant to emphasize and explicitly affirm this, for had he done so his materialist contemporaries might have dismissed the importance of the work. We suggest that Rousseau's understanding of *amour propre* rests implicitly on men's consciousness of their freedom of will.

Dualism and *Amour Propre* in the *Lettre à Beaumont*

This view is supported by Rousseau's *Lettre à Beaumont*, written to the Archbishop of Paris in protest against the censure of *Emile*. The letter contains one of Rousseau's most important statements of his principle of natural goodness; in it he explains his conception of natural goodness through two different interpretations of *amour propre*. The first is monistic, the second is dualistic:

> The fundamental principle of all morality, on the basis of which I have reasoned in all my writings, and which I have developed in this most recent work [i.e., *Emile*] with all the clarity of which I was capable, is that man is a being that is naturally good, loving justice and order; that there is no original perversity in the human heart, and that the first motions of nature are always right. I have shown that the only passion that is born with man – namely *l'Amour propre*[77] – is a passion indifferent in itself to good and evil; that it does not become good or bad except by accident and according

> to the different circumstances in which it develops. I have shown that all the vices that are imputed to the human heart are not natural to it; I have said in what manner they are born; I have, so to speak, followed their genealogy, and I have shown how, by the successive alterations of their natural goodness, men finally become what they are.
>
> I have further explained what I understood by this original goodness, which does not seem to follow [*se déduire*] from the indifference to good and evil natural to self-love [*l'amour de soi*]. Man is not a simple being; he is composed of two substances. If everybody does not agree on this, you and I agree on it and I have tried to prove it to others. Once this is proven, *amour de soi* is no longer a simple passion, but has two principles – namely, the intelligent being and the sensitive being – whose well-being is not the same. The appetite of the senses tends to the well-being of the body and the love of order to that of the soul. This latter love, developed and rendered active, is called conscience.

One reading of this passage would be to take the two interpretations it presents as incompatible alternatives. The first alternative is a monistic understanding of *amour de soi*: it grounds the argument for natural goodness in a materialist understanding of the accidental circumstances that lead man off the track. The second, dualistic understanding of *amour de soi* is at odds with this monistic alternative. As Rousseau himself points out, the second understanding of natural goodness based on a conscience 'does not appear to follow from the indifference to good and evil natural to *amour de soi*.' Those sceptical of Rousseau's belief in free will would argue that Rousseau only believes the monistic understanding and that this dualistic reinterpretation of *amour de soi* is intended simply to prop up healthy politics and cannot be taken at face value.[78] A fuller consideration of this question will follow in our chapter on *Emile*, but for the moment, consider two initial objections.

First, this argument that Rousseau presents the dualistic interpretation of *amour de soi* merely because it is salutary would be stronger if Rousseau had presented a historicist, materialist monism on the one hand and contrasted it to a traditional dualism of unchanging substances on the other. But this is not the case. Instead Rousseau applies the historical method to the dualism of body and soul itself. The functioning of man's intelligent soul changes over historical time. In the next few paragraphs, Rousseau gives a historical and moral account of the emergence and progressive silencing of conscience, which he presents as the principle of the intelligent substance of the soul. The counter-interpretation would have to explain why Rousseau supplements and thereby alters his monism in such an unusual and original way.[79]

This brings us to our second objection to the reading that Rousseau did not truly stand behind the dualistic interpretation of *amour propre* in this passage. This objection turns on an examination of the subsequent part of his argument in the *Lettre à Beaumont*. For there Rousseau goes on to describe the development of morality and *amour propre* through man's consciousness of his relations to other men in terms that echo and recall the interpretations we have offered about the relation between *amour propre* and free will in *Emile* and the *Second Discourse.* The passage continues as follows:

> But the conscience only develops and acts with man's enlightenment [*lumières*]. It is only through this enlightenment that he arrives at knowledge of order and it is only when he knows it that his conscience leads him to love it. Conscience is therefore nothing in the man who has compared nothing, and who has not seen his relations. In this state, man knows only himself; he sees his well-being as neither opposed to nor in conformity with the well-being of anyone else; he neither loves nor hates anything; limited to physical instinct alone, he is nothing, he is stupid [*il est bête*]; this is what I have shown in my *Discours sur inegalité.*
>
> When, by a development of which I have shown the progress, men begin to cast their eyes on their fellows, they also begin to see their relations and the relations of things, to acquire ideas of preferences, of justice and order; they begin to be sensitive to moral beauty [*le beau morale*] and the conscience stirs [*agit*]. (*OC* 4:936)

In keeping with his position in *Emile* and the *Discourse,* Rousseau stresses that man begins with a kind of tunnel vision; he 'knows only himself.' He does not judge his well-being on the basis of relations to others that he has not yet perceived: '*borné au seul instinct physique, ... il est bête.*'[80] In this account, Rousseau again presents man's observations of other people and a consciousness of their relations to him as a crucial moment in his development beyond the tutelage of physical instinct alone. It is true that there is no specific mention in this passage of man's consciousness of free will. But it is germane to remember that the French word *conscience* can mean both conscience and consciousness. In the *Discourse,* Rousseau's argument is that it is the '*conscience de la liberté*' that above all reveals the spirituality of man's soul.[81] It may even be that in the present passage, *conscience* stands in for '*conscience de la liberté.*'[82] But for the moment it suffices to note here that Rousseau's treatment of the emergence of *amour propre* based on casting one's eyes on others and considering 'their relations and the relations of things' not only echoes and recalls our interpretations of the development of *amour propre,* but also is explicitly presented as part of a dualistic understanding of the soul. Rousseau is implying that the conscience and ideas of justice, morality, and even vice cannot be adequately explained if they are understood as being fully determined by material causes and physical instinct.[83]

Rousseau's argument about how men attribute free will to other men helps him explain what leads them outside of animal, instinctual, determined nature. Once human beings see themselves and others as free from determination by external forces, they become caught up in a dialectic of human interaction, often at the expense of natural need. Eventually they can become obsessed by the judgments of other humans, depraved by inflated and overactive *amour propre.* 'As soon as *amour propre* has developed, the relative I is constantly in play' (*Emile,* trans. Bloom, 243).[84] The transformation of the natural passion of *amour de soi* into unnatural, conventional *amour propre* is possible because human beings realize they can will independently of natural causality.

Free will is not jettisoned from the argument of the *Discourse.* It is needed to explain how a naturally good being develops unnatural vice. Moreover, what had initially seemed to be a major liability of the free will argument – the fact that it is incompatible with the materialist understanding of natural causation – no longer appears to be merely a disadvantage. Free will's separateness from natural necessity helps explain how men leave the path of nature.

Jean de Castillon, the contemporary critic of Rousseau whose views we dicussed in chapter 1, had objected to Rousseau's characterization of the faculties in the *Second Discourse* as 'artificial faculties.' Castillon pointed out that the term 'artificial faculties' is a kind of oxymoron. In his response to the *Discourse,* Castillon wrote: 'Art can very well facilitate the exercise of the faculties; but it does not produce [*donne*] them; it can very well extend them; but not create them. An artificial faculty is a contradiction, unless one confuses the faculty with its perfection.'[85]

Rousseau deals with the problem of the artificial/natural divide by beginning his psychology from the passions. The key problem, as he sees it, is not so much to explain how we acquire artificial faculties as to explain how unnatural passions are produced by factitious *amour propre.* To do so requires an understanding of something outside nature

– the recognition of man's independence from natural necessity enjoins a dialectic that renders man a depraved animal.

Rousseau has a Hobbesian starting point in the *Second Discourse,* but his minimalist conception of man as a being guided by *amour de soi* is just that – a starting point. His description of man's sociality, his genealogy of vice and dysfunction, depends on a conception of man as a being who can see himself as independent of nature's compulsion. The Hobbesiansim of Rousseau's theory itself points towards Kant and Hegel.

Section 3: Free Will, the Rhetoric of Freedom, and the Problem of Immoral Freedom

The Objection That Consciousness of Freedom Is an Illusion

Our reading so far raises an important question that we have not yet treated directly: Does Rousseau think that the consciousness of free will he describes expresses a *true* perception about human nature? Most people think that humans have free will, but this, of course, does not *prove* they have it. People in Rousseau's time were of the opinion that it was a good idea to wrap infants in swaddling clothes, but he argues forcefully and persuasively against this erroneous opinion. The consciousness of freedom could be similarly based on a popularly accepted error.[86] Interpreters who view Rousseau as a materialist could argue that he in fact implies that *amour propre* is based on the illusion that men will freely. They could add that this flattering illusion that we have free will has a salutary use in that it can be employed to inspire us towards a willed mastery of the passions, that is, toward virtue.[87]

In response to this objection, we concede, in the first place, that Rousseau often appeals to his readers' pride in self-mastery in order to inspire them to virtue. Examples of this can be found in the *Profession of Faith of the Savoyard Vicar* and in the tutor's last speeches to Emile and in 1.8 of *Du contrat social.* Moreover, these moralizing appeals often repress or gloss over the possibility that one can will freely to adopt an unwise or unethical course of action. (And this, as we will see at the end of the chapter, is a possibility that Rousseau fully acknowledges elsewhere.) But our main argument in this section is that some of Rousseau's exhortations to self-mastery based on free will are actually rhetorical versions of a stronger argument in which he *does* believe – the argument that that the dynamic of the consciousness of freedom provides evidence for the existence of freedom of the will.

Probing the Rhetoric of Freedom

Consider two passages in which Rousseau describes the self's consciousness of freedom in the process of moral decision making. One is from the *Lettre à Franquières,* the other from the *Profession of Faith of the Savoyard Vicar.*

In the *Lettre à Franquières,* Rousseau combats his correspondent's determinism through an appeal to the sentiment of free will:

> How can you not appreciate that this same law of necessity that alone, according to you, rules the working of the world, and all events, also rules all the actions of men, all the thoughts in their heads, all the feelings of their hearts, that nothing is free, that everything is forced, necessary, inevitable, that all the movements of man, directed by blind matter only depend on his will because his will itself depends on necessity; that there are in consequence neither virtues, nor vices, nor merit, nor demerit, nor morality in human actions, and that the words 'honorable man' or 'villain' must be, for you, totally devoid of sense. They are not, however, I am very sure. Your honest heart, despite your arguments, declaims against your sad philosophy. The sentiment of freedom, the charm of virtue, are felt within you despite yourself, and that is how this strong and salutary voice of interior sentiment calls, from all parts, every man misled by his badly directed reason to the bosom of truth and virtue. Bless, Monsieur, this holy and beneficent [*bienfaisante*] voice which brings you back to the duties of man that your fashionable philosophy will end up making you forget. Surrender yourself to your arguments only when you feel they agree with the dictamen of your conscience, and every time that you feel the contradiction, be sure that it is your arguments that deceive you. (*OC* 4:1145)[88]

In this important statement in favour of free will, Rousseau is arguing that determinism is incompatible with the belief that we are morally accountable for our actions.[89] He suggests that free will anchors the idea of virtuous moral conduct: Franquières's honest heart is to be swayed by the moral need for free will, or at least by the moral vacuity of determinism.[90] But this reminds us that, as the counter-interpretation suggests, Rousseau has a motive to extol man's free will whether he believes in it or not. We have to grant this point.

At the same time, it is important to note that here Rousseau bases his argument for free will not on an appeal to the public opinion that we will freely but to the internal sentiment that we do. This inner sentiment, he holds, can be muffled by the arguments that emerge from prevailing intellectual fashion. He advises M. de Franquières to use a critical method of introspection that will allow him to understand that his internal sentiment of freedom supports a morality of virtue against the reasonings of predominant philosophical discourse.[91] So while Rousseau may imply in this passage that free will serves as the basis for conventional public morality, he does not present the sentiment of free will as being based upon these conventions.

Thinkers who favour the counter-interpretation might respond, however, that Rousseau's appeal to inner sentiment in this passage has a rhetorical bent – in particular, that he blurs the distinction between the good conscience oriented towards virtue, on the one hand, and the sentiment that one is free to do *either* the good or the bad, on the other. The passage creates the impression that these two are melded into the 'strong and salutary voice of inner sentiment.'

Nonetheless, the fact that Rousseau colours his argument for polemical effect should not distract us from its more plausible foundation. The defensible core of his argument is that comprehensive materialism does not sufficiently explain the inner sentiment of freedom that Franquières will feel as he contemplates his moral decisions. Simply put, the dynamic of the consciousness of freedom is evidence for the existence of free will. Similarly, Hans Jonas suggests that the reflexive process within the will distinguishes it from mere appetite and provides evidence for its freedom: 'All the phenomena of morality – freedom, choice, responsibility, conscience, guilt – are rooted in this primordial reflexiveness. Its *a priori* presence is the ontological basis of freedom.'[92]

The statement in the *Lettre à Franquières* bears some marked similarities to one of the Savoyard vicar's most famous arguments. In the next chapter we will thoroughly discuss the issue of whether one can safely consider the pronouncements of the vicar, a character in *Emile*, to be Rousseau's own. Here we critically analyse one of the vicar's arguments about free will. Like the passage from the *Lettre à Franquières*, here the vicar provides a description of how the sentiment of free will supplies evidence for free will's existence. Moreover, the vicar's argument similarly involves a rhetorical embellishment of a more credible underlying claim:

> No material being is active by itself, and I am. One may very well argue with me about this; but I sense it, and this sentiment that speaks to me is stronger than the reason combating it. I have a body on which other bod-

> ies act and which acts on them. This reciprocal action is not doubtful. But my will is independent of my senses; I consent or I resist; I succumb or I conquer; and I sense perfectly within myself when I do what I willed to do [*voulu faire*] or when all I am doing is giving way to my passions. I always have the power to will, I do not always have the force to execute. When I abandon myself to temptations, I act according to the impulsion of external objects. When I reproach myself for this weakness, I listen only to my will. I am enslaved because of my vices and free because of my remorse. The sentiment of my freedom is effaced in me only when I become depraved and finally prevent the voice of the soul from being raised against the law of the body.[93]

This paragraph contains two separate movements of thought. In the first of these, the vicar asserts that free will, understood as the ability to act independently of the senses or passions, exists. In the second, the vicar adduces a proof of this ability – the proof is the consciousness of freedom and, in particular, the sentiment of freedom that one feels in self-mastery or remorse.[94] The paragraph is tricky because this second movement of thought, which supports the first, is expressed so rhetorically: the vicar moralizes the consciousness of free will. His rhetoric about the consciousness of free will at once makes and stretches the point that free will exists.

The vicar suggests that the interior dialogues of both self-mastery (when I sense that I do what I wanted or willed to do) and remorse (when I sense that I have given way to my passions) support the inference that one has an undetermined choice. He is particularly insistent about remorse, and perhaps this is for a good reason. For proponents of the existence of free will often suggest that because remorse consists of a feeling that one could have acted otherwise but did not, its existence supports the inference that some of our choices are undetermined. It is difficult for determinists to give an account of remorse that does it justice.[95] Nonetheless, the vicar's statement involves a number of sleights of hand. These can be seen most clearly if we examine his changing use of the term 'will' within the passage.

As noted above, the vicar begins by stating that 'my will is independent of my senses.' Here he understands will simply as the capacity to decide to act upon the senses or to resist them. (And this is in keeping with Rousseau's description of man's ability to freely acquiesce in or resist nature's command in the *Second Discourse*.)[96] But he then proceeds to identify the passions (which seem to stand in for the senses) as 'external objects' that could impel him and so interfere with the exercise of his free will: 'When I reproach myself for this weakness,' he concludes, 'I listen only to my will.' When the vicar claims that in reproaching himself for giving in to the passions, he listens 'only' to his will, he is implying that the temptations and passions are not just external to the will: were they to get mixed up in it, they would *adulterate* it. The voice of moral reproach appears to be a pure or isolated form of will. Whereas at first he describes the will as the capacity to decide whether to acquiesce in or to resist the senses or passions, here he identifies the will solely with the voice of resistance to the passions, with the consciousness of freedom as it is oriented towards virtue. And this is a problem insofar as the consciousness of this freedom to resist the passions, which acquires the exclusive name of will, is adduced as proof of the existence of free will to resist *or to acquiesce* in the passions. To this extent, the proof or illustration of the argument is at odds with its premise.[97]

It is true that the vicar takes an interesting step in support of his conception that the unmixed or pure will is the will to will virtue when he contends that 'I always have the power to will but not the force to execute.' Executing free will is having the strength to be virtuous: vice is weakness of will. But it is hard to see how his assertions that one is enslaved by vice and impelled by desires support the idea that we are undetermined in our ability to choose virtue or vice – unless our enslavement to vice is a voluntary and spontaneous enslavement. But this is the very possibility that the vicar's rhetoric represses. If the will is really independent of the senses, then the free decision to acquiesce in the senses or passions must also be an act of free will.[98] To completely identify the free will with the virtuous will would conflate free will with moral strength, the power to will with the force to execute.

This is not to dispute that Rousseau's understanding of moral freedom is a significant and legitimate one. Rousseau defines moral freedom as obedience to self-prescribed law rather than to appetite alone (*DCS* 1.8). This is a useful definition: to govern the appetites is to be independent of them, and to resist acting from base motives is an admirable form of moral self-rule.[99] But the free will to spontaneously decide on a course of action is not identical with such moral freedom. Someone who considers the alternatives and decides to acquiesce in the passions or desires may well be exercising freedom of will, but not moral freedom. Free will is a necessary but not a sufficient condition of moral freedom.

Given these objections, and given that Rousseau never makes a complete argument for this identification of true free will with moral freedom, it is plausible that he does not truly endorse the identification. There is a strong case, then, that he presents the view for its salutary moral benefits. Some of his polemical formulations may create the impression that his entire teaching about free will is rhetorical. But our argument indicates that a distrust of the vicar's edifying exaggerations about the virtuous will need not translate into a distrust of their free will basis.

In fact, Rousseau very frequently disassociates free will and moral freedom. He often acknowledges and indeed emphasizes that free will entails the freedom to decide to act badly, to indulge in the passions, or to do evil.[100] In the concluding section of this chapter, we discuss the evidence for this. Rousseau's reflections about the misuse of free will are not only frequent but, we would suggest, genuinely philosophical. These searching statements would need to be explained by the countercase, as they do not contribute in an obvious way to a salutary teaching about free will.

Rousseau on the Moral Ambiguity of the Free Will Capacity

The vicar himself repeatedly shows his keen awareness that men may freely will virtue or vice and that they may freely make choices based on truth or error. Regarding error, in the paragraph directly following his declaration that he is free by his remorse, he acknowledges that having free will often entails making poor decisions: 'One chooses the good as he has judged the true; if he judges wrong, he chooses badly' (trans. Bloom, 280; *OC* 4:586).[101] And as for the freedom to will vice or evil, the vicar argues that man rather than God is responsible for evil because man does good or evil through active, free will. He contends that men have freedom so that they can do the *'bien par choix'* (*OC* 4:587).[102]

Lastly, consider the decisive way in which the vicar distinguishes the conscience from the freedom to govern one's conduct in this famous passage:

> Conscience, conscience! Divine instinct, immortal and celestial voice, certain guide of a being that is ignorant and limited but intelligent and free; infallible judge of good and bad which makes man like unto God; it is you who make the excellence of his nature and the morality of his actions. Without you I sense nothing in me that raises me above the beasts, other

> than the sad privilege of leading myself astray from error to error with the aid of an understanding without rule and a reason without principle. (trans. Bloom, 290; *OC* 4:600–1)

The passage begins with a vaunted description of the conscience of man in general, only to turn to the vicar's wistful first-person account of the freedom of decision he senses within himself. The vicar sees how his unprincipled reasoning and his unruly understanding distort the judgment that informs his will. He senses that he is free to lead himself astray; he is free to ignore the divine instinct of conscience, just as he can ignore the pull of bodily instinct.[103] In the silence of conscience, there is still freedom. The freedom to make his decisions is, in his striking phrase, a 'sad privilege.'

Rousseau originally wrote this paragraph distinguishing conscience from the sad privilege of freedom in his own name. It formed the denouement of the fifth letter of the *Lettres Morales* that he wrote for Sophie D'Houdetot.[104] Rousseau's own introspection leads him to a deep ambivalence about the implications of free will for the human species. Rousseau's descriptions of free will are not consistently or straightforwardly flattering to man's *amour propre*.

It is certainly the case that Rousseau sometimes expresses pride in men's capacity for free will. In the *Discourse*, he suggests that freedom is 'the noblest of man's faculties.' He describes men's freedom as 'a gift they receive from nature by being men [*en qualité d'homme*]' (*OC* 3:184; Masters, 168). Freedom confers morality on men's actions, distinguishes them from the beasts, and opens up possibilities for justice, virtue, and nobility. To give it up is to degrade oneself. But in assessing how flattering Rousseau's portrayal of free will is, one needs to distinguish between the capacity for free will and the use that human beings make of it. For while Rousseau sometimes voices pride in man's potential for free will, this pride is tempered by his disappointment in its actual use.

Man's misuse of free will leads him to vice. Recall Rousseau's remark in his *Lettre à Voltaire* of 16 August 1756: 'I do not know how one can look for the source of moral evil [*mal morale*] elsewhere than in free, perfected and thereby corrupted man.' He elaborates this thought in the letter to M. de Franquières, written about eleven years later: 'But moral evil! Work of man in which God has no other part than to have made him free and in this similar to himself.' Free will provides an opportunity for self-mastery, but all too often men use it for self-abasement. As we argued above, men's consciousness of free will in particular contributes to their corruption through its role in the development of *amour propre*. Rousseau's ambivalence about freedom of the will contributes to his ambivalence about human nature. His view that the will is free fosters his sense of lost opportunity, his acute perception of the discrepancy between man's noble potential and his debased condition.[105]

It is true that Rousseau often bases a powerful rhetoric on this very discrepancy. He tries to use men's pride or *amour propre* to infuse them with contempt for their present condition and a longing for a nobler estate. He is a preacher of both self-improvement and societal improvement. Much of his political radicalism is in this vein. But these polemical positions are not based on an overly optimistic view of human nature. Instead, they are grounded on an honest and sadly wistful assessment of man's predicament: 'All the animals,' he writes in *Emile*, 'have exactly the faculties necessary to preserve themselves. Man alone has superfluous faculties. Is it not very strange that this superfluity should be the instrument of his unhappiness?' (trans. Bloom, 81; *OC* 4:305).

This passage provides an interesting perspective on Rousseau's relation to a traditional teleological view of nature and man's nature. The context of his question is his discussion of the relation between the faculties and desires in Book II of *Emile*. There he observes that it is when man's desires outstrip his faculties or powers to obtain them that unhappiness results. If the desires do not exceed the capacity to fulfil them through the faculties, man is well ordered. He then remarks:

> It is thus that nature, which does everything for the best, constituted him in the beginning. It gives him with immediacy only the desires necessary to his preservation and the faculties sufficient to satisfy them. It put all the others, as it were, in reserve in the depths of his soul, to be developed there when needed. Only in this original state are power and desire in equilibrium and man is not unhappy. (*OC* 4: 304; Bloom, p. 80)

Nature constitutes men well initially, but when men's superfluous faculties, such as imagination, develop, men begin to desire to pursue objectives (beyond the necessary) that outstrip their abilities. In this way the superfluity of men's faculties becomes the 'instrument' of their unhappiness.

Rousseau's question implicitly grants that man's misuse of his superfluous faculties creates a puzzle about nature. Given that man's superfluous faculties are the vehicle of his unhappiness, why would nature be set up in such a way that man has them? Unsure of nature's goals, he turns an implicit objection about the logic of the system of nature into a wistful, searching question.[106] In assessing Rousseau's relation to teleological approaches, I think this passage should be weighed alongside his statement in the *Discourse* that the potential faculties required 'the chance combination of several foreign causes which might never have arisen' (*OC* 4:162; Masters, 140).

3 Free Will in *Emile*: Interpreting the *Profession of Faith of the Savoyard Vicar*

Emile is only beginning to receive the scholarly attention it deserves. But Rousseau himself thought it was his best work. He even went so far as to say that the *Profession of Faith of the Savoyard Vicar* contained within it was the 'best and most important work' written in the eighteenth century (*OC* 4:960). Readers in the eighteenth century disputed the work's merits but had no trouble seeing its significance. *Emile* was condemned and burned in Paris and Geneva and censured in Holland. Authorities in Paris and Geneva ordered Rousseau's arrest. *Emile's* reception turned Rousseau into a wandering exile. Nonetheless, there were those in the eighteenth century who agreed with his favourable assessment of it. 'Perhaps,' wrote Chateaubriand, 'in the entire world there are only five works to read: *Emile* is one of them.'[1]

Emile is a rich but complex source for our argument. Much of our interest centres on the extended philosophical meditation that is the *Profession of Faith of the Savoyard Vicar:* not only does the vicar present an enterprising critique of comprehensive materialism, but he also makes a forceful and detailed defence of the idea that men have free will. Moreover, as I suggest below, the vicar attempts to establish the foundations of a natural religion that could serve as a new civil religion. Freedom of the will is the *sine qua non* of that natural religion. But interpretation of the *Profession* is complicated because Rousseau presents these ideas through the character of the vicar rather than in his own name. And some interpreters add that the vicar's metaphysical dualism conflicts with the monistic approach that Rousseau takes towards Emile's education generally. Interpretation of the *Profession* is, in fact, a vexed question in Rousseau scholarship. Later in the chapter, we will examine the general question of whether Rousseau endorses the *Profes-*

sion of Faith as well as the particular argument that since the *Profession of Faith* conflicts with the teaching of the rest of *Emile,* it cannot reflect Rousseau's true opinions about matters metaphysical. But before tackling these questions we need to understand more about the *Profession of Faith* itself. More precisely, we need to understand its meaning and significance and the role of free will within it. The first section of the chapter is devoted to this task.

Section 1: *The Profession of Faith of the Savoyard Vicar*

In the second section of the chapter, we will take our own position in the controversy about Rousseau's endorsement of the *Profession of Faith;* in this section we show what is at stake in the question. Here we confine ourselves to considering the *Profession* in relative detachment from its context, in order to better situate it in within *Emile* in our subsequent argument. This section's argument proceeds as follows: we begin with an exegesis of the teaching about free will in the first part of the *Profession of Faith.* Following this, we analyse the larger purpose of the Profession as a whole; we suggest that through it Rousseau attempts to found a new civil religion.

The First Part of the Profession of Faith: *Man's Free Will Reasserted*

'The Profession of the Savoyard Vicar,' writes Rousseau in his *Lettre à Beaumont,* 'is composed of two parts. The first, which is the longest, the most important, the most filled with new and striking truths, is destined to combat modern materialism, to establish the existence of God and natural religion with all the force of which the Author is capable' (*OC* 3:996).[2] The vicar's meditation is a reply to the empiricist materialism of Locke, Condillac, and Helvétius. In response, Rousseau establishes an anti-materialist natural religion. Free will is its foundation; almost every argument in the first part of the *Profession* either affirms or depends on the notion of free will.

The primary goal of this section is exegesis of the *Profession of Faith,* but we will also be indicating which of the vicar's arguments Rousseau affirms elsewhere in his own name. We are particularly interested in the ways in which the vicar debates, reaffirms, and extends the presentation of free will in the *Second Discourse.* It is of particular importance that the vicar echoes and develops Rousseau's statements in the *Discourse* that the consciousness of free choice reveals a spirituality that physical laws of mechanics cannot explain. In this way, he elaborates and confirms what is most compelling in Rousseau's original exposition of free will in the *Second Discourse.*

This section contributes to our overall argument in another way. For in it we probe Rousseau's description of a dualism of two principles within human nature – an active principle that orients man towards order and justice and a passive principle through which man simply fulfils his appetite. This dualism of two principles within human nature, which is based on the metaphysical dualism of two substances, helps the vicar respond to the problem of evil. Furthermore, as we suggest at the end of the section, it plays a role in the sublime morality of virtue that the tutor advocates in the rest of *Emile.*

THE CONTEXT OF THE *PROFESSION OF FAITH*

Emile is Rousseau's imaginary pupil, and Rousseau presents the *Profession of Faith of the Savoyard Vicar* in the context of a discussion of how to approach the religious education of the young. Up to this point in the book, Rousseau has explicated a theory of natural education. Too often, he believed, the educational practices of his time rendered men dependent, twisted, alienated, and confused. Rousseau sets out to elucidate the kind of education that would allow people to remain self-sufficient, honest, and whole. He imagines himself to be Emile's tutor, teaching him to rely upon himself and to understand the workings of nature.

In the first stages of his education, Rousseau wants Emile to observe natural necessity and to learn from it, instead of having recourse to the judgments and caprices of men. Rousseau thinks a child should be instructed in the 'laws of the possible and the impossible alone' (*OC* 4:321; trans. Bloom, 92). Thus, Emile's early education is based on physical exercise, games, and experiments that will help him cultivate his senses. At this stage, he is able to form simple ideas by combining his sensations. This is what Rousseau calls 'sensual or childish reason' (OC 4:417; trans. Bloom, 157–8). It, in turn, will be the foundation for intellectual reason, which involves the combination of ideas.

Emile is taught the art of self-reliance. As a child, he will read only one book – *Robinson Crusoe* – a story about how a man's strength prevails over physical obstacles, a story of self-sufficiency. But Rousseau does not expect that Emile will spend his life alone: instead he will live in the company of others. Therefore he must be educated so as to develop his faculty of judgment.

For example, Rousseau thinks that during adolescence, Emile should perform charitable actions so that he can learn about human suffering. Undertaking good works will also help to draw him out of himself and to channel his *amour propre* into pride in his benevolent accomplishments: 'Let us extend *amour propre* to other beings. We shall transform it into a virtue and there is no man's heart in which this virtue does not have its root' (*OC* 4:547; trans. Bloom, 252). This experience of beneficence will help Emile to live harmoniously among other men and to judge more reliably of their ways.

But Emile's moral education would be incomplete without contemplation of higher things. Therefore, he will be expected to reason about the extremely important but complex question of religion.[3] Religious judgment requires reflection about such matters as the separation of spirit from matter, and, before the *Profession,* Rousseau provides an argument in his own name deducing this separation (*OC* 4:553, trans. Bloom, 256). The challenges of abstract thought are substantial, but Rousseau writes that he wants Emile to be prepared to choose the religious faith or sect 'to which the best uses of his reason ought to lead him' (*OC* 4:558; trans. Bloom, 260). He then introduces the character of the Savoyard vicar. Rousseau contends that he presents the Savoyard vicar's profession as 'an example of the way one can reason with one's pupil in order not to diverge from the method I have established' (*OC* 4:635; trans. Bloom, 313). Rousseau suggests that he himself met the vicar during his youth.[4] On an appointed day, on a high hill outside Turin, the vicar presented the young Rousseau with his *Profession of Faith.* Rousseau recounts the vicar's speech.

EXEGESIS OF PART 1 OF THE *PROFESSION OF FAITH*: THE VICAR'S INITIAL CRITIQUE OF HELVÉTIUS'S SENSATION-BASED MATERIALISM

In the initial passages of the first part of the *Profession,* the vicar offers an alternative to the materialist view that human judgments can be explained through the effects of the sensations alone. In particular, Rousseau gives indications that he wrote this section against Helvétius's principle that 'judgments are purely passive.' In the margins of his copy of Helvétius's *De l'esprit,* Rousseau wrote of this principle as follows: 'I tried to combat it and to establish the activity of our judgments, both in the notes that I wrote at the beginning of this book and above all in the first part of the profession of faith of the Savoyard vicar' (*OC* 4:1129).[5]

The vicar's argument for the activity of human judgments centres on an introspective investigation of his own abilities – in particular, of his capacity to compare the bodies he senses outside of himself: 'I reflect on the objects of my sensations; and, finding in myself the faculty of comparing them, I sense myself endowed with an active force which I did not before know I had' (*OC* 4:571; trans. Bloom, 270). In comparing objects, the vicar maintains, he moves them around, superimposes them, and evaluates their relationships. These are not simply passive operations. He also contends that errors in judgment attest to the activity involved in the process: in judging the relations between sensations, the understanding 'mixes its errors in with the truth of the sensations, which reveal only the objects' (*OC* 4:573; trans. Bloom, 271). He concludes with his most nuanced and forceful arguments for the activity of human judgment:

> Let this or that name be given to this force of my mind which brings together and compares my sensations; let it be called *attention, meditation, reflection*, or whatever one wishes. It is still true that it is in me and not in things, that it is I alone who produce it, although I produce it only on the occasion of the impression made on me by objects. Without being master of sensing or not sensing, I am master of giving more or less examination to what I sense.
>
> Therefore I am not simply a sensitive and passive being but an active and intelligent being. (*OC* 4:573; trans. Bloom, 271–2)

The vicar's specific arguments in this section do appear to bear the imprint of the first chapter of *De l'esprit*. For there Helvétius maintains that judgment is the key operation of thinking, suggests that judgment should be understood as comparing objects, and draws our attention to the problem of errors in judgments. It has to be said that Helvétius's reasoning is less subtle and skilful than that of the vicar. Nonetheless, whatever Rousseau owes to Descartes, Clarke, and Fontenelle in writing the vicar's argument in these initial pages of the *Profession*,[6] in terms of the originality of his argument, he is also very greatly obliged to a philosophical opponent.

Having reflected on his own capacities, the vicar then turns to examine bodies outside of himself, trying to determine how they move. In fact, the vicar's argument about how to explain the motions of matter will lead to his first article of faith – that a will moves the universe as a first cause. He argues that there are two kinds of motion – communicated motion, which occurs when the body is moved by something outside it, and spontaneous motion, which happens when the body moves itself. The existence of spontaneous motion is illustrated by his own sentiment of free will:

> You will ask me ... how I know there are spontaneous motions. I shall tell you that I know it because I sense it. I want to move my arm and I move it without this movement's having another immediate cause than my will. It would be vain to try to use reason to destroy this sentiment in me. It is stronger than any evidence. One might just as well try to prove to me that I do not exist. (*OC* 4:574; trans. Bloom, 272)[7]

Inanimate bodies cannot move themselves. Instead, the vicar suggests that they are naturally at rest.[8] As a result, some conception of a first spontaneous cause is needed to explain the origins of motion in the universe:

> The first causes of motion are not in matter. It receives motion and communicates it, but it does not produce it. The more I observe the action and reaction of the forces of nature acting on one another, the more I find that one must always go back from effects to effects to some will as first cause; for to suppose an infinite regress of causes is to suppose no cause at all. In a word, every motion not produced by another can come only from spontaneous, voluntary action. Inanimate bodies act only by motion, and there is no true action without will. This is my first principle. I believe therefore that a will moves the universe and animates nature. This is my first dogma, or my first article of faith. (*OC* 3:576; trans. Bloom, 273)

As the editors of the Pléiade note, arguments from the first cause date back to Aristotle, but since the vicar grounds his argument about it on the felt experience of free will, he understands this first cause as will.[9] The first article of faith of this natural theology is grounded on the sentiment of free will.

The vicar's second article of faith is that 'if moved matter shows me a will, matter moved according to certain laws shows me an intelligence' (*OC* 4:578; trans. Bloom, 275). He admits that he does not know the purpose of the world, but he asserts that it exhibits an order and artistry consistent with some purpose:

> I judge that there is an order in the world although I do not know its end;

> to judge that there is this order it suffices for me to compare the parts in themselves, to study their concurrences and their relations, to note their harmony. I do not know why the universe exists, but that does not prevent me from seeing how it is modified, or from perceiving the intimate correspondence by which the beings that compose it lend each other mutual assistance. I am like a man who saw a watch opened for the first time and, although he did not know the machine's use and had not seen the dial, was not prevented from admiring the work. 'I do not know,' he would say, 'what the whole is good for, but I do see that each piece is made for the others; I admire the workman in the details of his work; and I am quite sure that all these wheels are moving in harmony only for a common end which it is impossible for me to perceive.' (*OC* 4:578; trans. Bloom, 275)

Here the vicar adopts a radically open view of the whole. Some end may exist in nature but he cannot know or perceive it. He is agnostic, so to speak, as regards any particular teleology; but at the same time, he is affirming the working of intelligence and intention in nature.[10]

The vicar then states an important objection to his assertion that an intelligence governs the workings of the world:

> I should not, I agree, be surprised that a thing happens, if it is possible and the difficulty of its occurrence is compensated for by the number of throws of the dice. Nevertheless, if someone were to come to me and say that print thrown around at random had produced the *Aeneid* all in order, I would not deign to take a step to verify the lie. 'You forget,' I shall be told, 'the number of throws.' But how many of those throws must I assume in order to make the combination credible? As for me, seeing only a single throw, I can give odds of infinity to one that what it produced is not the result of chance. (*OC* 4:579; trans. Bloom, 275–6)

The vicar's tone is decisive, but evidence in Rousseau's letters shows that his own response evolved through repeated rumination on this question. As he notes in one manuscript of the *Lettre à Voltaire* of 18 August 1756, his thinking had been provoked by the objection as stated by Diderot in his *Pensées philosophiques*:

> I remember that what has struck me most forcefully in my whole life, on the fortuitous arrangement of the universe, is the twenty first *pensée philosophique*, where it is shown by the laws of analysis of chance that when the quantity of the throws is infinite, the difficulty of the event is more

> than sufficiently compensated by the multiplicity of throws, and that consequently the mind ought to be more astonished by the hypothetical combination of chaos than by the real birth of the universe. This is, while assuming motion necessary, what has never been said with more force to my mind on this dispute; and, as for me, I declare that I do not know the least response that common sense might have, whether true or false, if not to deny as false what one cannot know, that motion might be essential to matter. From another perspective, I do not know whether the generation of organic bodies and the perpetuity of seeds have ever been explained by materialism; but there is this difference between these two opposed positions, that, while both the one and the other seem equally convincing to me, the last alone persuades me. As for the first, let someone come to tell me that, from a fortuitous throw of letters the *Henriade* was composed, I would deny it without hesitating; it is more possible for chance to bring it about than for my mind to believe it, and I feel that there is a point where moral impossibilities are for me equivalent to a physical certainty.[11]

A year and a half after sending his *Lettre à Voltaire* of 18 August 1756, on 18 February 1758, Rousseau wrote to the Swiss pastor Jacob Vernes on the same subject:

> I have passed my life among unbelievers without allowing myself to be shaken. I loved them, esteemed them very much, and yet I could not stand their doctrine … I left them arranging their 'chances,' their 'lots,' their 'necessary motions,' and whilst they were constructing their universe from a throw of dice I was looking at that unity of purpose which showed me … a single author. It was just as if they had told me the *Iliad* had been composed merely by a chance throw of letters, whereas I said to them very resolutely: Such things are possible, but they are not true; and I have no reason for not believing them except the fact that I do not believe. That's prejudice, they say. Very well. But what can reason do, rude though it be, against a prejudice that is more persuasive than itself. Another endless argument against that distinction of the two substances from each other; another conviction on my part that there is nothing common to a tree and my thought; and it has amused me in all this to see them driven by their own sophisms to the point of preferring to endow stones with consciousness rather than concede a soul to man.[12]

We see, then, that in responding to the objection about the number of random combinations that could produce the universe, the vicar makes thoughtful arguments in support of a position Rousseau takes in his own name in private letters.

Having attempted to meet Diderot's objection, the vicar then presses his point that the order and harmony he observes in the laws that govern the world are hard to account for on a purely materialist view:

> How many absurd suppositions are needed to deduce all this harmony from the blind mechanism of matter moved fortuitously! Those who deny the unity of intention manifested in the relations of all the parts of this great whole can try to cover their nonsense with abstractions, coordinations, general principles, and symbolic terms. Whatever they do, it is impossible for me to conceive of a system of beings so constantly ordered without conceiving of an intelligence which orders it. I do not have it within me to believe that passive and dead matter could have produced living and sensing beings, that a blind fatality could have produced intelligent beings, that what does not think could have produced thinking beings. (*OC* 4:580; trans. Bloom, 276)

It is not easy, he reasons, to explain the generation of intelligent beings on the basis of comprehensive materialism.[13] Rousseau makes this point in his own name in his *Lettre à Franquières*. There he challenges his correspondent to explain the purely material genesis of organized, intelligent life as follows:

> You, Epicurean, you would compose the soul of subtle atoms. But what do you call *subtle*, I ask you? You know that everything is big or small relative to the eye that looks at it. By way of supposition, I take a microscope and I look at one of your atoms. I see a big piece of crooked rock. From the dancing and collisions of similar pieces, I expect to see thought result. You, Modernist, you show me an organic molecule. I take my microscope and see a dragon as big as half my room: I expect to see them shape themselves [*se mouler*] and twist around other dragons until I see, as a result of all this, a being not only organized but intelligent, a being who is not aggregative and who is rigorously one, etc. You note, Monsieur, that the world was fortuitously arranged like the Roman Republic. In order for the parallel to be accurate, the Roman Republic should not have been composed of men but rather of pieces of wood. Show me clearly and sensibly the material generation of the first intelligent being, I will ask you nothing more. (*OC* 4:1140)[14]

There is evidence, then, that the vicar's arguments for his second article of faith, that the laws of the universe reveal an intelligence, embody some of Rousseau's actual reservations about a purely materialist view of the universe.

We should also note how voluntarist is the vicar's presentation of that intelligence. In fact, the vicar combines the ideas of intelligence and will: 'I believe,' he says, 'that the world is governed by a powerful and wise will' (*OC* 4:580; trans. Bloom, 276). Thus, the development of the second article of faith depends on the first article of faith – that a will moves the universe – and on the arguments for free will that it required. Indeed, the vicar interprets the deity as will:

> This Being which wills [*veut*] and is powerful, this Being active in itself, this Being, whatever it may be, which moves the universe and orders all things, I call *God*. I join to this name the ideas of intelligence, power and will which I have brought together, and that of goodness which is their necessary consequence. (*OC* 4:581; trans. Bloom, 277)

The third article of faith is that 'man is ... free in his actions and as such is animated by an immaterial substance' (*OC* 4:586–7; trans. Bloom, 281). The vicar works up gradually to this conclusion. In his first argument he contemplates human nature within the cosmos:

> After having discovered those attributes of the divinity by which I know its existence, I return to myself and I try to learn what rank I occupy in the order of things that the divinity governs and I can examine. I find myself by my species incontestably in the first rank; for by my will and by the instruments in my power for executing it, I have more force for acting on all the bodies surrounding me, for yielding to or eluding their actions as I please, than any of them has for acting on me against my will by physical impulsion alone; and by my intelligence I am the only one that has a view of the whole. What being here on earth besides man is able to observe all the others, to measure, calculate, and foresee their movements and their effects, and to join, so to speak, the sentiment of common existence to that of its individual existence? (*OC* 4:582; trans. Bloom, 277)

The vicar contends that men's wills allow them to be more independent of instinct than the beasts who are governed by 'physical impulsion alone.' To this extent he confirms or reiterates Rousseau's position in the *Discourse*. In addition, he holds that man's will and his inventive use of the instruments in his power confer a competitive survival advantage upon him. Therefore, one might argue that he understands the will here as a distinctive power that operates in conjunction with perfectibility (given that Rousseau understands the latter as a form of malleability or flexibility).

But the vicar alleges that in addition to being freer of instinct because of his will, man is distinguished from the animals by the scope of his intelligence. And this view differs in several respects from Rousseau's position in the *Discourse on Inequality*. These differences deserve our attention. In the *Discourse* Rousseau alleges that animals can form and combine ideas and that 'in this regard, man differs from a beast only in degree' (*OC* 3:142). There he also suggests that his view that understanding is not the species distinction follows from his contention that the formation of ideas involved in understanding can be explained mechanistically. He contends that 'it is not so much understanding that is the specific distinction of man as his quality of being a free agent' (*OC* 3:142).

The Savoyard vicar, on the other hand, argues that man is distinguished from the beasts by the range and character of his intellectual abilities:

> Show me another animal on earth who knows how to make use of fire and who knows how to wonder at the sun. What! I can observe and know the beings and their relations, I can sense what order, beauty, and virtue are, I can contemplate the universe and raise myself up to the hand which governs it and I would compare myself to the brutes? Abject soul, it is your gloomy philosophy which makes you similar to them. Or rather, you want in vain to debase yourself. Your genius bears witness against your principles, your beneficent heart gives the lie to your doctrine, and the very abuse of your faculties proves their excellence in spite of you. (*OC* 4:582; trans. Bloom, 278)

The vicar appears to step away from Rousseau's teaching in the *Discourse* that understanding cannot distinguish man from the beasts. But is man's superior intelligence a difference of degree or of kind? The vicar appears to suggest that such a difference of degree amounts to a difference of kind.[15]

Moreover, unlike Rousseau in the *Discourse*, the vicar argues that thought cannot be explained mechanistically: 'whatever Locke says about it,' he says, 'I need only know that matter is extended and divisible in order to be sure that it cannot think' (*OC* 4:584–5; trans. Bloom, 279).[16] The denial that thought is material is a view in keeping with traditional Christian doctrine. This may lead some readers to think that while the vicar supports it, Rousseau himself does not. But this does not simply follow. In the *Lettre à Franquières,* he writes in his own name that 'regardless of what Locke says the supposition of thinking matter is a veritable absurdity' (*OC* 4:1136). The vicar's position on immaterial thought reflects the evolution of Rousseau's own views from the *Discourse* to *Emile.* Consider how he criticizes the view that there is thinking matter in his *own name* before the *Profession:*

> Once the abstract idea of substance has – I know not how – been arrived at, one sees that, in order to admit of only one substance, this substance must be assumed to have incompatible qualities, such as thought and extension, which are mutually exclusive since one is essentially divisible and the other excludes all divisibility. One conceives, moreover, that thought or, if you wish, sentiment is a primary quality inseparable from the substance to which it belongs, and that the same is the case for extension in relation to its substance. From this one concludes that beings that lose one of these qualities lose the substance to which it belongs; that consequently death is only a separation of the substances; and that beings in which these two qualities are joined are composed of the two substances to which these two qualities belong. (*OC* 4:553; trans. Bloom, 256)[17]

It seems that Rousseau was more willing or able to articulate his disagreement with the *philosophes* on the question of whether thought is of the same substance as matter by the time he wrote *Emile.* The case of his response to Condillac's view of the understanding is of particular interest here. Understanding or *entendement* is a key term for the followers of Locke, such as Condillac. As we saw in chapter 1, Condillac in his *Traité des Animaux* thoroughly criticizes Buffon's view that humans have a monopoly on *understanding,* but he accords humans 'that degree of intelligence we call reason.' In the *Second Discourse,* Rousseau takes a similar approach to that of Condillac – he asserts that the animals share in understanding, but in the Preface he writes that animals cannot participate in natural law because they are 'devoid of enlightenment [*lumières*] and freedom.' He leaves open the question of whether enlightenment and reason can be understood in material terms alone, while he states that the understanding can be understood mechanically.

In *Emile*, as we have seen, the case is quite different: both Rousseau and the vicar criticize the view that understanding can be explained in this way.[18] We surmise that by the time Rousseau wrote *Emile*, either he had begun to disagree more with materialist contemporaries such as Condillac on this question or he had became more assertive in articulating his disagreement.[19]

The vicar's argument that as compared to the understanding, the will is a derivative power, also deviates from Rousseau's position on mechanical understanding and spiritual will in the *Discourse*. The vicar acknowledges that the understanding shapes judgments that shape will. He concludes that 'if one clearly understands that man is active in his judgments, and that his understanding is only the power of comparing and judging, one will see that his freedom is only a similar power or one derived from the former.'[20] But as we noted in chapter 1, the vicar's position here on the relation between the two powers is much easier to defend than the view Rousseau takes in the earlier work. It may also be that Castillon's critique of Rousseau's view of this point influenced him to refine his position in *Emile*. Our own view, at any rate, is that Rousseau refined his opinions on this matter as his thinking about it matured.[21]

Rousseau develops and hones his views over time, but this, we have argued, is compatible with his claim to have a unified system. The unity is not always revealed in an absolute uniformity of argument and detail; in this case, it is revealed in the consistency of Rousseau's search for a teaching about reason, understanding, and will that provides a plausible alternative to a fully materialist understanding of human nature. That is to say, he employs different means towards the same goal or result, but the goal is consistent and is better achieved by the revised position in his later work.

At any rate, the overall movement of the vicar's argument for the third article of faith, that man has free will, is guided by his contention that free will allows him to choose how to behave and to do so with decidedly mixed results. Whereas initially, the vicar presents man's will as a competitive survival advantage, there is a dramatic shift in his argument when he contemplates man's actual use of this freedom:

> The picture of nature had presented me with only harmony and proportion; that of mankind presents me with only confusion and disorder! Concert reigns among the elements, and men are in chaos! The animals are happy; their king alone is miserable! O wisdom, where are your laws? O

providence, is it thus that you rule the world? Beneficent Being, what has become of your power? I see evil on earth. (*OC* 4:583; trans. Bloom, 278)

With this turn in the argument, the vicar presses one of Rousseau's most persistent messages: that men are distinguished by their unhappiness and their evil. If one only considers men's endowments or capacities, they might seem to be the luckiest of creatures. The expectation might therefore be that they could also be the happiest and the best. Instead, they alone are miserable and bad.

In fact, observation of these circumstances leads the vicar to articulate a teaching about man's contribution to evil through his free will. Its major elements are as follows: man's fate is not passively determined by the influence of instinct, appetites, senses, passions, or external forces. Instead, he is active in his decision making: 'No material being,' says the vicar, 'is active by itself, and I am.' The vicar is conscious of the independence of his will from his senses. And when he feels the torment of remorse, this instructs him that he chose the worse course but had the free will to act otherwise. He has the consciousness that since he can be independent of instinct and appetite, he freely chose to do the bad.[22] Largely on the basis of this evidence as well as of his critiques of the materialist view that matter moves itself, the vicar concludes that 'man is ... free in his actions and as such is animated by an immaterial substance.' This is the third article of faith.

But if we look at these responses to the presence of evil on earth in more detail, we find that in order to make them, the vicar formulates another, more original version of dualism:

Would you believe, my good friend, that from these gloomy reflections and these apparent contradictions there were formed in my mind the sublime ideas of the soul which had not until then resulted from my researches? In meditating on the nature of man, I believed I discovered in it two distinct principles; one of which raised him to the study of eternal truths, to the love of justice and moral beauty [*le beau morale*], and to the regions of the intellectual world whose contemplation is the wise man's delight [*les délices du sage*]; while the other took him basely into himself, subjected him to the empire of the senses and to the passions which are their ministers, and by means of all these hindered all that the sentiment of the former inspired in him. In sensing myself carried away and caught up in the combat of these two contrary motions, I said to myself, 'No, man is not one. I want and I do not want; I sense myself enslaved and free at

> the same time. I see the good, I love it, and I do the bad. I am active when I listen to reason, passive when my passions carry me away; and my worst torment, when I succumb, is to sense that I could have resisted.' (*OC* 4:583; trans. Bloom, 278–9)

Here the vicar claims that there is a dual movement within human nature – an active aspiration towards truth, justice, and moral beauty[23] and a passive orientation towards the material body, its senses, and the passions that feed them. As the vicar's subsequent argument makes clear, he does not think that the aspiration towards justice and moral beauty can be explained in material terms. But this passage raises a substantial question: is man's spiritual or immaterial aspect exhibited in his aspiration towards justice and moral good or is it exhibited in the freedom to choose between justice and injustice, good or bad? In an important sense, the vicar is suggesting that it is exhibited in both. Man is spiritual both in his ability to choose how to behave in independence of instinct and in the elevation of soul revealed by his identification with justice and moral beauty. He may be suggesting that the consciousness of freedom that perceives the ability to resist instinct and appetite best demonstrates immateriality of soul. In it, these two senses of spirituality reinforce each other. It is plausible that Rousseau stands behind the argument to this extent.

But the vicar is also suggesting that the good will is the active will and that determination by the senses implies passivity. In that case, how should malicious or spiteful decisions be understood? They would seem to be equally free in the metaphysical sense. Moreover, the vicar's conception of badness is ambiguous: What does it mean to say 'I do the bad'? If it is following the appetites, why are the animals who follow their appetites not bad? Defining badness simply as following appetites requires more explanation since he has just explained how man introduces for the first time '*mal sur terre.*'

Consider, as well, a revealing change that Rousseau made in working on the drafts of the first part of this passage, in which the vicar explains the sort of dualism he conceives in response to the problem of evil. In the first draft, instead of 'sublime ideas of soul,' Rousseau had the vicar speak of the 'sublime ideas of the divinity about which I had up to that time had only unformed ideas' (*OC* 4:1538n1). Moreover, in preparing the manuscript for printing he considered returning to the first draft version. In fact, there is compelling evidence that Rousseau does ground his own response to the existence of evil on a conception of God as the active element in a dualism of active and passive principles. In an important passage of the *Lettre à Franquières,* he responds as follows to M. Franquières's questions about the origin of evil:

> But moral evil! Work of man in which God has no other part than to have made him free and in this similar to himself! ... Why, you will say, make man free if he must abuse his freedom? ... All that I know is that the ease I had in resolving these questions came from the opinion I have always had of the eternal co-existence of two principles, an active one, which is God, the other passive, which is matter; that the active being combines and modifies with a full power, but without having created matter and without the power to annihilate it. This opinion made me subject to the hoots of the *philosophes* to whom I spoke of it: they decided it was absurd and contradictory. Perhaps, but it did not appear to me as such, and I found [in it] the advantage of explaining without difficulty and clearly, according to my inclination, so many questions with which they were entangled, among others the one you have proposed here as insoluble. (*OC* 4:1141–2)

Here Rousseau is suggesting that he was able to resolve the problem of moral evil through recourse to the idea he had 'always had' of a dualism between an active God and passive matter. This dualism appears to be the basis of the 'sublime ideas of divinity' he refers to in the drafts of the *Profession.*

A passage from the *Lettre à Beaumont* supports the view that Rousseau is serious about this dualism of two eternal principles of things and about the critique of creation that helps justify it. In his *mandement,* Beaumont had accused Rousseau of implying in the *Profession of Faith* that there are 'several Gods.' In reply, Rousseau debates the question of whether the cause of all things is better conceived as one or two principles: 'There are,' he wrote, 'two manners of conceiving the origin of things; namely, either through two diverse causes, one alive and the other dead, one active and the other passive, one efficient and the other instrumental; or through one unique cause which derives from itself alone [*qui tire d'elle seule*] everything that is, and everything that is done' (*OC* 4:955). He thinks that the hypothesis that one cause creates everything from nothing is implausible. Therefore, he leans strongly towards the idea of two principles: 'The co-existence of two principles seems to explain better the constitution of the universe and to remove the difficulties that one has trouble resolving without it, amongst others, that of the origin of evil' (*OC* 4:956–7).[24]

Why, then, does Rousseau decide to have the vicar defend a dualism of two principles within human nature rather than a dualism of active God and passive matter? In the same discussion in the *Lettre à Beaumont*, Rousseau handles the question of the vicar's position on the two principles in the *Profession* warily: he points out that the vicar does not admit 'two principles of things.'[25] Perhaps, then, he has the vicar explicitly elaborate only the dualism within human nature to avoid a more obvious conflict with Church doctrine. But note that with such a move, he seeks to avoid the repercussions for publishing his unconventional but metaphysical beliefs. This dualism of active divinity and passive matter puts Rousseau on the other side of the Christian orthodoxy of Beaumont, but he is not, for all that, in the same place as his materialist contemporaries.

At any rate, the vicar defends a dualism of two principles within human nature, and it is clear that this has an effect on Rousseau's teaching about *amour de soi* (in the *Profession* and, as we will suggest in the next section, in the rest of *Emile*). As we have seen, in the *Lettre à Beaumont*, Rousseau describes two principles of *amour de soi* as part of his interpretation of natural goodness: 'Man is not a simple being; he is composed of two substances. If everybody does not agree on this, you and I agree on it and I have tried to prove it to others. Once this is proven, *amour de soi* is no longer a simple passion, but has two principles – namely, the intelligent being and the sensitive being – whose well-being is not the same. The appetite of the senses tends to the well-being of the body and the love of order to that of the soul. This latter love, developed and rendered active, is called conscience. But the conscience only develops and acts with man's enlightenment [*lumières*]. It is only through this enlightenment that he arrives at knowledge of order and it is only when he knows it that his conscience helps him to love it' (*OC* 4:936). Rousseau explains that as the conscience becomes active, men begin to acquire ideas of justice and order; the morally beautiful begins to have a hold over them.[26] Applying two principles within human nature to *amour de soi* leads Rousseau to argue that the conscience is innate.

If we return to the *Profession of Faith*, we find that in the paragraph directly following his introduction of two principles within human nature, Rousseau suggests that *amour de soi* entails an innate conscience.

> If conscience is the work of prejudices, I am doubtless wrong and there is no demonstrable morality. But if to prefer oneself to everything is an inclination natural to man, and if nevertheless the first sentiment of justice

> is innate in the human heart, let him who regards man as a simple being overcome these contradictions, and I shall no longer acknowledge more than one substance. (*OC* 4:584; trans. Bloom, 279)[27]

Here the vicar might be accused of circular reasoning. The metaphysical dualism of two substances underlies these two principles. Therefore an assumption of the argument (metaphysical dualism) is used in proving its conclusion – that there is more than one substance. But the vicar only leaves himself open to this accusation because he pushes his argument a step too far. And it is only by pushing it too far that he is able to show us how it all fits together. He applies a substance dualism to *amour de soi* and this results in a dualism of two principles, which provides an anchor for just action as well as a response to the problem of evil that avoids relativism.[28]

This innate conscience or sentiment of justice grounds morality and serves as a guide for the will. But although its orientation towards the good may be infallible, its hold over man is not. As we saw at the end of chapter 2, the vicar distinguishes conscience from 'the sad privilege of leading myself astray from error to error with the aid of an understanding without rule and a reason without principle' (trans. Bloom, 290; *OC* 4:600–1). And this is a distinction that Rousseau had already made in his own name in the *Lettres Morales* (*OC* 4:1111). The sense of justice within human beings guides them through the heady and precarious experience of becoming moral beings. But the conscience is a guide rather than a panacea for man. Moreover, something beyond conscience is obviously required to explain the presence of evil on earth. Recall the vicar's puzzle: the most intelligent of creatures are the only unhappy and twisted ones. And why would a divine power have allowed this to happen? These are the puzzles to which free will is the vicar's solution. Free will affords men the means to do bad things and cause themselves misery.

As the vicar sees it, man's power of free will allows him to choose between good and bad or evil courses of action and so confers moral responsibility upon him rather than upon God:

> If man is active and free, he acts on his own. All that he does freely does not enter into the ordered system of providence and cannot be imputed to it. Providence does not will the evil man does in abusing the freedom it gives him; but it does not prevent him from doing it, whether because this evil, coming from a being so weak, is nothing in its eyes, or because

> it could not prevent it without hindering his freedom and doing a greater evil by degrading his nature ... It has put him in a position to make this choice by using well the faculties with which it has endowed him ... What more could divine power itself do for us? Could it make our nature contradictory and give the reward for having done well to him who did not have the power to do evil? What! To prevent man from being wicked, was it necessary to limit him to instinct and make him a beast? No, God of my soul, I shall never reproach You for having made him in Your image, so I can be free, good and happy like you! (*OC* 4:587; trans. Bloom, 281)

The vicar holds that the misuse of free will underlies man's decline and corruption.[29] It is easy for a modern reader to accept a version of this reasoning: the misuse of our freedom causes our vices and errors. It may therefore seem most reasonable to take the position that Rousseau may have thought some version of free will accounted for our misery but that he did not endorse the vicar's exalted expressions of allegiance to a sublime dualism of active and passive principles. In this exegesis of the first part of the *Profession*, we have, however, presented evidence that indicates that Rousseau understood the two problems together.

The Profession of the Savoyard Vicar as a New Civil Religion

In giving us the *Profession of Faith,* Rousseau sets out to do nothing less than to found a new civil religion. The *Profession of Faith* has puzzled some interpreters because it contains both an argument establishing the core beliefs necessary to theism (in the first part) and a radical critique of revelation that seems to undermine the foundation of all existing Western religions (in the second part). It appears to be an odd combination: one part reverence, one part irreverence. But this combination no longer seems odd; instead it appears entirely necessary if one accepts the hypothesis that Rousseau is establishing the basis for a new civil religion. If the order were reversed, if the critique of the basis of the traditional religions and especially Christianity came first, preparing the way for the proclamation of what Rousseau calls 'new and striking truths destined to combat modern materialism and to establish the existence of God and natural religion,'[30] his project would have been more transparent. But by commencing with the arguments for the existence of God and against materialism, and by putting the entire *Profession of Faith* in the mouth of a Catholic priest, Rousseau makes his endeavour look more orthodox than it is.

The evidence that through the *Profession of Faith* Rousseau is seeking to found a new civil religion is compelling. In the famous chapter 'On the Civil Religion' in Book 4, Chapter 8, of the *Social Contract*, Rousseau makes two crucial arguments about the relation between religion and politics: namely, that 'a State has never been founded without religion serving as its base, and ... that Christian law is fundamentally more harmful than useful to the strong constitution of a State.'[31] Every state requires a religion, Rousseau argues, but Christianity is too otherworldly to serve as a solid bond among the citizens of a this-worldly state.[32] These two pivotal points are the ones he reiterates in his letter to Isaac-Ami Marcet de Mézières, a Genevan who sought to defend Rousseau when the Petit Conseil was considering his case:

> As regards the *Social Contract*, the Author of this writing claims that a Religion is always necessary for the good constitution of a State. This sentiment may well displease the poet Voltaire, the juggler Tronchin and their Satellites but it is not from that side that they would dare attack the book in public. The Author then examines which is the civil Religion Without which no State can be well-constituted. It is true that he seems not to believe that Christianity, at least that of today, is that civil Religion, indispensable to all good legislation.[33]

These passages establish that Rousseau clearly thought there was a need for a new civil religion. In fact, a few years earlier, in his *Letter to Voltaire* of 16 August 1756, Rousseau had called on Voltaire to write a kind of '*civil profession of faith*' (*OC* 4:173, emphasis mine). He begins by describing what he means: 'There is ... a sort of profession of faith that the laws can impose, but beyond the principles of morality and natural right, it ought to be purely negative.' In its negative dimension, this civil profession would proscribe religions that 'attack the foundations of society,' especially intolerant religions. Rousseau would even proscribe 'intolerant believers who wish to force the people to believe nothing.' Having risked offending the famously anti-clerical Voltaire, he then proposes that the poet might undertake the writing of such a profession:

> I would therefore wish that in each State one might have a moral code, or a sort of *civil profession of faith*, which contained positively the social maxims that everyone would be bound to admit, and negatively the fanatical maxims that one would be bound to reject, not as impious, but as seditious.

> Thus every Religion which could not agree with it would be proscribed; and everyone would be free to have none other than the code itself. Done carefully, this work would, it seems to me, be the most useful book ever composed, and perhaps the only one necessary for men. There, sir, is a subject for you.[34]

He goes on to suggest that if Voltaire were to write such a 'Catechism of the Citizen,' it would be a fitting cap to a brilliant career.[35]

Did Rousseau execute the project he once urged on Voltaire? The *Profession of Faith of the Savoyard Vicar* resembles his proposal to Voltaire insofar as it contains, positively, a series of articles of faith, presented as the essential maxims of religion, in the first part, and a negative argument against religious imperialism and intolerant religions, in the second part. In his chapter 'On the Civil Religion' in the *Social Contract*, Rousseau's suggestions for the articles of a 'purely civil' profession of faith also have a positive and a negative dimension:

> The dogmas of the civil religion ought to be simple, few in number, stated with precision, without explanations or commentaries. The existence of a powerful, intelligent, beneficent, foresighted and providential divinity; the afterlife; the happiness of the just; the punishment of the wicked; the sanctity of the social contract and the laws. These are the positive dogmas. As for the negative ones, I limit them to a single one: intolerance. (Masters, 131)[36]

The Savoyard vicar's *Profession*, with its affirmation of the existence of an intelligent diety, the afterlife, the happiness of the just, the torment through remorse of the wicked, and its condemnations of intolerance, does, we would suggest, set out the basis for key dogmas of such a 'purely civil profession of faith.'[37]

Moreover, that Rousseau had audacious views about the possible political effects of the creed of the Savoyard vicar is plain from his comment in the Third Reverie. There he refers to the *Profession of Faith* as 'a work vilely prostituted and profaned among the present generation but which may one day make a revolution among men, if good sense and good faith are ever reborn among them' (*OC* 1:1018; trans. Butterworth, 34). As we noted above, in the *Lettre à Christophe de Beaumont*, defending *Emile* and the *Profession*, Rousseau writes that the *Profession* is the 'best and most useful writing in the eighteenth century' (*OC* 4:960) (a remark that recalls his suggestion that if Voltaire were to write a civil profession of faith, it would be 'the most useful book ever composed'). And should there remain any doubt about the boldness and grandeur of Rousseau's intentions regarding *Emile* as a whole, we would do well to recall Rousseau's ringing statement at the end of the *Lettre à Beaumont*: 'Yes, I am not afraid to say it, if there is a single truly enlightened government in Europe, a government whose views were truly useful and healthy, it would have given public honours to the author of *Emile*, it would have erected statues to him' (*OC* 4:1003).

It is also striking that in the summary of the *Social Contract* in *Emile*, Rousseau does not mention the need for a civil religion.[38] The absence of any mention of this, the subject of the longest, most controversial chapter in the work, is conspicuous, to say the least. In fact, the political-religious teachings of *Emile* and the *Social Contract* complete each other. In Book 4, Chapter 8, of the *Social Contract*, Rousseau's analysis of the need for the civil religion and the inadequacy of traditional Christianity to the task is followed by the description of a 'purely civil profession of faith' that we have just described. Ronald Beiner has suggested that after a 'very thorough critical analysis' of the problem of civil religion in the first part of the chapter, in the final paragraphs Rousseau offers only an 'anemic religion,' or, as he also puts it, a 'watered-down quasi-religion.' Thus, he argues, 'the problem of the civil religion presents ... an aporia' with which the *Social Contract* concludes.[39] But perhaps the aporia at the end of that bold chapter is filled by the *Profession of Faith of the Savoyard Vicar*, just as the intended political significance of the *Profession of Faith* can only be fully grasped by reading the political-religious descriptions in the chapter on the civil religion.

Rousseau's civil religion is intended to negotiate the tensions between particularistic religious affiliations (the religion of the citizen) and universal religious principles (see especially *Emile*, OC 4:607–9; trans. Bloom, 295–6).[40] It is to feature core religious truths available to all national religions. In the *Lettre à Beaumont* defending *Emile* and the *Profession*, Rousseau gives an example of a speech that 'men of sense' among the Christians, the Jews, and the Turks would use to address an assembly of the human race established in order to find 'a Religion common to all peoples.' The speech explores their agreement about the core principles of 'essential religion' – for example, about the creator of Heaven and Earth, about the idea that man is composed of two substances, and about the existence of the afterlife. The speech concludes with the following words: 'For the rest, no more disputes amongst you about the merits (*préferénces*) of your cults. They are all good when they are prescribed by the laws and the essential Religion is found in them; they are bad when it is not. The form of the cult is the administration [*la police*] of religions and not their essence, and it is up to the Sovereign to regulate the administration of the country.' Directly after this, Rousseau writes as follows: 'I thought, Sir, that the one who reasoned this way would not be a blasphemer, an impious person, that he proposed a means of peace that was just, reasonable and useful to men; and that does not prevent him from having his own religion as the others do or his being as sincerely attached to it' (*OC* 4:977). Rousseau is defending himself against charges of blasphemy and impiety in this letter. He begins his comment with the phrase 'I thought,' referring to his own former thought.[41] If Rousseau is 'the one who reasons this way,' then it appears his religious vision attempts to be both particularist and universal. In the chapter 'On Civil Religion,' Rousseau argues that 'there is no longer and can never again be an exclusive national religion' (*OC* 3:469; Masters, 131). In the face of this fact, he champions a minimalist core of religious belief. The substance is to be common, to be mutually agreed upon, but the expression can be parochial, or national. It is a kind of religious federalism.[42]

If this reading is correct, Rousseau is attempting to reduce, although he does not resolve, the tension between the religion of man and the religion of the citizen.[43] For one thing, a monotheistic essential religion remains in tension with polytheisms. For another, the core religious beliefs are to be ecumenical, but this is a Christian notion. Therefore, while its articulation may be explicitly impartial, it may be implicitly Christian. Furthermore, one has to stand outside *some* – and perhaps, finally, outside *all* – religious traditions to believe that the administration or external expressions of a religion can be separated from its core beliefs. Perhaps here Rousseau betrays Enlightenment assumptions that are incompatible with serious belief in a religious tradition.

This argument that Rousseau attempts to found a new civil religion through the vicar's natural religion of course supplies him with a strong motive to present the salutary teachings it contains as true, whether or not he believes them to be such. Sceptics would suggest that Rousseau thinks the *Profession of Faith* and the defences of free will within it are salutary but not true. We therefore need to examine this case and respond to it. This is the subject of section two, which constitutes the rest of the chapter.

Section 2: The Question of Rousseau's Endorsement of the Vicar's Profession

This section, in turn, has two parts. In the first part, we examine the general question of whether Rousseau endorses the *Profession of Faith.* In the second part, we investigate the specific argument that since the *Profession* conflicts with the teaching of the rest of *Emile,* it cannot reflect Rousseau's true opinions about matters metaphysical.

Rousseau's Endorsement of the Vicar's Profession: The Overall Debate

If Rousseau does seek to found a new civil religion with the vicar's creed, he does so to inculcate healthy politics based on salutary teachings, so if anything, this interpretation underscores the fact that Rousseau has an ulterior motive for defending the salutary positions such as man's possession of free will. As we argued in relation to the *Second Discourse,* however, a position can be both true and salutary.[44] But this merely imposes on us a further question: Does Rousseau consider the *Profession of Faith* to be true? Does he endorse the vicar's views? This question is important to our investigation. If we can show that Rousseau probably does endorse these arguments, it strengthens our overall case that he endorses his discussion about man's free will in the *Second Discourse.* But, as noted, if Rousseau is using the *Profession* to introduce a new civil religion that is essential to political life, then he has a powerful motive for lying about any elements of it that he might regard as salutary but not true. In the Third Walk of the *Reveries,* he relates that the result of his attempt to determine his principles 'was just about [*un peu près*] that of the profession of faith of the Savoyard vicar' (*OC* 1:1018). But the Fourth Walk of the *Reveries* contains a discussion of lying, which can be read as a defence of salutary lying. Thus, in the next chapter, through a reading of the Third and Fourth Reveries, we will be considering whether Rousseau means to indicate that he is lying about free will or about his endorsement of the *Profession of Faith.* In this section, we discuss some key objections to the idea that Rousseau stands behind the vicar's teaching; we also carefully consider Rousseau's own statements about the question. Our overall view is that the *Profession of Faith* embodies much of Rousseau's own personal position about both metaphysics and religion.

Let us begin by reviewing some objections. We concede that it has to be borne in mind that the vicar is a character in *Emile,* a fact that should lead interpreters to hesitate before taking the vicar's positions for those of Rousseau. Rousseau might be using the device of presenting a character to offer up edifying views that he does not share.

Another important aspect of the position that Rousseau does not endorse the vicar's creed is the argument that there are significant contradictions between the positions the vicar takes and those Rousseau states elsewhere. For example, the vicar's position relies on metaphysical dualism, while in the rest of *Emile,* Rousseau's psychology seems to assume that Emile 'should as much as possible be one' (*OC* 4:636). We will return to this objection soon.

It is further argued that the vicar's positions contradict those that Rousseau takes in his other philosophical works. But each supposed contradiction is open to debate. One can dispute whether the contradictions can be reconciled or explained. And even if a contradiction is genuine, there are rival hypotheses about its cause. After all, as we noted above, Rousseau changed his mind about a number of issues, such as the naturalness of the family and the character of *amour propre* itself. Rousseau's contradictions therefore do not necessarily point to his duplicity in making one of the assertions.[45]

As to the important question of whether the other *philosophes* saw Rousseau as endorsing the vicar's creed, here, too, the evidence is ambiguous. According to Mark Hulliung, if the *philosophes* 'overcame their fears that [Rousseau] would join the dévot party, they did so on the grounds that his religiosity was a cover for his attacks on them.' As evidence, Hulliung says that 'Voltaire consistently interpreted Rousseau's religious beliefs as nothing more than an occasion to attack the philosophes.'[46] But Rousseau complains in the Third Reverie that 'the whole present generation ... finds truth and evidence in the system opposed to mine. It even seems incapable of believing that I adopt my own in good faith.' This may have been true of Voltaire, but Diderot (who knew him so well) concluded that Rousseau held principles opposed to those of the *philosophes*. Peter Gay tells us that in a commentary on Helvétius, Diderot 'apostrophized his dead acquaintance' as follows: 'The difference between you and Rousseau is that Rousseau's principles are false, and the consequences are true, while your principles are true and the consequences false. In exaggerating his principles, Rousseau's disciples will be nothing but madmen; yours, moderating your consequences, will be wise men.'[47] And Helvétius himself takes the vicar's criticism of his conception of judgment as Rousseau's own opinion in his discussion of *Emile* in *De l'homme*.[48]

The question of Rousseau's real views about the vicar's speech is a complex one. In adopting the device of character, Rousseau is able to use the vicar as a mask. But what sort of mask is it? Allan Bloom argues that the *Profession of Faith* 'is clearly not Rousseau's final reflection about metaphysics or the question of God because it is explicitly put in the mouth of another and is less radical than reflections pronounced in Rousseau's own name.'[49] It is true that the *Profession of Faith* is more regimented and less mystical than the reflections on religion contained in the *Lettre à Malesherbes*. It is more decisive and uniform than the stabbing assertions and troubled vacillations in Rousseau's account of his metaphysical journey in the Third Reverie. In the *Lettre à Beaumont*, Rousseau writes that in the *Second Discourse, Julie,* and the *Lettre à D'Alembert,* his principles were expressed with 'less reserve' than in the vicar's *Profession of Faith* (*OC* 4:933). But Rousseau suggests in this passage that it puzzled him that it was the relatively tidy, circumspect *Profession of Faith* that shocked his contemporaries. And shock them it did. Largely because of the second part of the *Profession,* Rousseau was accused of blasphemy and impiety. *Emile* was condemned and burned chiefly because of the assertions made by the Savoyard vicar.

Nonetheless, when Rousseau defends himself against these charges, he often uses the character of the vicar as a protective shield against the consequences of stating his real opinions. Thus the device of characterization cuts two ways. While certain of the vicar's orthodoxies may dissimulate the unconventional character of Rousseau's religious aspirations, it is also true that if attacked, he could play on the fact that the vicar was a character in the work. The vicar's condemnations of reliance on revelation, his criticisms of Catholicism, and his questioning of miracles could be presented as the vicar's personal opinions and not necessarily as those of Rousseau.[50] (All the more so since Rousseau presents the vicar as an actual man he met in his youth.) This is precisely the strategy that Rousseau used repeatedly in his own defence. During the heat of the controversy caused by the publication of *Emile,* Rousseau often described himself as the 'editor' of the vicar's creed rather than its 'author.'[51] To one of his would-be defenders in Geneva, Rousseau exhibited a cagey evasiveness that revealed how much he expected to rely on the protective mask of the vicar's character:

> The Author of the book does not present himself as that of the profession of faith; he declares that it is a writing he transcribes in his book, and in the preamble this writing appears to be addressed to him by one of his fel-

> low citizens. There is all one can infer from the work itself, to go further is to divine and if even once one gets involved in divining in the Tribunals, what will happen to private individuals who do not have the good fortune to be pleasing to Magistrates?[52]

Rousseau consistently defended the vicar's views, but he also played on the fact that his opponents could not ascribe the vicar's views to him with certainty. The vicar is more tight-laced than Rousseau, but at least in his public statements, Rousseau was still determined to keep him at arm's length.[53] As Rousseau himself put it in a draft fragment of the *Lettre à Beaumont*, one cannot attribute to an editor 'the sentiments he publishes unless he expressly adopts them' (*OC* 4:1028).

This leads us to the next step in our inquiry: does Rousseau 'expressly adopt' the *Profession of Faith*? What is his own direct testimony about whether he stands behind the vicar's creed? As we noted above, Rousseau tells us that after examining all his principles in an attempt to settle them 'once and for all,' the 'result ... was just about [*un peu près*] that which I have since set down in the profession of faith of the Savoyard vicar' (*OC* 1:1018). Here Rousseau seems to be expressly indicating that he adopts most of the vicar's views. But to get a fuller picture of his intention, we need to compare this remark with two other key statements that Rousseau makes about the *Profession*. In the *Letters Written from the Mountain*, which was written in the throes of controversy, Rousseau is more coy about his real relationship to the *Profession*. He comments on the similarities between Julie's profession on her deathbed and the vicar's profession as follows:

> These two pieces are enough in agreement that one can explain the one by the other, and from this accord one can presume with some plausibility [*vraisemblance*] that if the Author who published the books where they are contained does not adopt the one and the other in their entirety, he favors them a lot. Of these two professions of faith the first being the most extended and the only one where one finds the incriminating evidence [*corps de delit*] should be examined in preference. (*OC* 3:694)[54]

Here Rousseau is introducing a distinction between favouring and adopting; he strongly *favours* the vicar's profession, but he also implies that he does not *adopt* it in its entirety. While in the *Reveries* statement, Rousseau implies that he adopt most of the vicar's views, this statement leaves open the possibility that he does *not* adopt some portions.

On the other hand, in his letter to his close friend Moultou of 23 December 1761, Rousseau appears to endorse the vicar's profession as a whole. In this letter, written after an accident with a catheter that acutely aggravated his urinary complaint, Rousseau speculates that he may soon die. He also informs Moultou that he will send him a copy of the *Profession of Faith of the Savoyard Vicar* in the next day's post: 'Adieu, dear Moultou, you will easily conceive [*concevrez*] that the profession of faith of the Savoyard Vicar is mine [*la mienne*]. I desire too much that there be a God not to believe it, and I die with the firm confidence that I will find in his bosom the happiness and peace which I could not enjoy here below.'[55]

The preponderance of evidence indicates, we surmise, that the *Profession of Faith* really does contain much of Rousseau's own position about metaphysics and religion. But, as these words to Moultou also indicate, the key to a fuller understanding of Rousseau's intentions regarding these matters lies in attending to the changing nature of his hopes and doubts, and his reasons and feelings. Rousseau hopes that God and free will exist, and he tries to ground these hopes on reason – in effect, to turn them into reasonable hopes.[56] In the next chapter we will closely examine the evolution of these dimensions of Rousseau's intention. But before we do so, another inquiry awaits us. We now turn to the place of the *Profession of Faith* in the teaching of *Emile* as a whole.

The Profession *in* Emile

In this section we examine and reply to the objection that because the vicar's teaching in the *Profession of Faith* is so different from Rousseau's teaching in the rest of *Emile*, it is unlikely that he endorses the vicar's views about metaphysical dualism – in particular, his views about free will.

To see its full pertinence, it is best to begin by drawing out the reasoning behind this objection. Emile, Rousseau writes after the *Profession*, is to be 'as much as possible one' (*OC* 4:636, trans. Bloom, 314). But this approach appears to be at odds with the vicar's teaching, which contrasts man's immaterial soul with the needs of his material body. As Allan Bloom puts it, 'the Vicar teaches the dualism of body and soul, which is alien and contradictory to the unity which Emile incarnates.'[57]

Advocates of the counter-case also suggest that while the psychology of *Emile* is based on the duality of *amour de soi* and *amour propre*, this duality is compatible with comprehensive materialism, which, in turn, is incompatible with the metaphysical dualism of the vicar. They maintain that the main text of *Emile* (as well as the *Second Discourse*) is based on this monistic understanding. That is to say, human nature is not split or divided between a material body and an immaterial soul animated by free will.[58]

In reply to these interpretations, we suggest that *Emile* is a two-level response to the empiricist materialism of Rousseau's day. Associated with the work of Condillac, Helvétius, and Locke, this school often goes by the name 'sensualism.' Sensualism denies that there are innate ideas and explores the ways in which human thought is shaped by sense impressions. Rousseau shares some of the assumptions of the 'sensualist' school regarding the impact of sense impressions on learning, but he sees the limitations of a sensualist approach to ethics and human agency.[59]

There are two lines or tracks of argument in *Emile,* just as there are two in the *Second Discourse.* In the main body of *Emile,* Rousseau argues chiefly on the ground of the sensualist camp. It is fair to say that he begins from their key premise that sense experience shapes the understanding. He does so both because he concedes it and agrees with it and because he does not want *Emile* to be dismissed by the materialists of his time.[60] (Condillac and Helvétius were both materialist thinkers; the case of Locke is more contested.) At the same time, however, through the *Profession of Faith,* Rousseau offers a more uncompromising critique of materialism: he offers an anti-materialist theism grounded in free will.

That said, two further points require attention. First, outside of the *Profession,* in his own name, Rousseau makes a number of arguments that go beyond the premises of the sensualist approach, including, notably, a clear dualist argument asserting that there are two substances.[61] Second, the Savoyard vicar accepts many of the premises of the sensualist school.[62] This is important, because it reveals that we are faced with two different *layers* that run through the entire text of *Emile* rather than two strictly compartmentalized sections.

Designing a text with two layers is a conscious strategy on Rousseau's part. One layer of the text of *Emile* might be called metaphysically neutral in the sense that it would not be controversial to the determinist materialist thinkers of his time, including those of a sensualist bent. The other layer of text reflects a commitment to dualism and free will; it might be called metaphysically *engagé.* The sensualist layer of argument in *Emile* is compatible with materialism, but it is less a metaphysical argument than an epistemological one; it brackets metaphysical controversies while it is epistemologically *engagé*.

The metaphysically neutral account of how Emile is shaped by natural forces is couched in a vocabulary that engages eighteenth-century materialist and sensualist thinkers. This two-track strategy allows Rousseau to present his arguments for free will in a context that gives them to fairer hearing. Nonetheless, both layers of the text are genuine reflections of Rousseau's views. He thinks that sensualism is insightful up to a certain point. It is a rich epistemological approach that combines very well with his purpose of providing Emile with a natural education.

Rousseau's canny, two-track strategy is similar to the one (we have argued above) he uses in the *Second Discourse*. Rousseau's strategic but sincere use of sensualism in *Emile* is comparable to his strategic but sincere use of perfectibility in the *Discourse*.

Sceptics might respond that Rousseau does not fully reconcile these two lines of argument and further that this is an indication that he only really believes in the materialist line. We would concede that Rousseau does not fully reconcile metaphysical dualism with comprehensive materialism; he certainly does not claim to have done so. But we believe that to see what he does accomplish, one has to take into account his two understandings of the dualism within human nature. He understands humanity both through a basic or plain metaphysical dualism of spiritual soul and material body and, as we suggested earlier in the chapter, through a second dualism – a dualism within *amour de soi* between a principle that orients the soul to justice and order and a principle that directs the body to fulfil its material desires. It is on the basis of this second dualism of two principles within *amour de soi* that Rousseau makes his (albeit partly rhetorical) appeal to the development of sublime sentiments in the pupil Emile. In the *Lettre à Beaumont*, Rousseau suggests that this second dualism is grounded on the metaphysical dualism of material body and spiritual soul.[63] It is this second (still metaphysically based) dualism of two principles within *amour de soi* that Rousseau combines with a broadly empiricist account of man's historical development.

The summary of his teaching about natural goodness that Rousseau offers Beaumont contains the clearest statements both of the relation between the two dualisms and of the sort of reconciliation he envisions between the dualism of two principles within *amour de soi* and historicist empiricism. It will be worth our while to look more closely at its key elements before we investigate the extent to which this proposed reconciliation is embodied in *Emile*. In this passage, Rousseau defends himself against Beaumont's censure by explaining his principle of natural goodness. He begins as follows: 'The fundamental principle of all morality about which I have reasoned in all my writings and that I developed in this last one with all the clarity of which I was capable is that man is a naturally good being, loving justice and order; that there is no original perversity in the human heart, and that the first movements of nature are always right [*sont toujours droits*].' Rousseau suggests that *amour propre* is 'the only passion born with man' and is 'indifferent in itself' to good and evil. Evil and vice are not original to human nature; rather, they arise through the circumstances that Rousseau tells Beaumont he has tried to describe. But he then argues that his interpretation of natural goodness has another dimension:[64]

> I have further explained what I understood by this natural goodness, which does not seem to follow [*se déduire*] from the indifference to good and evil natural to self-love. Man is not a simple being; he is composed of two substances. If everybody does not agree on this, you and I agree on it and I have tried to prove it to others. Once this is proven, *amour de soi* is no longer a simple passion, but has two principles – namely, the intelligent being and the sensitive being – whose well-being is not the same. The appetite of the senses tends to the well-being of the body and the love of order to that of the soul. This latter love, developed and rendered active, is called conscience. (*OC* 4:936)

Rousseau then explains that conscience is a disposition that develops gradually as man's enlightenment progresses. Once men become capable of making comparisons and judging their relations with one another, they become open to the morally beautiful and to ideas of order and justice.[65] At this point, the conscience becomes active, only to be thwarted and silenced as men's ambitions increase and their interests conflict. This presentation of the emergence and progressive suppression of an innate conscience joins a metaphysically based principle within human nature and a natural history of the human soul inspired by modern empiricism.

In both the Profession and the *Lettres Morales*, the conscience is presented as a source of morality rooted in our natures. Starting from the vocabulary of the empiricists, both Rousseau and the vicar suggest that conscience is not an acquired idea, instead it is a natural sentiment:

> We sense before knowing, and since we do not learn to want what is good for us and to flee what is bad for us but rather get this will from nature, by that very fact love of the good and hatred of the bad are as natural as the love of ourselves. The acts of conscience are not judgments but sentiments. Although all our ideas come to us from outside, the sentiments evaluating them are within us, and it is by them alone that we know the compatibility or incompatibility between us and things we ought to seek or flee. (*OC* 4:599; trans. Bloom, 289–90)[66]

In addition to the natural self-love that directs one to protect oneself, man has an innate conscience: 'There is in the depths of our souls, then, an innate principle of justice and virtue according to which, in spite of our own maxims, we judge our actions and those of others as good or bad. It is to this principle that I give the name *conscience*' (*Lettres Morales, OC* 4:1108; *OC* 4:598; trans. Bloom, 289).

Our next task is to examine to what extent the text of *Emile* illustrates or supports the reconciliation or combination of two strands of thought he outlines in his *Letter to Beaumont*. In this vein, consider Rousseau's comments (in his own name) in the first part of Book IV about how the impulses towards justice and goodness might be understood as natural needs within us:

> If this were the place for it, I would try to show how the first voices of conscience arise out of the first movements of the heart, and how the first notions of good and bad are born of the sentiments of love and hate. I would show that *justice* and *goodness* are not merely abstract words [*ne sont point seulement des mots abstraits*] – pure moral beings formed by the understanding – but are true affections of the soul enlightened by reason, are hence only an ordered development of our primitive affections; that by reason alone, independent of conscience, no natural law can be established; and that the right of nature is only a chimera if it is not founded on a natural need in the human heart. But I am reminded that my business here is not producing treatises on metaphysics and morals or courses of study of any kind. It is sufficient for me to mark out the order and the progress of our sentiments and our knowledge relative to our constitution. Others will perhaps demonstrate what I only indicate here. (*OC* 4:522–3; trans. Bloom, 235)[67]

Here Rousseau is signalling the limits of what he accomplishes in *Emile*. He does not claim to be accomplishing the sort of reconciliation of metaphysics and physics that Kant undertook. On the contrary, he is pointing out that the assumptions he makes, and the reconciliation he favours or envisions, are in need of further demonstration by subsequent thinkers. Nonetheless, his view that justice and goodness are an 'ordered development of our primitive affections' shows that he is seeking a basis for morality that starts from the modern empirical view of human nature and the body. His argument that conscience is a natural need in the human heart is an ingenious combination of Malebranche and Nietzsche.[68]

In his treatment of the transformation of *amour propre* through compassion, Rousseau provides one example of how primitive affection might be guided towards justice: Emile's active beneficence will engender 'sublime sentiments' within him and help him understand ideas of justice and order and 'true models of the beautiful' (*OC* 4:547–8; trans. Bloom, 252–3).[69]

Importantly, it is a moral version of the dualism within human nature that Rousseau attempts to reconcile with the teaching of *Emile*. If we compare the elements of each type of dualism, we see that both in the basic dualism of immaterial soul and material body and in the more original dualism of one principle oriented towards justice and order and another principle oriented towards bodily appetites, the material body is the basis of the lower term. But what we might call the upper term differs more substantially, and this has implications for our free will argument. In the dualism of two principles, since the upper term is directed towards justice and order, it is already moralized, as it were. In the basic dualism of immaterial soul and material body, the upper term (i.e., the immaterial soul) is characterized by free will. But this free will is, of course, free to choose justice and order (fulfilling the active principle) or to choose disorder and injustice (presumably transgressing it). The vicar contends that resisting determination by the appetites is active, whereas giving in to them is passive. Whether disorder and injustice are passive is arguable, but what is clear is that the *perception* that they are is instantiated or frozen in Rousseau's second dualism – that is, in his dualism of two principles within human nature. This dualism is the picture of a moment in the life of the virtuous human being – during this moment, free will and the active principle cooperate in the choice of justice and order.[70] There is a difficulty here in that, as we have argued, free will is a key element in the origin of vice. But in the dualism of two principles, this fact is repressed, and free will is marshalled in service of virtue. Free will is suppressed yet at the same time used in the sublime sentiments that the tutor instils in Emile.

Here it could be objected that even this partial reconciliation of the strands of metaphysical dualism and empiricism should be viewed with scepticism. For it could be argued that both the passages that embody this reconciliation and the statements in Rousseau's name advocating metaphysical dualism are *ad hoc*. They do not seriously affect the basic contrast between the dualism of material body and spiritual soul of the vicar and the monism of *Emile* as a whole. According to this view, Rousseau presents the metaphysical dualisms he does because he thinks they are salutary but not because he thinks they are true. Instead, he thinks that the monistic duality of *amour de soi / amour propre* is true.

We favour another explanation, one that is grounded on Rousseau's developmental theory of education. In *Emile,* Rousseau repeatedly states that his goal is to articulate a method of education that is appropriate to the actual capacities of the developing child at each stage of his life. He puts it eloquently in the Preface:

> Childhood is unknown. Starting from the false idea one has of it, the farther one goes, the more one loses one's way. The wisest men concentrate on what it is important for men to know without considering what children are in a condition to learn. They are always seeking the man in the child without thinking of what he is before being a man. This is the study to which I have most applied myself, so that even though my entire method were chimerical and false, my observations could still be of profit. (*OC* 4:241–2; trans. Bloom, 33–4)

Thus, we concede that Emile's early education is based on a development of the senses, and of his responses to the material universe (Books I to III). This is what is appropriate to the abilities of a young child. But Emile will be exposed to ideas such as the immateriality of the soul, free will, and a first cause once he is in a position to understand them. In this manner, Rousseau justifies his decision to delay Emile's exposure to reasoning about religion.

He also criticizes Locke's method of beginning to teach a pupil about spirits and subsequently introducing the concept of matter because he contends that this method only 'establishes materialism.'[71] Similarly, in his second-to-last speech to Emile, the tutor says regarding virtue, 'I have waited for you to be in a position to understand me before explaining this much profaned word to you' (*OC* 4:817; trans. Bloom,

444). This interpretation also explains Rousseau's lack of reference to virtue or self-mastery in his discussion of what the immediate effect will be on Emile of hearing the vicar's profession.

The basic dualism of material body and immaterial soul conflicts with Emile's education as a young child, but Rousseau claims that the goal of the early education is the formation of the physical being, prior to the formation of the moral being. The metaphysical dualism of two principles within human nature, however, is compatible with the education of the mature Emile, whose freedom consists of mastery of his appetites and the exercise of virtue.

In one of his last speeches to Emile, the tutor argues that because Emile has not yet learned to rule on the appetites of his heart, he must undertake 'another apprenticeship, more painful than the first' (*OC* 4:818; trans. Bloom, 445). This new apprenticeship is more painful than Emile's earlier apprenticeship to nature because it involves a struggle against ills that 'come from ourselves.' Up to this time, Emile has been good in the sense that he is independent of unnatural vices; but the mature Emile will live among others and will feel very passionately about some of them. He needs an apprenticeship in virtue in order to learn how to use his will to control his affections. 'Virtue,' the tutor suggests, belongs to a being that is 'strong by will.' The virtuous man 'knows how to conquer his affections; for then he follows his reason and his conscience; he does his duty; he keeps himself in order, and nothing can make him deviate from it' (*OC* 4:818; trans. Bloom, 444–5). Reason and conscience are to guide Emile's will in the control of his affections. The Savoyard vicar's position that reason and conscience condition the will in its mastery of the affections and passions finds an important echo in the main text of Emile.

According to this reading, both the metaphysical dualism in Rousseau's own name in *Emile* and the passages that suggest a natural base for Emile's sublime sentiments would not be *ad hoc* but would be an integral part of his education and one in keeping with its developmental logic. This argument is strengthened by the fact that it stems from one of Rousseau's primary goals in *Emile.*

4 The Quality of Rousseau's Intention and the *Reveries of the Solitary Walker*

In this chapter, we turn to Rousseau's last work, the *Reveries of the Solitary Walker*. The work itself, the chapters of which are organized as a series of walks or reveries, is beautifully written and often very profound. But two of the Reveries within it are particularly relevant to our case that Rousseau *believes* his teaching about free will. Through readings of the Third and Fourth Reveries, we uncover new dimensions of Rousseau's intention. The Third Reverie, which we examine in a first section, provides us with an opportunity to present a richer, more nuanced view of Rousseau's intention with regard to free will and metaphysical issues than we have so far been able to do. As we will see, it also yields important insights into his own understanding of his method for examining those issues. The Fourth Reverie, which we consider in the second section, helps us understand how he *presents* his intention with regard to metaphysical issues; it allows us to gauge how much confidence we can have in his presentation of his belief in free will.

In the Third Reverie, Rousseau describes his desire to combat atheistic materialism and to provide sound reasons for his alternatives to it. As he describes it, this effort involves a complex interplay of reasoning, sentiment, hope, and doubt. We trace the evolution of Rousseau's own understanding of his method over time, and we find that he develops an increasingly solid and sophisticated defence of it. Although he had some nagging doubts about the success of his endeavour, he consistently desired to provide a reasonable alternative to atheistic materialism, and he made a very carefully reasoned case for his adherence to it.

The Fourth Reverie, however, is about lying. Is Rousseau, as some interpreters have thought, lying about his belief in a metaphysical alternative to the views of the *philosophes*? Here we confront the question of

Rousseau's use of esoteric writing and its impact on our case. After all, it is because Rousseau writes esoterically that the controversy about his belief in free will arises. We concede that Rousseau sometimes writes esoterically; therefore, the fact that he justifies certain kinds of lying needs to be taken very seriously in interpreting his work. But, after analysing the principles that he says have guided him in telling truth and lies, we argue that his principles would never have permitted him to lie about the issue of freedom of the will.

Section 1: Of Hope and Doubt, Reason and Sentiment: Rousseau's Multi-Sided Intention and His Defence of His Method in the Third Reverie

In this study of Rousseau's belief in free will we have so far focused primarily on the meaning of *free will* in his texts. In this section we focus on what it means to say he *believes* in the free will teaching. We document Rousseau's statements about his hopes for an alternative to atheistic materialism. But hope is merely a feeling, and Rousseau's philosophic project requires reasons. Therefore we trace the stages of his endeavour to ground his hopes on reason, to turn his hopes into *reasonable* hopes.

In matters of religion and metaphysics, Rouseau's method is to combine reasoning and sentiment in the face of his hopes and fears. He consistently defends this method; when we compare his defences of it over a period of many years, we find that he produces progressively sounder justifications of it. This, we argue, indicates that he had both a lasting attachment and a reasoned commitment to the teaching he generated through it.

Reasoned Hopes and Direct Convictions: Rousseau's Metaphysical Method

As we saw in the previous chapter, Rousseau wrote to his dear friend Moultou about the role his hope played in his judgments about divinity: 'I desire too much that there be a God not to believe it.' But this statement does not tell us much about the *character* of Rousseau's hope. In fact, Rousseau's position about the place of hope in his religious and metaphysical thinking evolved over time. To see this, and to interpret his defences of his method for investigating matters of faith and metaphysics, we will compare several works. We will move from his initial efforts in the *Lettre à Voltaire* of 16 August 1756, through formulations in the *Lettre à D'Alembert*, the vicar's *Profession of Faith*, and the *Dialogues*, to a more extended analysis of his justification of his method in the Third Reverie.

In the *Lettre à Voltaire* of 16 August 1756 – which is sometimes called the Letter on Optimism because in it, Rousseau defends the goodness of God and the Universe – Rousseau writes that in spite of insoluble objections pro and con about the existence of God,

> I believe in God quite as strongly as I believe in any other truth because to believe or not believe are not things that depend on me, because the state of doubt is too violent for my soul, because when my reason wavers, my faith cannot for long remain in suspense, and is determined without it and finally because a thousand alluring considerations attract me to the most consoling side and join the weight of hope to the equilibrium of reason. (*OC* 4:1070–1; *Collected Writings*, vol. 3, 117)[1]

Here Rousseau tries out a number of different formulations for describing the relations among faith, hope, and reason; some of these are more respectful of reason than others. One formulation seems particularly anti-rationalistic: 'when my reason wavers,' he writes, 'my faith cannot long remain in suspense and is determined without it.' Here Rousseau flirts with the idea of abandoning reason when it does not produce the desired result, of simply siding with his feeling instead of basing his position on his reason.[2] It is true that, as Pascal put it, '*le coeur a ses raisons que la raison ne connait point*.' But to decide a question in the absence of reason is a different matter altogether. Since each of us has different feelings, endorsing feelings instead of reason undermines the basis of debate. A simple rejection of reason is counterproductive. Rousseau himself argues this point effectively in a footnote to the *Lettre à D'Alembert*. There he suggests that religious mysteries that are based on evident absurdities must be rejected: 'Otherwise, reason giving witness against itself would force us to renounce it. And far from making us believe this or that, it would prevent us from believing anything at all, considering that every principle of faith would be destroyed.'[3]

Determining one's faith without reason, then, is problematic. But Rousseau had offered a more defensible formula at the end of the same paragraph in the *Lettre à Voltaire* quoted above: 'a thousand alluring considerations attract me to the most consoling side and join the weight of hope to the equilibrium of reason.' When reason manifests itself on both sides and judgment equivocates, hope can be the deciding factor.

A passage from the *Dialogues*, written nearly twenty years later, reiterates and clarifies this idea:

> My practice in my judgment about this man is like that in my belief concerning matters of faith. I yield to direct conviction without stopping at the objections I cannot resolve; as much because these objections are founded on principles that are less clear, less solid in my mind than those that determine my persuasion, as because in yielding to these objections, I would come up against others still more invincible. In making this change, I would therefore lose the strength of evidence without avoiding the obstacle of difficulties. You say that my reason chooses the sentiment that my heart prefers and I don't deny it. That is what happens in all deliberations where judgment is not enlightened enough to reach a decision without the help of the will.[4]

Rousseau declares that when his judgment is at such an impasse, 'my reason chooses the sentiment that my heart prefers' and, he claims, so would everyone else's. Now, it is not entirely clear why it is reason that chooses, but it is important that it not be put aside. Instead, reason chooses the side of sentiment and 'direct conviction.'

Rousseau's description in the Third Reverie of the process that led to the writing of the *Profession of Faith of the Savoyard Vicar* presents the clearest, most mature statement of the role that his hopes and doubts, his heart and his reason, play in his deliberations. There he writes that he was disturbed by the 'dismal doctrine' of the atheistic modern philosophers, but when he tried to respond to their arguments, 'my heart responded to them better than my reason.'[5] Therefore, he began to seek his own philosophy in order to provide himself with principles to govern his conduct. He admits that his hopes might have swayed him at the outset:

> to be sure, I have no doubt but what the prejudices of childhood and the secret wishes of my heart made the scale lean to the side most consoling for me. It is difficult to keep ourselves from believing what we so ardently desire, and who can doubt that most men's interest in admitting or rejecting the judgments of the next life determines their faith and does so according to their hope or fear. All of that could dazzle my judgment, I agree, but not alter my good faith, for I feared deceiving myself about anything. (*OC* 1:1017; trans. Butterworth, 33–4)

Here Rousseau clearly acknowledges the dangers of believing consoling illusions, of 'wishful thinking,' but he denies that this is his method.[6] His proof is an extended description of his procedure:

> Resolved to settle once and for all these matters human intelligence has so little hold over and finding impenetrable mysteries and insoluble objections on all sides, I adopted for each question the sentiment which seemed to me best established by direct means and most believable in itself without paying attention to objections I could not resolve, but which were refuted by other no less strong objections in the opposite system. A dogmatic tone about these matters is suitable only to charlatans but it is important to have one's own feeling [*sentiment*] and to choose it with all the maturity of judgment one can put into it. (*OC* 1:1018; trans. Butterworth, 34)

Here Rousseau is relying on a procedure that draws on both reason and sentiment and that attempts to give both their due. Sentiment plays a significant but regulated role in the process. It is not enough to have a sentiment: it must be chosen with one's considered judgment, and judgment presumes reason. Moreover, when he says that he determines to accept the 'sentiment' that is 'best established by direct means and most believable in itself,' he is implying that he will accept the sentiment based on a form of reason. We can see this more clearly if we turn to the discussion of methodology in the *Profession of Faith* itself.

Just as Rousseau says in the Third Reverie that he decides to accept the sentiment 'best established by direct means,' the Savoyard vicar says that his initial dispositions and sentiments were supported by 'direct' forms of evidence:

> Then, going over in my mind the various opinions which had one by one drawn me along since birth, I saw that although none of them was evident enough to produce conviction immediately, they had various degrees of verisimilitude, and inner assent was given or refused to them in differing measure. On the basis of this first observation, I compared all these different ideas in the silence of the prejudices, and I found that the first and most common was also the simplest and most reasonable, and that the only thing that prevented it from gaining all the votes was that it had been proposed last. (*OC* 4:569–70)

The vicar initially gauges the degrees of 'inner assent' warranted by the various systems; he finds that the theistic system is the 'simplest and most reasonable.' He explains that he finds the system proclaiming the 'Being of beings,' articulated by the English theologian Samuel Clarke, to be not merely more reassuring but less obscure, and given to fewer 'incomprehensible' ideas than any materialist system.[7] In particular, its comprehensiveness provides evidence that he finds compelling enough that it justifies his decision not to be distracted by insoluble objections:

> I said to myself, 'Insoluble objections are common to all systems because man's mind is too limited to resolve them. They do not therefore constitute a proof against any one in particular. But what a difference in direct proofs! Must not the only one which explains everything be preferred, if it contains no more difficulties than the others?' (*OC* 1:570; trans. Bloom, 269)

It would be misleading to simply say that the vicar appeals to reason rather than sentiment as a standard for judgment. On the contrary, it must be granted that he champions the idea of a sincere reckoning with one's inner sentiment. 'I am resolved,' he says, 'to accept as evident all knowledge to which in the sincerity of my heart I cannot refuse my consent' (*OC* 1:570; trans. Bloom, 269–70). But if we are right in our reading so far, his appeal to sincerity is itself justified by an appeal to simplicity – to the simplicity of direct proofs and readily believable arguments rather than the complicated abstractions or metaphysical sleights of hand of, say, some professional philosophers. One example of such a direct proof is the harmony of the universe. Another is the feeling of having freedom of the will itself, of making a spontaneous choice.[8] The vicar resolves to accept the evidence his heart cannot deny, but it is, after all, evidence. Rousseau's sentiments are consoling, but they are also grounded on an appeal to a specific form of reason. The vicar's appeal to simplicity and to 'direct proofs' might be taxed as anti-intellectual, but it is not for all that anti-rational. In fact, in the last instance, it might be better to criticize the vicar for undue modesty. For the vicar uses some complex metaphysical arguments to shore up his side. He relies on reason in its various forms and reason no less than sentiment. As Arthur Melzer puts it, the *Profession* 'unites reason and sentiment, head and heart, by putting conscious thought and reasoning in harmony with the belief that inexorably wells up from within us.'[9]

In the Third Reverie, it is on the basis of this dialectic of inner sentiment and reason that Rousseau allows himself to evade or at least forestall the insoluble objections on each side. There, he relates that after he had recorded the reflections that formed the basis of the vicar's creed, sometimes objections, both familiar and unforeseen, would come to trouble his peace of mind. These, however, he refuses to accept as decisive. Of such objections, he would say to himself:

> those are all only metaphysical quibbles and subtleties which have no weight next to the fundamental principles adopted by my reason, confirmed by my heart, and which all carry the seal of inner assent in the silence of the passions. In matters so much greater than human understanding, will an objection I cannot resolve overturn a whole body of doctrine so solid, so well integrated and formed with so much meditation and care, so very suited to my reason, to my heart, to my whole being, and reinforced by the inner assent I feel to be lacking in all the others? No, vain arguments will never destroy the congruity I perceive between my immortal nature, the constitution of this world, and the physical order I see reigning in it. In the corresponding moral order, whose arrangement I discovered by my seeking, I find the supports I need to endure the miseries of my life.[10] (*OC* 1:1018–19; trans. Butterworth, 35)

We have seen how Rousseau's thinking about his relation to his hopes develops from the experimental efforts of the *Lettre à Voltaire*, to the vicar's resolution to accept the direct evidence he cannot reject in the sincerity of his heart, to this fervent justification of hope through a contrapunctual combination of reason and feeling. Together these passages confirm the reading that Rousseau has sincere hopes about the viability of his alternative to the atheistic system of the *philosophes*. Here Rousseau argues that he finds consolation in the compatibility of the physical order of the world, of his immortal nature and the arrangements of the moral order. He proposes a moral/physical dualism as an alternative to materialism. Moreover, this statement in the *Reveries* is Rousseau's most mature statement and most convincing defence of the method that culminates in the *Profession of Faith*. In it, Rousseau appeals to reason a number of times. His basic principles are 'adopted' by his reason and 'suited' to it. The entire teaching is 'solid' and 'well-integrated.' But what makes this statement so striking is his description of the different elements that contribute to produce his conviction: the whole doctrine is 'so very suited to my reason, to my heart, to my whole being and reinforced by the inner assent I feel to be lacking in all the others.'[11]

There is, however, a problem with Rousseau's description of his method in this passage. The purpose of the passage is to justify his decision to avoid a more extended consideration of the objections to his argument. He tells himself that the objections that sometimes bothered him are 'only metaphysical quibbles and subtleties.' But this seems too dismissive. Were the objections of the other *philosophes* simply 'vain arguments'? The nature of this problem becomes clearer if we recall Rousseau's attempt to justify the decision to avert an extended examination of the objections a few paragraphs earlier in the Third Reverie. There he wrote that he decided to accept the sentiment 'most believable in itself without paying attention to the objections I could not resolve, but which were refuted by no less strong objections in the opposite system' (*OC* 1:1018; trans. Butterworth, 34).

But this solution is unsatisfactory at least insofar as it does not allow Rousseau to prevent the objections from troubling his peace of mind. On the contrary, in the rest of this walk, he describes the 'intervals of worry and doubt' that sometimes undermined his confidence in the consoling system he had earlier established:

> The powerful objections I had not been able to resolve then presented themselves to my mind more forcefully to finish striking me down precisely at those times when, overburdened by the weight of my fate, I was ready to give way to discouragement. Frequently, new arguments I heard came back to mind in support of those which had already tormented me. Ah! I said to myself then, when my heart was constricting so as to suffocate me, who will keep me from despair if my lot is so horrible that I no longer see anything but idle fancies in the consolations my reason furnished me; if thus destroying its own work it overturns the whole support of hope and confidence it had stored up for me in adversity?

This passage is interesting not least because in it Rousseau separates himself into two I's – the I that identifies with his hope and the I that identifies with his sceptical reason. In identifying with his hopes, Rousseau explains that 'powerful objections' torment him and beat down his courage and his heart. Here he distrusts the reason that ruins the consoling work 'it had stored up for *me* in adversity' (emphasis mine). Reason is the enemy of the sanguine Jean-Jacques. But this reason is also his own, or, better, it is also him. It is the reasoning Jean-Jacques who grasps the shortcomings of his system, who begins to distrust his principles, and who suspects he may be 'a dupe, a victim and a martyr of a vain error' (*OC* 1:1021; trans. Butterworth, 37).

In these moments of discouragement there is a dangerous schism between reason and hope: 'If ever I had spent an entire month in this state,' Rousseau tells us, 'my life and I would have been done for' (*OC* 1:1021; trans. Butterworth, 37). To extricate himself from these 'discouraging doubts and faltering hopes,' he tells himself that his reason is not as agile as it was when he undertook his extensive review of his principles. He recalls that at that time he had decided not to get involved with objections that went beyond human comprehension. And he adds that new objections that crop up 'are the sophisms of a subtle metaphysics which is unable to weigh the eternal truths admitted at all times by wise men, recognized by all nations and engraved on the human heart in indelible characters' (*OC* 1:1021; trans. Butterworth, 38).

Finally, he considers whether it would be better to adopt the position of the *philosophes* who ostracized him and the morality that accompanies it. He suggests that behind this 'rootless and fruitless morality which they pompously display in books or in some striking scene on the stage' lies another, secret morality that excuses wickedness and harm to others, 'this secret and cruel morality, the inner doctrine of all their initiates, for which the other serves only as a mask.'[12] Rousseau notes that in taking up wickedness he would acquire nothing and lose his innocence and good opinion of himself in the bargain. He concludes this series of arguments as follows:

> Reasoning in this way with myself, I succeeded in no longer allowing myself to be shaken in my principles by captious arguments, by insoluble objections, or by difficulties which went beyond my reach and perhaps beyond that of the human mind. My own mind remains as firmly tempered as I was able to make it and has become so well accustomed to resting there in the shelter of my conscience that no foreign doctrine, old or new, can any longer move it or trouble my rest for an instant. Fallen into mental languor and heaviness, I have forgotten even the reasonings on which I grounded my belief and my maxims, but I will never forget the conclusions I drew from them with the approval of my conscience and of my reason, and I hold to them henceforth. (*OC* 1:1022; trans. Butterworth, 39)

In effect, Rousseau is saying that he overcame the schism between reason and hope by splitting his reason in two and choosing the reason allied with his hopes. Here we see that he sides with a justificatory process of reasoning ('Reasoning this way with myself') that allows him to accept his former principles against the reason that destroys 'its own work.' He accepts the conclusions that he sanctioned with his conscience and his reason in the past rather than undertake the 'mental operations' required to review his former arguments and respond to the objections anew (*OC* 1:1023; trans. Butterworth, 39). He sides with the consolations of his 'full and vigorous reason' against the doubts of his 'declining reason.'[13]

Reason is the dynamic element in the Third Reverie: it is reason that moves between hope and doubt. As we have seen, Rousseau justifies the method that culminates in the *Profession* by arguing that it is based on reason as well as feeling. He uses reasoned argument to justify his persistence in his system in spite of the objections that troubled him. But he knows that it is reason – indeed, sometimes his reason – which underlies the objections as well. He decides to resist foreign doctrines and to remain confined 'within the sphere of my former knowledge.' But this decision itself betrays the threatening power of his doubts. As such it is an incomplete and unstable resolution of his dilemma.[14]

The crux of the problem is this: in writing the *Profession of Faith of the Savoyard Vicar,* Rousseau transformed his hopes into reasonable hopes; but at the same time, he transformed his doubts into reasonable doubts. In articulating his system, he became wholly conversant in the opposing case. Although this represents an advance in terms of the greater reasonableness of the debate, it also means that any progress of hope over doubt is not solid enough to secure Rousseau's unwavering conviction. However much Jean-Jacques extols the feelings of his heart, his heart listens to his reasoning about his hopes and doubts. Accordingly, at the end of his life his doubts are in his heart along with his hopes.

How does this reading affect the competing interpretations of Rousseau's positions on metaphysics and materialism that we have been considering? In my view, a detailed understanding of Rousseau's 'discouraging doubts and faltering hopes' is at once the place where both readings meet and a stumbling block to dogmatic readings on either side. For example, taking Rousseau's descriptions of his doubt in the Third Reverie seriously precludes one from overconfident assertion that he had a stalwart and unwavering belief that humans have free will. But careful attention to the Third Reverie also discourages overconfident assertion that he merely pretended to have this belief.

Rousseau's statements about his hopes for an anti-materialistic, theistic alternative are echoed in the *Lettre à Voltaire*, the *Lettre à Franquières*, and the *Profession of Faith* itself. The counter-case would have to argue that all of these statements are *ad hoc*. The counter-case would also have to account for the progress in sophistication from his earlier statements about his method to his later ones. Reading the Third Reverie in the context of his repeated defences of his method elsewhere raises the question of whether it is credible that he would have made all of these efforts as part of an elaborate ruse.

The subject of the Third Reverie is not a justification of the content of his metaphysical teaching but a rigorous re-examination and justification of the method that yielded the content. Rousseau rejects the sophistry of the *philosophes;* he criticizes their use of reason as a mere technique to be used cynically for achieving morally dubious ends. He himself uses an introspective reasoning process to defend his approach of using rational argument based on 'direct proofs' allied with sentiment.[15] There is, however, a final and very substantial objection to the case that Rousseau truly believes that we have free will and an immaterial soul. This one arises from the Fourth Reverie, which is Rousseau's account of lying.

Section 2: Truth and Consequences: A Reading of the Fourth Reverie

In the previous section we examined Rousseau's determined defences of his method in metaphysical matters. We also described the inner divisions that underlie Rousseau's intention: his reasoned hopes for a moral life based on the principles of the *Profession of Faith of the Savoyard Vicar* and his reasoned doubts about these principles based on his inability to refute all the objections to them. A reading of the Fourth Reverie confirms that Rousseau's intention is complex, while deepening and developing our understanding of that complexity. In this reading, we concede that Rousseau's moral code did not always force him to render the truth to others, but we argue that the terms of this moral code indicate that it is very unlikely that he lied about the specific question of his belief in free will. Rousseau condemns the telling of falsehoods that lead to any harm whatsoever, but he tolerates telling truths that may entail some harm to some people. We suggest that free will is a potentially harmful idea that Rousseau is nonetheless able to endorse because he thinks it is not a falsehood but a truth.

Rousseau describes the occasion of the Fourth Reverie as follows: while organizing some pamphlets, he found a journal sent to him by a naturalist of his acquaintance named Father Rozier, and on the title page Rozier had written '*Vitam vero impendenti*, Rozier.' This is an acknowledgment of Rousseau's own motto, '*Vitam impendere vero*,' or 'to consecrate one's life to the truth.' Rousseau interprets this as a slight on Rozier's part, but the incident affords him the opportunity to probe the question of his own truthfulness and of his lies.

In his ruminations, Rousseau initially recalls a lie he told about fifty years before, when, while working as a servant, he accused another servant of stealing the pink and silver ribbon he himself had pocketed. This lie continues to fill him with remorse. Then, after some further reflection, Rousseau admits that in spite of having adopted his motto, 'I was quite surprised at the number of things of my own invention I recalled having passed off as true at the same time that, inwardly proud of my love for truth, I was sacrificing my security, my interests, and myself to it with an impartiality of which I know of no other example among human beings' (*OC* 1:1025; trans. Butterworth, 44). Moreover, he finds that his conscience did not reproach him for these fabrications: 'by what strange inconsistency did I thus lie with gaiety of heart, unnecessarily, without profit, and by what inconceivable contradiction did I feel not the least regret, I, who for fifty years have not ceased to be afflicted by remorse for a lie?' (*OC* 1:1025; trans. Butterworth, 44). It is in order to come to terms with this problem that Rousseau undertakes his complex meditation on truth and lying.

Rousseau begins his description of this meditation by presenting a definition of lying:

> I remember having read in a Philosophy Book that to lie is to conceal a truth we ought to make manifest. From that definition, it indeed follows that to withhold a truth we have no obligation to declare is not to lie: but does he who, not content with not telling the truth in such a case, says the opposite, lie or not? According to the definition, we could not say that he lies. For if he gives counterfeit money to a man to whom he owes nothing, he undoubtedly deceives this man, but he does not rob him. (*OC* 1:1026; trans. Butterworth, p. 45)

From the philosophy book definition, Rousseau extracts a matter of interest to our overall case: the prospect of saying the opposite of the truth when there is no obligation to declare it. If we presume, for the sake of argument, that Rousseau actually thinks that determinism is true, his reasoning above would allow him to say that he does not lie when he says the opposite of the determinist truth, as long as he does not have an obligation to declare the determinist truth.[16]

Rousseau does not leave it at that, however. Instead he raises two questions that arise from his initial reflection on the philosophy book definition: 'The First, when and how we owe the truth to another, since we do not always owe it. The second, whether there are cases in which we may innocently deceive' (*OC* 1:1026; trans. Butterworth, 45).

When and How We Owe the Truth to Another

Rousseau answers his first question about when and how we owe the truth to another by saying that this depends on the usefulness of the truth. He starts off his response by describing the kinds of truths that are owed:

> General and abstract truth is the most precious of all goods. Without it, man is blind; it is the eye of reason. By it, man learns to direct himself, to be what he ought to be, to do what he ought to do, to head toward his true end. Particular and individual truth is not always a good; it is sometimes an evil, very often an indifferent thing. The things important for a man to know and of which he must be aware to achieve happiness are perhaps not very numerous. But however numerous they are, they are a good which belongs to him, which he has a right to demand wherever he may find it, and which we cannot keep from him without committing the most iniquitous of all robberies, since it is one of those goods common to all and one whose disclosure does not deprive the person who makes it. (*OC* 1:1026; trans. Butterworth, 45)

General truths that lead both to right conduct and to happiness are owed, but truths that are useless, Rousseau suggests, are not owed to another: 'As for truths which have no usefulness whatever, neither for instruction nor in practice, how could they be a good which is owed, since they are not even a good? And since property is founded only on usefulness, where there is no possible usefulness, there can be no property' (*OC* 1:1026; trans. Butterworth, 46). It is by now obvious that Rousseau has introduced a very specific vocabulary into the discussion. He repeatedly refers to truth as a good or property that is owed, compares it to money and land, and twice has considered whether withholding the truth is a robbery. This striking terminology calls to mind the discussion of justice as 'what is owed' and returning property in Book 1 of Plato's *Republic*. Indeed, later in the Fourth Reverie, Rousseau becomes preoccupied with the truths owed as a matter of justice. His position can be illuminated, I think, by a brief backward glance at the terms of discussion in Book 1. There Polemarchus argues that 'It is just to give each what is owed' (331e). Polemarchus had jumped into the argument to defend the position of his father, Cephalus. When Cephalus suggests that justice is both telling the truth and giving back what has been taken from another, Socrates responds by raising a difficulty:

> [E]veryone would surely say that if a man takes weapons from a friend when the latter is of sound mind, and the friend demands them back when he is mad, one shouldn't give back such things, and the man who gave them back would not be just, and moreover, one should not be willing to tell someone in this state the whole truth. (331c)[17]

Socrates raises a question that is of immediate relevance to Rousseau's discussion. If a weapon should not be given to someone who is mad, should 'the whole truth' be given to a mad person? In fact, Rousseau's question of 'when and how we owe the truth to another' also raises the question of whether dangerous or harmful truths are owed. But, significantly, Rousseau sidesteps this question.[18] His discussion turns instead on the distinction between useful and useless truths. He determines that one does not owe 'an idle fact, indifferent in all regards and without consequence for anybody.' Since such a useless truth is not even a good, one has no obligation to make it manifest.

This discussion of useless truths, however, is more important than it appears, for one of the most notable features of the Fourth Walk is Rousseau's association of utility with conduct and justice.[19] In what is perhaps the best statement of the thrust of its argument, Rousseau shows that his idea of usefulness implies above all utility for just human conduct: 'The truth that is owed is that which concerns justice, [*la verité due est celle qui interesse la justice*] and this sacred name of truth is debased if applied to vain things whose existence is indifferent to all and knowledge of which is useless for anything' (*OC* 1:1027; trans. Butterworth, 46).

But if utility, defined in terms of justice, is the criterion for rendering truth, the argument implies that one owes moral usefulness rather than truthfulness. If the truth is owed only for the sake of moral utility, rather than for its own sake, moral utility could trump truthfulness. And if one should render the truth that concerns justice, does Rousseau also think that one should also render the *lies* that concern justice?[20] Such a conclusion would admittedly weaken our case that he tells the truth when he says that men are distinguished by having free will.

In the subsequent part of our discussion of the Fourth Reverie, we consider the possibility that Rousseau thinks that moral utility rather than the truth is owed. We also consider the question of whether Rousseau entirely abandons the standard of the truth for its own sake. We respond that although Rousseau rejects telling lies that may harm anyone, he is willing to entertain rendering truths that may be harmful to some. If such truths are allowable, it is because of their status as truths rather than lies. Free will serves a salutary moral purpose but it also has the potential to harm people. We suggest that Rousseau can only in good conscience advocate a volatile idea like freedom of the will because he believes it to be true.

Whether There Are Cases in Which We May Innocently Deceive

In order to tease out the elements of our argument, we need first to carefully examine Rousseau's response to his second question of 'whether there are cases in which we may innocently deceive.'[21] In response, he begins by asking whether one can innocently disguise useless truths. He determines that a person who says the opposite of an indifferent and inconsequential truth has done no harm:

> Wherever the truth is indifferent, the opposing error is also indifferent; from whence it follows that in such a case he who deceives by saying the opposite of the truth is no more unjust than he who deceives by not declaring it; for with useless truths, error is no worse than ignorance. Whether I believe the sand at the bottom of the sea to be white or red matters no more to me than being unaware of what colour it is. How could we be unjust when we harm no one, since injustice consists only in the wrong done to someone else? (*OC* 1:1027; trans. Butterworth, 46)

One problem with this argument is that it focuses exclusively on consequences rather than on intentions. For example, the one who says the sand is red knowing that it is white may intend to depart farther from the truth than the one who falls silent and 'deceives by not declaring it.'[22] But Rousseau asks: 'How could we be unjust when we harm no one since injustice consists only in the wrong done to someone else?' Socrates, for his part, concludes his discussion with Polemarchus by saying that 'it is never just to injure anyone' (335d). But both Socrates and Rousseau know that to understand whether one may innocently deceive, one must go beyond the consequences. After noting that judgments about the usefulness of the truth are complicated by the demands of distributive justice and by the requirements of public good, Rousseau asks the further question: 'In examining what we owe to others have I sufficiently examined what we owe to ourselves and what we owe the truth for its own sake?' (*OC* 1:1028; trans. Butterworth, 47). Not unlike Glaucon, who complains that the discussions in Book I praised justice merely on the basis of its effects and who asks Socrates to describe the power of justice 'all alone by itself when it is in the soul – dismissing its wages and its consequences,' Rousseau inquires whether we can endorse the truth without regard to its consequences:

> How many embarrassing discussions we could easily extricate ourselves from by saying: let us always be truthful, whatever comes of it. Justice itself is the truth of things; a lie is always iniquity; error is deceit whenever we set forth that which is not as the rule of what we ought to do or believe. And whatever consequence result from the truth, we are always blameless when we have told it, because we have put nothing of our own into it.[23]

Rousseau avoids endorsement of the view that the truth should always be told regardless of the consequences. Saying that to so choose the truth regardless of its effects is to 'settle the question without answering it,' he shifts the attention back to his original definition of lying as concealing truths that ought to be made manifest. Unsatisfied with the results of the discussion so far, he seeks a rule for judging the cases in which one may innocently deceive. 'In all difficult questions of morality like this,' he notes, 'I have always found myself better off answering them according to the dictamen of my conscience than according to the insights of my reason.'[24] As it turns out, the rule he settles on takes into account both the intention of the speaker and, in a certain way, the consequences of the statement:

> To judge men's discourses by the consequences they produce is usually a poor way to assess their worth. Apart from the fact that these consequences are not always perceptible or easy to recognize, they vary infinitely, as

> do the circumstances surrounding these discourses. Only the intention of the speaker gives them their worth and determines their degree of malice or goodness. To say what is false is to lie only when there is an intent to deceive; and even an intent to deceive, far from always being joined to an intent to harm, sometimes has an entirely different goal. Still, to make a lie innocent it is not enough that there be no express intent to harm; there must, in addition, be certainty that the error into which one throws those to whom one speaks can harm neither them nor anyone in any way whatever. It is rare and difficult to come by such certainty; thus it is difficult and rare for a lie to be perfectly innocent. (*OC* 1:1028–9; trans. Butterworth, 48)[25]

To judge the blameworthiness of a lie, Rousseau now argues that one must consider not only the consequences of the lie alone but also the intention of the speaker who lies. But one has to consider the speaker's intention with regard to the consequences of the lie, which is to say the effects the speaker intends to produce (or could anticipate producing) through the lie.

For the act to be a lie, there must be an intention to deceive, but even this intention to deceive does not always stem from an intention to harm others: the intention 'sometimes has an entirely different goal.' Here Rousseau is implying not only that the absence of an intent to harm others helps excuse a lie, but also that the presence of an intent to benefit others helps excuse one as well. The intent to benefit others would seem to be the 'entirely different goal,' which is far from the goal of harm to others. And when reading this entire discussion about a person's responsibility for the consequences of their misleading discourses, it is useful to remember that in many circles, Rousseau is chiefly remembered for his bad influence on politicians, who used duplicitous and violent means to attain egalitarian political goals. A passage in which Rousseau contemplates excusing deceptive discourses intended to bring about good consequences raises the question of his dubious influence on the demagogues of the French Revolution and on sundry propagandists of the Left in subsequent times. The idea that Rousseau is partly responsible for the deceptions of his followers gains credibility when one considers that in the *Du contrat social* he implies that the legislator should manipulate public opinion in order to inculcate the requisite social spirit. But Rousseau's second criterion for making a lie innocent in the present passage is so stringent as to cast doubt on this line of argument. To lie innocently one must not only have no intent to harm others, 'there must, in addition, be certainty that the error into which one throws those to whom one speaks can harm neither them nor anyone in any way whatever' (*OC* 1:1029; trans. Butterworth, 48). To demand certainty that a lie will harm no one in any way whatsoever – this is an extremely exacting standard for innocent lying.

But it is nonetheless Rousseau's standard.[26] As he himself notes, it is extremely hard to be certain that a lie will harm no one at all; therefore, it is rare that a lie is 'perfectly innocent.' This admission raises the possibility that although this is Rousseau's ideal standard for innocent lying, he did not always live up to it. At the end of the *Reverie*, however, after admitting that he has sometimes told fables and lied, he writes, 'but I have wronged no one at all' (*OC* 1:1038; trans. Butterworth, 57).

Note how different this stringent condition for innocent lying is from Rousseau's discussion of the conditions for judging the usefulness of the truth. Whereas in the case of lying there can be no harm to anyone whatsoever, in the case of truth Rousseau is willing to entertain the idea of weighing of the harm and benefit that may result. He does so in the passage in which he discusses the difficulty of judging the utility of the truth:

> Very often, what is to one person's advantage is to another person's prejudice; private interest is almost always opposed to public interest. How should we conduct ourselves in such cases? Must what is useful to an absent person be sacrificed to what is useful to the person to whom we are speaking? Must the truth which profits one person while harming another be kept quiet or uttered? Must we weigh everything we say only on the scale of the public good or only on that of distributive justice? (*OC* 1:1027–8; trans. Butterworth, 47)

Rousseau's point, of course, is to underline the difficulty of such judgments. But my suggestion is that it is only in the case of the truth that this dilemma arises for him. While he does not go so far as to say that one should always tell the truth regardless of the consequences, he considers the possibility of tolerating some harm to some people in the name of a truth that also carries some benefit. There are no cases in which lies that cause harm to others are allowed, but it is at least possible that there are cases in which the truth should be told, although it might cause harm to some. If it is unacceptable to tolerate any harm resulting from a lie, the bar is lower in the case of truth.

This is important, because it would mean that Rousseau could only justify diffusing some of his most dangerous teachings because he thought they were true. Rousseau after all, undertook the risk of harm to some others in taking the part of the starving multitude, defending the strangling of a sultan, and declaring all existing regimes illegitimate.[27] But the main question that concerns us is this: Would Rousseau have believed that his teaching about free will could cause harm to some people? If so, according to his own standards, he could only justify diffusing this teaching because he believed it to be true.

In what sense could propagating the idea of free will be harmful? In the preceding chapters, we have conceded that free will is, on the whole, a salutary idea for political life: determinism carries a political danger in that it undermines the notion of moral responsibility in its usual sense. But it does not follow that there is no harm to be incurred by claiming determinism's opposite. The affirmation of free will can have bad consequences as well as good.

Rousseau was well-positioned to see this. After all, as we have argued above, he suggests that when humans begin to believe that the actions of other humans are based on free will, they are liable to become part of an entrenched dialectic of warring egos. His defence of free will as the species characteristic could, in some cases, exacerbate the dysfunction: vain and ambitious souls could, seizing on the more rhetorical aspects of Rousseau's account, appeal to their spiritual freedom of will to justify their tyrannical or capricious doings. Rousseau, who calls freedom a 'sad privilege,' and who holds up the goodness and innocence of the natural and savage man as a contrasting standard, was aware of this possibility. By the same token, he would have been acquainted with the argument that an acceptance of determinism should foster cheerfulness.[28]

Moreover, Rousseau's doctrine of free will might cause harm in conjunction with his other doctrines, and in particular with his political teaching about will. Hegel famously suggests that the general will contributed to the violence of the Terror during the French Revolution because the concept precludes particular, pluralistic forms of political action.[29] Now, free will is not the same thing as the general will. Even so, Rousseau's teaching about free will influences and inflects his teaching about the general will.[30] It also seems quite unlikely that Rousseau's discourse of will would have had as powerful an impact on political actors had it been explicitly determinist.

Obviously, speculation in hindsight is all too easy, and Rousseau would have been horrified by the blood that was shed in his name. But these historical discussions do serve to show that the stakes regarding these issues were extremely high. Moreover, Rousseau was not naive about the possible implications of his ideas. (Recall, for example, his remark in the Third Reverie that the *Profession of Faith* 'may one day make a revolution among men, if good sense and good faith are ever reborn among them.') He was canny enough to have been aware that his teaching on such an important question could possibly cause harm as well as good.

We concede that, on balance, Rousseau might reasonably expect his teaching about free will to be more beneficial than harmful to humanity. But it is not the kind of teaching about which one could confidently say that it would harm no one 'in any way whatsoever.' His own standards, then, would not have allowed him to lie about this issue and call those lies innocent.

In this chapter, we have examined Rousseau's attempts to ground his hopes for a viable alternative to atheistic materialism in reason. He consistently defends his method for doing so over many years, and his defences of it become sounder and more reasonable over time. This, we have argued, suggests his reasoned commitment to the teaching he articulated through it. We concede that his ardent wish for an alternative to the doctrine of comprehensive materialism gives him a strong motive to tell pious lies that he believes in free will when he does not. But by his own account, his principles would not have allowed him to do so. Instead, he was only willing to run the risks entailed by his fervent defences of free will because he believed that men truly have it.

Conclusion

Both free will and perfectibility, we have suggested, describe man's independence of instinct. But while free will requires the controversial doctrine of metaphysical dualism, perfectibility is compatible with materialism; as Rousseau notes, perfectibility is the species distinction 'about which there can be no dispute.' In fact, perfectibility is such a flexible concept that in principle it is compatible not only with materialism but with dualism as well. Buffon gives perfectibility an immaterial interpretation in his 'De la nature de l'homme.'[1] Rousseau, on the other hand, interprets perfectibility in materialist terms alone. For him, perfectibility may make man a tyrant of nature, but it does not take him beyond the material order of nature. Still, in principle, perfectibility is amenable to either a dualist or a materialist interpretation. By contrast, Rousseau believes that a defence of free will, even a free will latent in man's nature, commits him to move beyond comprehensive materialism. But now we see that this is not necessarily only a liability for his argument. Instead, it is consciousness of free will that allows Rousseau to explain how *amour propre* arises along with morality and vice. We have argued, then, that Rousseau believes his free will doctrine and that he uses it; although the teaching of the *Discourse on Inequality* is based on perfectibility, free will plays a significant role in its argument.

Rousseau's position is best characterized not simply as metaphysical neutrality but as metaphysical ambivalence. His strategy is to use different lines of defence on different fronts. He uses materialist perfectibility to insulate himself against attacks on dualism, but he also uses dualism to protect against the assimilation of human to animal nature. As we suggested in the introduction, Rousseau uses his different interpretations of man as the free animal with consummate skill.

Now let us consider some of the implications of this argument for Rousseau's moral and political teaching. As we have seen, Rousseau's critique of arbitrary government later in the *Discourse on Inequality* rests in part on an argument about the wrongness of selling oneself into slavery. There he opposes Pufendorf's view that one can transfer one's liberty to someone else 'just as one transfers his goods to another by conventions and contracts' (167). He criticizes this analogy between divesting oneself of property and divesting oneself of liberty as follows:

> ... the goods I alienate become something altogether foreign to me, the abuse of which is indifferent to me; but it matters to me that my freedom is not abused, and I cannot, without making myself guilty of the evil I shall be forced to do, risk becoming the instrument of crime ... But if one could alienate his freedom like his goods, there would be a very great difference for children, who enjoy the father's goods only by transmission of his right; whereas since freedom is a gift they receive from nature by being men [*en qualité d'homme*], their parents did not have any right to divest them of it. (Masters, 167–8; *OC* 3:183–4)

For Rousseau, freedom is a vital endowment of men as such. Freedom is a gift each child receives from nature '*en qualité d'homme*.' If determinism were true, slavery would be a misfortune, but if we assume that the will is free, the loss is greater, for then slavery is not merely a hardship, it is morally degrading. As Rousseau says of the renunciation of freedom from slavery in *Du contrat social*, 'There is no possible compensation for anyone who renounces everything. Such a renunciation is incompatible with the nature of man and taking away all his freedom of will is taking away all morality from his actions.'[2] These formulations develop Rousseau's earlier claim that free will is a species characteristic of man.[3]

Even so, it should be said that beyond the statements quoted above, Rousseau does not explain and draw out the significance of free will to his teaching about political legitimacy. But there is a reason for this, and it lies in the requirements of his two-track strategy of metaphysical ambivalence. Like the *Second Discourse* and *Emile*, the *Social Contract* has a layer of text that is metaphysically neutral to the determinist materialists of Rousseau's time and as well as a layer of text that is metaphysically *engagé*. While Rousseau avoids explicitly founding his conception of political legitimacy and obligation on dualistic free will, his critique of slavery implicitly relies on the free will premise.[4]

In stating that Rousseau has a metaphysically ambivalent approach, we do not mean to suggest that he is merely of two minds and undecided about free will and dualism. Instead, metaphysical ambivalence is a conscious strategy on his part. His strategy of metaphysical ambivalence allows him to use the metaphysically neutral layer of his texts to ensure that his ideas get a fair hearing from determinist materialists, while the metaphysically *engagé* layer expresses his reasoned hopes for his alternative to deterministic materialism.

Interpreters who neglect the importance of Rousseau's anti-materialist arguments have at best an incomplete and at worst a distorted presentation of his view of human nature and of his moral and political psychology. In response to thinkers who suggest that Rousseau simply sees humanity as an entirely malleable product of history, we have argued instead that man, for Rousseau, is a partly natural being, an animal with significant natural endowments, some of which take him beyond nature. In response to the assertion that he has a lower view of human nature than does Hobbes, we have suggested that free will is a potential to choose lower or higher courses of action. But perhaps above all, those who dismiss the metaphysically *engagé* layer of his texts miss the importance of Rousseau's emphasis on the '*conscience de la liberté*' as a unique human characteristic.

We have argued that our awareness of the freedom of will of other humans accounts for the way in which we depart from natural independence and develop vice. Consider this argument in the context of Rousseau's notable discussion of the contrast between dependence on men and dependence on things in Book 2 of *Emile*. Rousseau explains this key point as follows:

> There are two sorts of dependence: dependence on things, which is from nature; dependence on men, which is from society. Dependence on things, since it has no morality [*n'ayant aucun moralité*], is in no way detrimental to freedom and engenders no vices. Dependence on men, since it is without order [*étant desordonnée*], engenders all the vices, and by it, master and slave are mutually corrupted. (*OC* 4:313; trans. Bloom, 85)

Why does dependence on men engender 'all the vices'? How does the morality that accompanies dependence on men harm their liberty? In Book 4 of *Emile*, Rousseau describes how individual children gradually acquire an awareness of the free wills of others. As children, he explains, we begin with 'purely mechanical' attachments to those who care for us. Our perception that another person freely wills to help us or harm us transforms our 'blind instinct' into feelings of love and hate: 'those from whom one expects good or ill by their inner disposition, by their will – those we see acting freely for us or against us – inspire in us sentiments similar to those they manifest toward us. We seek what serves us but we love what wants to serve us. We flee what harms us but we hate what wants to harm us.' Once the feeling of these 'connections with others' awakens, we respond emotionally to their freely willed dispositions towards us and the irascible passion of *amour propre* is born. Our *amour propre* engenders unrealistic expectations of others and makes us dependent on their attitudes towards us; ultimately, it 'demands others to prefer us to themselves, which is impossible' (*OC* 4:492–3; trans. Bloom, 213–14).

According to the *Discourse on Inequality, amour propre* does not exist in the true state of nature. Hate and the desire for revenge can only come from the feeling that one has been offended, and 'it is scorn or intention to hurt that constitutes the offence.' In the true state of nature, men who do not know 'how to evaluate themselves or compare themselves' are unable to feel scorn or to understand intentions to harm; therefore they cannot be offended. They consider the plunderings of others to be mere 'natural occurrences' (*OC* 3:218–20; Masters, 222). But once men attribute free will to others, they become self-conscious, insultable animals. *Amour propre* sparks the clash of *freely willing* egos – the clash of individuals who *recognize* one another as free to decide to act otherwise than they do. We become dependent on the attitudes and dispositions of other people towards us, and our awareness of our dependence on the free wills of other humans makes us vicious and unfree in a way that our dependence on nature does not.

Rousseau's keen sense of the moral tyranny and subjection entailed by dependence on the free wills of men helps explain why he imagines a radical alternative political scenario: 'If the laws of nations could, like those of nature, have an inflexibility that no human force could ever conquer, dependence on men would then become dependence on things again; in the republic all the advantages of the natural state would be united with those of the civil state, and freedom which keeps man exempt from vices would be joined to morality which raises him to virtue' (*OC* 4:313; trans. Bloom, 85). That such a vision is amenable to misuse by tyrants is, by now, all too clear. But this should not obscure the contribution that Rousseau makes through his diagnosis of our psychological ills. In particular, by explaining the causes of the genealogy of vice, he offers freely willing individuals tools for resisting the unnecessary suffering that misdirected *amour propre* engenders.[5]

Consider the question of moral indignation. If we are right in believing that mentally healthy adults can at least sometimes freely choose how to act and that they sometimes choose to act cruelly or unjustly, can we not hold them accountable for these actions? For example, if a person chooses to defraud a friend, is the person not responsible for this choice? Justice would seem to require it. But frustration about freely willed injustice often leads individuals not only to hold others accountable for unjust acts but also to develop powerful forms of moral indignation and resentment about such acts, and this indignation can have its own harmful (and sometimes unjust) effects. Moral indignation can also, of course, have important political implications – manifested, for example, when communities blame one another for freely chosen past actions.

Rousseau is certainly aware of the violent potential of moral indignation about freely willed injustice; however, he seeks to address it not by denying freedom of the will but rather by elucidating the sources of moral outrage. By excavating the sources of dependence and vice, he offers readers tools for understanding the role of *amour propre* in their moral and political relationships and for liberating themselves from excessive subjection to it.

The interpretation of the present work also has implications for our view of Rousseau's teaching as a whole. It leads, I think, to a view of Rousseau as a critic of materialism who partook in the modern scientific project and at the same time rejected it as a comprehensive understanding of the world. It lends weight to the view of Rousseau as both a member of the Enlightenment and the founder of the counter-Enlightenment.

Rousseau was also the founder of the Left, and as such, he is one of the most important and influential figures in modern thought and practice. He harshly criticizes Enlightenment society for its lack of equality and freedom and for its undemocratic practice. But his assertions about the liberty of our wills and his reservations about materialism make him an even more radical critic of Enlightenment. In this respect, he sets himself against the very foundation of modernity with its material view of the universe – a view of the universe that is, in George Grant's words, 'prodigious' but 'shallow.'

Notes

Introduction

1 Like the other philosophers mentioned above, Rousseau uses the term 'man' generically to describe all of humanity. I adopt his sexist language consciously – if his generic use of 'man' and 'he' represses female existence, the question of how it does so can only be examined if we retain the sexist terminology. Gender-neutral substitutions would only obscure the issue. For a persuasive discussion of the pitfalls of false gender neutrality, see Susan Moller Okin, *Justice, Gender, and the Family* (Chicago: Basic Books, 1989), 10–13.

2 Jean-Jacques Rousseau, *The First and Second Discourses*, ed. Roger D. Masters, trans. Roger D. Masters and Judith R. Masters (New York: St Martin's, 1964), 113–14. I use the French Pléiade edition: *Oeuvres complètes*, ed. Bernard Gagnebin and Marcel Raymond, 5 vols. (Paris: Editions Gallimard, 1959–95). Subsequent references to these texts will be embodied parenthetically within the text. I abbreviate the Pléiade edition as follows: *OC* 3:141–2 (for the passage quoted above). I refer to the Masters' translation simply as Masters and employ it most of the time. I have, however, on occasion, used the following translation by Victor Gourevitch instead: *The Discourses and Other Early Political Writings* (Cambridge: Cambridge University Press, 1997). In such cases, it seems to me that the Gourevitch translation has allowed for an additional nuance; I have indicated when his translation is used in the text.

3 Although I try to avoid reading Rousseau as if he were trying to be Kant, my description of the problem here derives from Kant's presentation of it. I follow Kant's formulation, rather than, for example, J.S. Mill's description of determinism as involving the predictability of human action in

principle, because Kant's descriptions are closer to Rousseau's own formulations of the matter. See Immanuel Kant, *Critique of Pure Reason*, trans. Norman Kemp Smith (London: Macmillan, 1986), 465 ff. (A534 ff.) Cf. Maurice Cranston, *Freedom: A New Analysis* (London: Longman's, Green and Company, 1954). The history of philosophical debate about the question of free will is, of course, a lengthy one. As Hannah Arendt has it, the debate features 'Descartes and Leibniz on one side of the argument, Hobbes and Spinoza on the other.' Arendt, *The Life of the Mind*, vol. II: *Willing* (New York: Harcourt Brace Jovanovich, 1978), 149. On the question of how determinism allows that our characters and attitudes shape our actions, see Isaiah Berlin, *Four Essays on Liberty* (Oxford: Oxford University Press, 1969), xiii.

4 I have drawn in part on Patrick Riley's translation in *The General Will before Rousseau: The Transformation of the Divine into the Civic* (Princeton: Princeton University Press, 1986), 255.

5 This is not to say that Rousseau completely rejects materialism. He accepts some materialistic explanations of the workings of nature (as presented by modern science) but rejects a comprehensive, deterministic materialism which holds that matter is the only cause. As we shall see, in the Letter to Franquières, he repeatedly indicates the limits of materialism. It is true that in the *Confessions*, Rousseau relates he had begun a manuscript titled *La morale sensitive, ou le matérialisme du sage* which would consider the influence of material causes on the state of the human mind and point to causes which could 'put or keep the mind in the state most conducive to virtue' (*OC* 1:381). But note that he refers to influences on the state of the human mind and not to the determination of the decisions of the mind. Matthew Simpson puts his finger on the crucial point: he writes that Rousseau 'believed that although one's nature and environment together determine the kinds of inclinations and passions that one has, human beings are uniquely able to use their judgment to choose whether or not to follow those inclinations.' *Rousseau's Theory of Freedom* (London: Continuum, 2006), 64. Rousseau later abandoned the project. Note, too, that in the final book of the *Confessions*, he suggests that it would be a mistake to infer that the projected work was a concerted defence of philosophical materialism. Upon discovering that a rough draft of the text (along with some letters) was missing from among his papers, he speculated that D'Alembert might have stolen the writings: 'My guess was that he had been misled by the title, *The Morals of Sensibility*, and had imagined that here was the plan of a real treatise on materialism, which he would have used against me in a manner easy to imagine. Feeling sure that he would soon be undeceived

on examining the manuscript, and having made up my mind entirely to give up writing, I did not worry much about these thefts, which were not the first I had sustained at his hands without complaining.' Trans. J.M. Cohen (London: Penguin, 1953), 562. For a discussion of Rousseau's early, unpublished fragment on freedom, see ch4n5. In addition to evidence that he thinks men have free will presented throughout the book, see especially his statement about free will in the *Dialogues, OC* 1: 841–2, quoted in ch4n12.

6 Letter to G.H. Schaller, cited in Hannah Arendt, *Willing*, 24.

7 Isaiah Berlin, 'From Hope and Fear Set Free,' in *Concepts and Categories*, ed. Henry Hardy (New York: Viking Press, 1978), 13. I would like to thank Troy Riddell drawing this argument to my attention. For a comparison of Berlin and Rousseau on free will, see Robert Wokler, 'Rousseau's Two Concepts of Liberty,' in *Lives, Liberties, and the Public Good: New Essays in Political Theory for Maurice Cranston*, ed. George Feaver and Frederick Rosen (London: Macmillan, 1987). Cf. Wokler's 'Rousseau's Perfectibilian Libertarianism,' in *The Idea of Freedom: Essays in Honour of Isaiah Berlin*, ed. Alan Ryan (Oxford: Oxford University Press, 1979). The latter article contains a forceful and subtle response to critics of Rousseau's approach to negative liberty.

8 This is a position known in the contemporary philosophical literature as incompatibilism. For an especially clear overview, see 'Dualism,' in *A Companion to the Philosophy of Mind*, ed. Samuel Guttenplan (Oxford: Blackwell, 1994). Cf. J.S. Mill, 'The Freedom of the Will,' excerpted in *Free Will and Determinism*, ed. Bernard Berofsky (New York: Harper & Row, 1966).

9 Thomas Hobbes, *Leviathan*, ed. C.B. Macpherson (London: Penguin, 1985), ch. 34, 435.

10 Ibid., ch. 21, 262.

11 Kant, *Critique of Pure Reason*, 465, A534.

12 Ibid., 470, A543. Robert Kane, a leading contemporary proponent of free will, points out that advocates of free will have often reasoned that if agents have willed freely in choosing an action 'then some *additional* factor *not included among the past circumstances or laws* must account ... for an agent's acting or choosing in one way rather than the other.' Kane, *A Contemporary Introduction to Free Will* (Oxford: Oxford University Press, 2005), 39. This approach Kane calls an 'extra-factor strategy.' He explains that free will advocates have adopted various extra-factor strategies such as 'immaterial minds, noumenal selves outside space and time or non-event agent-causes.' Ibid., 132. But he notes that this strategy is open to the objection that such explanations of agency or causation are mysterious and hard to square with

the findings of modern science. He therefore proposes a free will theory, compatible with contemporary science, grounded on an idea of free will as the arbiter of conflicts in the will; according to the theory, in cases of 'self-forming' actions, the will is an arbiter between options that correspond to competing neural networks in the brain. See especially ch. 12.

13 Quoted in *OC* 3:1317n2.

14 See particularly Rousseau's discussion of natural man's eating habits: 'Men, dispersed among the animals, observe and imitate their industry, and thereby develop in themselves the instinct of the beasts; with the advantage that whereas each species has only its own proper instinct, man – perhaps having none that belongs to him – appropriates them all to himself, feeds himself equally well with most of the diverse foods which the other animals share, and consequently find his subsistence more easily than any of them can' (*OC* 3:135; Masters, 105–6. Cf. *OC* 3:142–3; Masters, 115). For an important interpretation of the *Discourse* that probes the importance of this passage, see Richard L. Velkley, *Being after Rousseau* (Chicago: University of Chicago Press, 2002), ch. 2.

15 See Jean Starobinski, 'Rousseau et Buffon,' in *Jean-Jacques Rousseau et son oeuvre,* edited by *Comité national pour la commémoration de Jean-Jacques Rousseau* (Paris : Klincksieck, 1964). Cf. Allan Bloom, 'Rousseau,' in *History of Political Philosophy*, ed. Leo Strauss and Joseph Cropsey (Chicago: University of Chicago Press, 1987), esp. 564, where Bloom writes that given free will and perfectibility as the species distinctions, 'it can be said that natural man is distinguished by having almost no nature at all, by being pure potentiality. There are no ends, only possibilities. Man has no determination; he is the free animal.' I am struck by the acuity of Bloom's phrase, 'the free animal,' and so have borrowed it for my title.

16 As we shall see, Rousseau took full advantage of the flexibility of his concept of perfectibility. But this does not mean he did not truly believe men are characterized by it. We suggest that Rousseau thought men are distinguished by perfectibility and that he therefore used it to build a history of men in the state of nature that was plausible in the light of the scientific knowledge of his time.

17 Jean Starobinski, 'Rousseau et Buffon'; Victor Goldschmidt, *Anthropologie et politique* (Paris: Vrin, 1974).

18 In his sceptical review of the *Second Discourse,* in *Edinburgh Review* no. 1, Adam Smith wrote that 'it is by the help of this style, together with a little philosophical chemistry, that the principles and ideas of the profligate Mandeville seem in him [i.e., Rousseau] to have all the purity and sublimity of the morals of Plato, and to be only the true spirit of a Republican

carried a little too far' (1755, 74–5). For Voltaire's scepticism see Mark Huilling, *The Autocritique of Enlightenment: Rousseau and the Philosophes* (Cambridge, MA: Harvard University Press, 1994) and our discussion in chapter 3.

19 Leo Strauss, *Natural Right and History* (Chicago: University of Chicago Press, 1953), 271–80 and note 48. Cf. John Charvet, *The Social Problem in the Philosophy of Rousseau* (Cambridge: Cambridge University Press, 1974); and Arthur Melzer, *The Natural Goodness of Man: On the System of Rousseau's Thought* (Chicago: University of Chicago Press, 1990). As Asher Horowitz points out, among scholars influenced by Leo Strauss, there are differences of opinion on this question. See Horowitz, *Rousseau, Nature, and History* (Toronto: University of Toronto Press, 1987), 19n51. Pierre Manent, Victor Goldschmidt, Luc Ferry, and Roger Masters have all suggested that Rousseau's account is to be taken at face value. My own approach is to use the method of a careful reading of Rousseau's texts to critique the sceptical view and to try to reveal the complexity of his intention and its evolution over time.

20 Mark Plattner, *Rousseau's State of Nature: An Interpretation of the Discourse on Inequality* (DeKalb: Northern Illinois University Press, 1979), 24. Subsequent references, cited as Plattner and a page number, will be integrated into the main text. My own argument originally evolved in response to Plattner's work but subsequently grew well beyond this initial starting point. Based on a reading of Strauss's interpretations of Rousseau on nature and history, John Marini has recently come to the following conclusions: 'Progressive political thought was dependent upon the idea of the state that grew out of the second wave of modern political thought, which replaced nature with History. It originated in the attack on nature and reason by Jean-Jacques Rousseau.' See his 'Progressivism, Modern Political Science, and the Transformation of American Constitutionalism,' in *The Progressive Revolution in Politics and Political Science: Transforming the American Regime*, ed. John Marini and Ken Masugi (Lanham: Rowman & Littlefield, 2005), 236. Although Rousseau thinks that forming a political community requires denaturing the citizens, he also asserts that the citizens of the city of the social contract should be 'as free as before' they entered into the social contract. A statement to the effect that Rousseau attacks nature ignores the fact that he argues repeatedly that we have physical drives, inclinations, and capacities that cannot simply be assimilated to the historically and artificially shaped sides of ourselves. For a more extensive critique of the idea that Rousseau renounces nature for history, see chapter 2 below.

21 According to Graeme Garrard, 'a decree of April 1757 in France sanctioned the death penalty for authors convicted of attacking religion.' Garrard, *Rousseau's Counter-Enlightenment: A Republican Critique of the Philosophes* (Albany: SUNY Press, 2003), 71.

22 See Judith Shklar, *Men and Citizens: A Study of Rousseau's Social Theory* (Cambridge: Cambridge University Press, 1969), 70, 185. Cf. 57. Cf. Horowitz, *Rousseau, Nature, and History,* and also his '"Laws and Customs Thrust Us Back into Infancy": Rousseau's Historical Anthropology,' *Review of Politics*, 52, no. 2 (1990): 215–41.

23 The Academy's question provides a clear organizing theme, but Rousseau's title to the work, *Discourse on the Origin and Foundations of Inequality Among Men,* drops any mention of natural law and adds in the mention of foundations of inequality.

24 Strauss, *Natural Right and History*, 265–6.

25 Jacques Derrida, *De la grammatology* (Paris: Les Edition de Minuit, 1967), 227. I have drawn upon but slightly altered the translation by Gayatri Spivak, *Of Grammatology* (Baltimore: Johns Hopkins University Press, 1976), 158.

Chapter 1

1 Victor Goldschmidt, *Anthropologie et politique* (Paris: Vrin, 1974), 281. See especially Buffon's 'Discours sur la nature des animaux,' in *Oeuvres philosophiques de Buffon,* ed. Jean Piveteau (Paris: PUF, 1954).

2 Cf. Marc Plattner, *Rousseau's State of Nature: An Interpretation of the Discourse on Inequality* (DeKalb: Northern Illinois University Press, 1979), 42.

3 Jean Morel, 'Recherches sur les sources du Discours de l'Inégalité,' *Annales de la Société Jean-Jacques Rousseau* 5 (1909): 119–98.

4 Michel de Montaigne, *The Complete Essays of Montaigne,* trans. Donald M. Frame (Stanford: Stanford University Press, 1958), 189. Several other passages in Rousseau recall this argument of Montaigne's. See footnote (10)(J) to the *Second Discourse, OC* 3:201, 213; *Lettres morales* (III); and *Du contrat social* I.II.

5 All of these references are cited in Morel, 'Recherches,' 144–5. The quotes appear on pages 358, 337, and 336 respectively of Frame's literal translation of the *Essays* cited in the previous note.

6 See especially *Emile, or On Education,* trans. Allan Bloom (New York: Basic Books, 1979), 85, *OC* 4:311. Subsequent references to this translation will be embedded parenthetically in the text.

7 For a discussion of Rousseau's sad wistfulness about man's misuse of free will see the end of ch. 2 below.

8 *OC* 3:146; Masters, 120; *OC* 4:343; *Emile*, trans. Bloom, 107.

9 Goldschmidt, *Anthropologie et politique*, 273–93; cf. 264 ff. Regarding the question of the influence of Condillac's 1755 *Traité des animaux* on Rousseau's 1754 *Discourse on Inequality*, Goldschmidt comments as follows: *'C'est un point d'histoire, sans doute impossible à élucider, que de savoir si les échanges de vues qu'il est légitime de supposer entre Rousseau et Condillac se sont étendus aux thèses qui feront l'objet, un an plus tard, du Traité des animaux.'* *Anthropologie et politique*, 281. Nonetheless, he concludes that whatever the difficulties of chronology may be, as regards doctrine, Rousseau defines his position in the *Discourse* in relation to both Condillac's *Traité des animaux* and Buffon's *Discours sur la nature des animaux*.

10 Etienne Bonnot de Condillac, *Oeuvres philosophiques*, ed. George Le Roy (Paris: Presses Universitaires de France, 1947), I:347.

11 Ibid., I:347.

12 Ibid., I:361.

13 *'Le moi d'habitude suffit aux besoins qui sont absolument nécessaires. Or l'instinct n'est que cette habitude privée de réflection.'* Ibid., I:363.

14 Ibid., I:379. See Rousseau's defence of the idea of instinct and his critique of Condillac's critique of it in his footnote to *La profession de foi d'un vicaire Savoyard*, *OC* 4:595; *Emile*, trans. Bloom, 286.

15 Goldschmidt, *Anthropologie et politique*, 284.

16 Ibid., 282–3.

17 Condillac, *Traité des animaux*, 378b. Cf. *Condillac's Treatise on the Sensations*, trans. Geraldine Carr (London: Favil Press, 1930). See especially Condillac's 'Dissertation on Freedom,' which appears as an appendix to the latter.

18 In his fine study, *Freedom* (London: Macmillan Education, 1991), Tim Gray points out that the scholars who define freedom as the *availability* of choice presume a subject capable of choice, 'thereby excluding both inanimate objects and animate creatures unable to make choices' (31). The same cannot be said, Gray observes, of the conception of freedom as the absence of impediments, which serves as the basis for Berlin's idea of negative freedom.

19 Consider also the possible impact on Rousseau of Buffon's statements about the '*substance spirituelle*' of man's soul in his fascinating *Discours sur la nature des animaux* of 1753. There, for example, Buffon poses a question about how we should understand the way that external objects modify the actions of animals. This leads him to comment about the relevance of the difference between humans and animals in deciding the following

question: '*Cette question est d'autant plus difficile à résoudre, qu' étant par notre nature différens des animaux, l'ame a part à presque tous nos mouvemens, & peut-être à tous, & qu'il nous est très-difficile de distinguer les effets de l'action de cette substance spirituelle, de ceux qui sont produits par les seules forces de notre être matériel : nous ne pouvons en juger que par analogie & en comparant à nos actions les opérations naturelles des animaux; mais comme cette substance spirituelle n'a été accordée qu'à l'homme, & que ce n'est que par elle qu'il pense & qu'il réfléchit; que l'animal est au contraire un être purement matériel, qui ne pense ni ne réfléchit, & qui cependant agit & semble se déterminer, nous ne pouvons pas douter que le principe de la détermination du mouvement ne soit dans l'animal un effet purement méchanique, & absolument dépendant de son organisation.*' He adds that while both man and beast have an internal sense (*sens intérieur*) that receives the impressions transmitted by the external senses such as sight and hearing, man has an additional sense: '*nous possédons de plus un sens d'une nature supérieure & bien différente, qui réside dans la substance spirituelle qui nous anime et conduit.*' Buffon, *Œuvres philosophiques*, 323, cf. 337. I have retained the eighteenth-century punctuation and spelling of this text.

20 Harry Frankfurt, 'Freedom of the Will and the Concept of a Person,' *Journal of Philosophy* 68, no. 1 (1971), 6.

21 Ibid., 7. Frankfurt's conception of second order volitions is much discussed in current free will debates. For an overview, see Robert Kane, *A Contemporary Introduction to Free Will* (Oxford: Oxford University Press, 2005), ch. 9.

22 Charles Taylor, 'What Is Human Agency?' in *The Self*, ed. Theodore Mischel (Oxford: Basil Blackwell, 1977). The quotations are from pages 107, 104, and 117 respectively.

23 In *The Future of Our Religious Past: Essays in Honour of Rudolf Bultmann*, ed. James M. Robinson (New York: Harper and Row, 1971).

24 Jonas writes that 'appetition is not concurrently an *appeto me appetere* as volition is a *volo me velle*' (337). This distinguishes his position from that of Frankfurt.

25 Ibid., 339–40.

26 In the *Social Contract*, Rousseau writes that 'for an arbitrary government to be legitimate, it would therefore be necessary for the people in each generation to be master of its acceptance and rejection. But then this government would no longer be arbitrary.' Bk 1, ch. 4, *OC* 3:356; *On the Social Contract with Geneva Manuscript and Political Economy*, ed. Roger D. Masters, trans. Judith R. Masters (New York: St Martin's, 1978), 49. For a useful discussion of Rousseau's use of the term 'arbitrary,' see Arash Abizadeh, 'Banishing

the Particular: Rousseau on Rhetoric, *patrie,* and the Passions,' *Political Theory* 29, no. 4 (2001): 556–82.

27 In the *Second Discourse,* Rousseau uses the language of contract to describe the institution of government; but in *Du contrat social* he insists that only the prior pact of civil association should be called a contract. On the importance of the distinction between the contract of association and the contract of government, see J.W. Gough, *The Social Contract: A Critical Study of its Development* (Oxford: Clarendon, 1957).

28 See Robert Derathé, *Jean-Jacques Rousseau et la science politique de son temps* (Paris: Vrin, 1950), 192–207. Derathé propelled me to look more closely at the relevant arguments of Pufendorf, Grotius, and Locke.

29 Hobbes and Grotius are defenders of absolute monarchy, but the case of Pufendorf is more ambiguous. On Pufendorf and Rousseau, see Derathé, *Jean-Jacques Rousseau et la science politique,* 78–84 and 209–216; and Morel, 'Recherches,' 160–79.

30 Baron Samuel de Pufendorf, *The Rights of War and Peace,* trans. A.C. Campbell (Washington: M. Walter Dunne, 1901), 1.2.8, 63. In I.IV of *Du contrat social,* Rousseau summarizes this argument of Grotius's in order to criticize it.

31 Consider Rousseau's criticism of Grotius in *Du contrat social*: 'Grotius denies that all human power is established for the benefit of those who are governed. He cites slavery as an example. His most persistent mode of reasoning is always to establish right by fact. One could use a more rational method but not one more favourable to tyrants.' *On the Social Contract with Geneva Manuscript and Political Economy,* ed. Roger D. Masters, trans. Judith R. Masters (New York: St Martin's, 1978), I.II, 47. Compare this with his introduction to his fourth argument in this section of the *Discourse*: 'Continuing thus to test the facts by right, one would find no more solidity than truth in the voluntary establishment of tyranny; and it would be difficult to show the validity of a contract that would obligate only one of the parties, where all would be given to one side and nothing to the other, and that would only damage the one who binds himself' (Masters, 166). Also, while Rousseau claims in *Du contrat social* that Grotius uses the method of establishing right by fact, he says his own method is to 'to test the facts by right' (*OC* 3:1354n2; *Du contrat social,* I.II; Masters, 47). On fact and right, cf. Plattner, *Rousseau's State of Nature,* 101–4; and Arthur M. Melzer, *The Natural Goodness of Man: On the System of Rousseau's Thought* (Chicago: University of Chicago Press, 1990), 168n28.

32 It is useful to think here of John Locke's definition of liberty as 'the power in any agent to do or forbear any particular action, according to the de-

termination or thought of the mind' in *An Essay Concerning Human Understanding* (London: Ward, Lock and Company, n.d.), Bk II, ch. XXI (Of Power), Section 8, 167. This is in keeping with Frederick Neuhouser's analysis of Rousseau's view of freedom. See his fine 'Freedom, Dependence and the General Will,' *Philosophical Review* 102, no. 3 (1993): 363–95.

33 Cf. Locke, *Second Treatise of Government*, ed. Richard Cox (Arlington Heights: Harlan Davidson, 1982), ch. 4.

34 Beyond his argument that voluntary slavery is unnatural, Rousseau claims that the involuntary slavery of the children of slaves is unnatural: 'But if one could alienate his freedom like his goods, there would be a very great difference for children, who enjoy the father's goods only by transmission of his right; whereas since freedom is a gift they receive from nature by being men [*en qualité d'hommes*], their parents did not have any right to divest them of it ... Just as to establish slavery, violence had to be done to nature, nature had to be changed to perpetuate this right; and the jurists who have gravely pronounced that the child of a slave would be born a slave, have decided in other terms that a man would not be born a man' (*OC* 3:184; Masters, 168). Rousseau directs this critique to the Roman jurists who maintained that that the children of slaves are 'born slaves.' As Rousseau would have known from reading Barbeyrac, the Roman jurists criticized voluntary slavery but allowed the involuntary slavery of the children of slaves. Barbeyrac relates in a note that according to Roman civil law 'no one could directly sell or transfer their liberty to another by any convention whatsoever.' In the same note, Barbeyrac cites the opinion of Roman jurists that 'the children of our servants are born slaves.' For an important discussion, see Robert Derathé, *Jean-Jacques Rousseau et la science politique*, 198. Derathé concludes that 'if the Roman jurists did not know how to draw all the conclusions of their principle, and allowed slavery without denying that it was contrary to nature, it is because they consider liberty as a right belonging to the dignity of the citizen, while with Rousseau it becomes a right of man'; ibid., 199–200. Cf. Gourevitch, *The Discourses and Other Early Political Writings* (Cambridge: Cambridge University Press, 1997), 367.

35 According to the editors of the Pléiade edition, in an initial draft of the sixth letter of *Lettres Ecrits de la Montagne*, when defending the argument of *Social Contract*, near a paragraph in which Rousseau asserts that the foundation of political obligation is the free engagement of those who are obliged, the following 'isolated passage' can found: '*Le débat sur le choix n'importe guères et l'autorité pourvu qu'on en reconnoisse un et qu'il soit solide n'en souffre point. J'ai donc fait en cela comme les autres.*' In the final text, instead of using this isolated passage, Rousseau follows his assertion about

the foundation of political obligation in the free engagement of the members with a paragraph that begins as follows: '*Mais par cette condition de la liberté, qui en renferme d'autres, toutes sortes d'engagemens ne sont pas valides, mêmes devants les Tribinaux humains.*' This statement in the final version points, I think, to the link between the 'condition of liberty' and the invalidity of the slave contract; but in the unused isolated passage Rousseau indicates he is not willing to explicitly base his teaching about the foundation of political obligation through free engagement of the members on a dualistic view of free choice. This suggests a strategy of metaphysical ambivalence in the *Social Contract* itself. See *OC* 3:806–7 and 1662n(a).

36 Plattner, *Rousseau's State of Nature*, 44.

37 A fuller interpretation of the relevance of *La profession de foi du vicaire savoyard* to my argument is contained in chapter 3 below. As we will see, while one cannot simply take the pronouncements of the vicar, a character, for those of Rousseau, nonetheless the vicar's reasoning does provide support for the arguments about free will and the limits of materialism that Rousseau makes in his own name elsewhere.

38 Rousseau continues the thought as follows: 'to the extent he had spoken to me according to his conscience, mine seemed to confirm what he had told me.' See *OC* 4:606; *Emile*, trans. Bloom, 294.

39 *OC* 3:694. For a discussion of the question of Rousseau's endorsement of the profession, see chapter 3.

40 C.E. Vaughan, for example, finds Rousseau's alleged dualism preferable to Condillac's virtually unmitigated materialism. He writes that 'the author of the *Discourse* is careful to avoid the rather gross materialism into which his friend is not seldom betrayed by the very brilliance of the mechanical image [of the living statue in the *Traité des Sensations*] which forms the groundwork of his argument.' Vaughan, *Rousseau's Political Writings* (Cambridge: Cambridge University Press, 1915), I:121.

41 *OC* 3:586–87; *Emile*, trans. Bloom, 280–1. As we discuss below, in *Emile*, Rousseau uses the term 'immaterial' rather than the term 'spiritual.'

42 Regarding changes in Rousseau's ideas about the naturalness of the family, compare endnote 12(L) of the *Discourse on Inequality* (*OC* 3:214–218) with Rousseau's assertion in Bk 1, ch. 2, of the *Social Contract* that 'the only natural' society is the family (*OC* 3:352). Consider also the differences between Rousseau's presentation of *amour propre* as unnatural and as simply problematic for human interaction in note 15(O) of the *Discourse on Inequality* with the different descriptions of it in *Emile* (*OC* 4:322 and *OC* 4:490–1). For more on this, see note 77 to chapter 2 below. As to the causes of the rise of civil society, compare the position he takes in the *Discourse on Inequal-*

ity (see, for example, *OC* 3:162) with his different account in the first two paragraphs of Bk 1, ch. 6 of the *Social Contract* (*OC* 3:360).

43 That Rousseau in the *Profession of Faith* accords reason a larger role in the will might also be related to the fact that he is generally less dependent on and more critical of Condillac in *Emile* than he was in the *Second Discourse*. Condillac, the reader will recall, argues against a human monopoly on understanding. Another possibility is that Rousseau was persuaded by Castillon's objections to alter his subsequent reflections about freedom and reason. Already in the preface to the *Second Discourse* he admits that the legitimacy of law depends on the understanding informing one's will when he writes that for a natural law to be a law 'the will of him who is bound by it [must] be able to submit to it with knowledge.' We re-examine this issue in our discussion of the *Profession of Faith* in chapter 3.

44 Goldschmidt takes a very different view of this passage. He writes that the 'allusion to the "difficulties surrounding these questions" does not betray the slightest doubt about whether the thesis is well-founded: it is the rhetorical device of the *concession*, destined to introduce a new "specific quality" which permits one to distinguish man from animal and "about which there can be no dispute": perfectibility.' The italics are his. *Anthropologie et politique*, 286. But Rousseau's assertion that there is 'room for dispute' about his argument at least implies that there are doubts to be raised about its sufficiency. The key question is about his relation to these doubts.

45 See Leo Strauss, *Natural Right and History* (Chicago: University of Chicago Press, 1953), 265–6; Aram Vartanian, 'Necessity or Freedom? The Politics of an Eighteenth Century Metaphysical Debate' in *Studies in Eighteenth Century Culture*, ed. Roseann Runte (Madison: University of Wisconsin Press, 1978), vol. 7; and Lester G. Crocker, ed., *The Age of Enlightenment* (New York: Harper & Row, 1969).

In the margin beside the passage describing the spirituality of free will in his copy of the *Discourse*, Voltaire jotted '*Voilà une assez mauvaise métaphysique*' (*OC* 3:1316n1). Incidentally, this would seem to indicate that Voltaire takes the passage at face value as an authentic expression of Rousseau's intention. Cf. his strongly worded arguments against the human possession of free will in the article '*De la liberté*' in his *Philosophical Dictionary*, trans. Theodore Besterman (Harmondsworth: Penguin, 1971). Voltaire struggled with the issue over his long career, moving from an endorsement of free will to a critique of it. I am grateful to Christian Hugenot for his research into this question.

46 Alexis Philonenko rightly notes the closeness of the term to its Latin root, *perfectum* or achievement. *Jean Jacques Rousseau et la pensée du malheur* (Paris: Vrin, 1984), I:191.

47 Immanuel Kant, *Critique of Pure Reason,* trans. Norman Kemp Smith (London: Macmillan, 1986), 475n(a).

48 Victor Gourevitch writes that 'Rousseau and all his contemporaries knew that 'orang-outang' means 'man of the woods' in Malay, and hence in Latin *homo sylvestris;* which is what, for example, Lucretius called the first men; thus the name alone tended to prejudice the question at issue, especially for all those who had never so much as seen a single great ape.' *The Discourses and Other Early Political Writing* (Cambridge: Cambridge University Press, 1997), 375n5. The editors of the Pléiade remark that Rousseau 'refuses' to refer to either orangutans or pongos by the term '*singe.*' *OC* 3:1371n. See, above all, Robert Wokler's 'Perfectible Apes in Decadent Cultures: Rousseau's Anthropology Revisited,' *Daedalus* 107, no. 3 (1978): 107–34.

49 For the 'social virtues,' see *OC* 3:162; Masters, 140; and Plattner, 46; on the faculties that perfectibility develops, see also Judith Shklar, *Men and Citizens: A Study of Rousseau's Social Theory* (Cambridge: Cambridge University Press, 1969), 37–8; and *OC* 4:1340n1.

50 Jean Starobinski, 'Rousseau and Buffon,' in *Jean-Jacques Rousseau et son œuvre,* ed. Comité national pour la commémoration de Jean-Jacques Rousseau (Paris : Klincksieck, 1964); cf. Edna Kryger, *La notion de liberté chez Rousseau et ses répercussions sur Kant* (Paris: Nizet, 1979); and Asher Horowitz, '"Laws and Customs Throw Us Back into Infancy": Rousseau's Historical Anthropology,' *Review of Politics* 52, no. 2 (Spring 1990): 215–41.

51 Goldschmidt detects an 'emptiness of content' in the concept of perfectibility: '*S'opposant à l'instinct animal, la perfectibilité est plus vide de contenu que celui-ci, elle n'est ni invention ni reflection, elle n'est pas raison, pas plus qu'elle n'est liberté. Elle est seulement la condition préalable et formelle qui rend possibles toutes ces facultés.*' *Anthropologie et politique,* 288. There is something almost tautological about perfectibility: perfectibility is that distinctive human characteristic which when activated allows man to become distinctively human. It is above all a concept that explains a process. Cf. Wokler's 'Perfectible Apes in Decadent Cultures,' 127; and Paul de Man's question: 'Where are we to find a structural description of perfectibility in what seems to be a self-enclosed genetic text in which perfectibility simply functions as an organizing theme?' In *Allegories of Reading: Figural Language in Rousseau, Nietzsche, Rilke, and Proust* (New Haven: Yale University Press, 1979), 141.

52 The term is Daniel Cullen's; see his *Freedom in Rousseau's Political Philosophy* (DeKalb: Northern Illinois University Press, 1993), 38. Cf. Plattner, *Rousseau's State of Nature;* and Melzer, *The Natural Goodness of Man.*

53 For example, in the *Lettre à Beaumont*: *OC* 4:936–7; cf. our discussion of *amour propre* and free will in *Emile* below.

54 There are passages in which Rousseau stresses instead that natural man is confined to instinct. '*Il avait dans le seul instinct tout ce qu'il lui falloit pour vivre dans l'état de Nature …*' *OC* 3:152; Masters, 127–8. Cf. *OC* 3:142–3; Masters, 115; and see *Beaumont,* where he contends that natural man is '*borné au seul instinct physique*' (*OC* 4:936). Our interpretation therefore assumes that natural man may have instinct but that he has a latent capacity to be relatively independent of it.

55 Regarding hunger, compare Rousseau's reference at the outset of Part 2 of the *Discourse* to 'hunger and other appetites,' which make man in the state of nature 'experience by turns various manners of existing' (*OC* 3:164; Masters, 142). Cf. Buffon's '*Discours sur la nature des animaux*' and *OC* 3:1316n3.

56 Later in the *Discourse* Rousseau refers to procreation in the state of nature as a 'purely animal act,' pointing out that it is 'devoid of sentiment' (*OC* 3:164; Masters, 142). Cf. his references to 'pure sensations' (*OC* 3:164, Masters, 143; and Gourevitch translation, 161).

57 This is how Rousseau puts it in the *Lettre à M. de Franquières* (*OC* 4:1139).

58 I owe this point and a general debt in my presentation of the counter-case in this section to Professor Clifford Orwin. Cf. Cullen, *Freedom in Rousseau's Political Philosophy*, esp. 42–3.

59 For his references to the faculties natural man has '*en puissance,*' see *OC* 3:152, Masters, 127; and *OC* 3:162; Masters, 140. For '*facultés virtuelles,*' see *OC* 3:208, Masters, 204.

60 Also, in *Emile*, Bk II, Rousseau refers to the faculties man has 'as it were, in reserve in the depth of his soul, to be developed there when needed.' *OC* 4:304; trans. Bloom, 80–1. Cf. Plattner's evidence in *Rousseau's State of Nature*, 48.

61 Compare *Essai sur l'origine des langues: 'Il parait encore … que l'invention de l'art de communiquer nos idées dépend moins des organes qui nous servent à cette communication que d'une faculté propre à l'homme, qui lui fait employer ses organes à cet usage, et si ceux-la lui manquoient lui en feroit employer d'autres à la même fin.'* *OC* 5:379.

62 Cf. Goldschmidt, *Anthropologie et Politique.*

63 Thus we are in agreement with Robert Derathé's admirably clear statement that 'by this perfectibility, Rousseau means the power to develop certain faculties that man in the state of nature possesses only "in potential."' *Le rationalisme de Jean-Jacques Rousseau* (Paris: Presses Universitaires de France, 1948), 10.

64 The first operations of savage man's soul are 'to will and not to will [*vouloir et ne pas vouloir*], to desire and to fear' (*OC* 3:143; Masters, 115).

Let us assume for the moment that savage man has a rudimentary ability to will or not to will that develops into a spontaneous freedom to choose between courses of action and to make judgments. Two possible hypotheses about free will and perfectibility stem from this assumption. According to one hypothesis, the dynamic of perfectibility contributes to the development of free will. That is, perfectibility develops free will, just as it develops the other faculties. Alternatively, it may be that free will and perfectibility simply exhibit a similar pattern of development: both free will and perfectibility act like enzymes that develop once triggered by the catalyst of outside circumstances.

65 *Emile*, trans. Bloom, 61, 63. For evidence that Rousseau has in mind a free will, see his discussion at the outset of Bk 4 of *Emile*, esp. 213.

66 Cf. his statement that 'the action of the soul on the body with respect to man's constitution is the abyss of philosophy.' *Geneva Manuscript*, I, IV; *OC* 3:296.

67 Perhaps this is one reason why Rousseau does not make his position clear on whether he considers free will to be a 'faculty.' While he has not explicitly referred to free will as a faculty in the foregoing passages, later in the *Discourse* he refers to freedom as 'the noblest of man's faculties' (*OC* 3:183; Masters, 167). Cf. our discussion on the faculties in chapter 2.

68 Thomas Hobbes, *Leviathan*, ed. C.B. Macpherson (Harmondsworth: Penguin, 1982), ch. 3, 95–6.

69 Cf. *OC* 3:125; Masters, 94.

70 *OC* 1:388. See also *The Confessions*, trans. J.M. Cohen (London: Penguin, 1953), but Cohen renders '*nu*' as naked. At the outset of the *Discourse*, Rousseau also says he approaches natural man by 'stripping this Being, so constituted, of all the supernatural gifts he may have received, and all the artificial faculties he could only have acquired by prolonged progress' (*OC* 3:134; Gourevitch, 134). Cf. the image of Glaucus, *OC* 3:122; Masters, 91; and his assertion in the first *Discourse* that 'the good man is an athlete who likes to compete in the nude' (*OC* 3:8; Masters, 37).

71 Here I use Gourevitch's translation from *The Discourses and Other Political Writings* (Cambridge: Cambridge University Press, 1997), 212. Cf. Rousseau's statement that 'the same cause which keeps savages from using their reason keeps them from abusing their faculties.'

72 Strauss writes in *Natural Right and History* that 'natural man is premoral in every respect; he has no heart. Natural man is subhuman.' See 271 ff. Consider Rousseau's statement that before man becomes enlightened and able to make comparisons '*il est bête*' (*Lettre à Beaumont*: *OC* 4:936). For a differ-

ent view see Gourevitch, 'Rousseau's Pure State of Nature,' *Interpretation* 16 (1988): 23–59 at 41n28; and Richard Velkley, *Being after Rousseau* (Chicago: University of Chicago Press, 2002), 41 ff. Velkley writes that 'it would be a mistake to take at face value any apparent assertion that natural man was merely an animal with only instinct and sensation. Rousseau will not turn his gaze toward the prehuman, except for the purpose of positing natural man as *apart* from it, not as identical with it or even derived from it' (41).

73 Clifford Orwin, 'Rousseau and the Discovery of Political Compassion,' in Clifford Orwin and Nathan Tarcov, eds., *The Legacy of Rousseau* (Chicago: University of Chicago Press, 1997). See also *OC* 3:153 ff; Masters, 130 ff.

74 See Melzer, *The Natural Goodness of Man*, 284–8, and Plattner, *Rousseau's State of Nature*, 128–32, for interesting discussions.

75 Hobbes, *Leviathan*, chs. 1, 6, and 21.

76 Ibid., chs. 10–11, 21, and 46.

77 Here I rely on Gourevitch's translation, 172. Cf. Masters, 157. The Savoyard vicar puts it this way: 'the very abuse of your faculties proves their excellence in spite of you' (trans. Bloom, 278). Cf. *Fragments politiques: 'Si l'homme vivait isolé, il aurait peu d'avantages sur les autres animaux. C'est dans la fréquentation mutuelle que se développent les plus sublimes facultés de sa nature.'* Quoted by Derathé, *OC* 3:xciii. Cf. Laurence D. Cooper's discussion of how, for Rousseau, 'the high evolves out of the low without being reducible to it' in his *Rousseau, Nature and the Problem of the Good Life* (University Park: Pennsylvania State University Press, 1999), 73 ff. Cf. Immanuel Kant, 'Idea for a Universal History with Cosmopolitan Intent,' Fifth Thesis: 'Thanks be to nature for the incompatibility, for the distasteful, competitive vanity, for the insatiable desire to possess and also to rule. Without them, all of humanity's excellent capacities would have lain eternally dormant.' *In Perpetual Peace, and Other Essays on Politics, History, and Morals*, trans. Ted Humphrey (Indianapolis: Hackett, 1983), 32.

Rousseau's famous statement about the natural goodness of man in his *Lettre à Beaumont* points both to man's original innocence and to his potential for just action: 'The principal statement about all morality, about which I have reasoned in all my writings ... is that man is a naturally good being, loving justice and order' (*OC* 4:935).

Chapter 2

1 See *Physics* 2; *Nicomachean Ethics* 1.1; and the *Politics* 1154a21. For Aristotle, a teleological cause focuses on that 'for the sake of which' something is. On Rousseau's rejection of a teleological approach to man's development,

see Leo Strauss, *Natural Right and History* (Chicago: University of Chicago Press, 1953); Arthur M. Melzer, *The Natural Goodness of Man: On the System of Rousseau's Thought* (Chicago: University of Chicago Press, 1990); Richard Velkley, *Freedom and the End of Reason* (Chicago: University of Chicago Press, 1989), ch. 2; idem, and *Being After Rousseau* (Chicago: University of Chicago Press, 2002), esp. 39; and Luc Ferry, *Political Philosophy I*, trans. Franklin Philip (Chicago: University of Chicago Press, 1990), ch. 1, esp. 40 ff. We concede, but with some reservations, that Rousseau in the *Discourse* has a non-teleological conception of the development of perfectibility and the faculties. For example, note the passage in which Rousseau states that 'it was by a very wise providence that [savage man's] potential faculties were to develop only with the opportunities to exercise them, so that they were neither superfluous and burdensome to him beforehand, nor tardy and useless when needed' (Masters, 127). Cf. Rousseau's remarks about man's soul in *Emile*, Bk II (OC 4:304; trans. Bloom, 80) and our discussion of them at the end of this chapter. For a recent and thought-provoking interpretation of perfectibilty as a teleological idea, see Jonathan Marks, *Perfection and Disharmony in the Thought of Jean-Jacques Rousseau* (Cambridge: Cambridge University Press, 2005).

2 Judith Shklar calls Rousseau a 'complete agnostic.' *Men and Citizens*, 108, quoted in Melzer, *Natural Goodness*, 30n1. But for compelling evidence about Rousseau's attachment to the idea of God, see his own description of the incident at the home of Mlle Quinault recounted in *OC* 3:clxxxiv. Cf. P.M. Masson, *La Religion de J.-J. Rousseau*, 3 vols. (Paris: Librairie Hachette, 1916); idem, *'Rousseau Contre Helvétius,' Revue d'histoire littéraire de la France* 18 (1911): 103–24; Ronald Grimsley, *Rousseau and the Religious Quest* (Oxford: Clarendon, 1968); Victor Gourevitch, 'The Religious Thought' in *The Cambridge Companion to Rousseau*, ed. Patrick Riley (Cambridge: Cambridge University Press, 2001); and Jeremiah Alberg, *A Reinterpretation of Rousseau: A Religious System* (New York: Palgrave Macmillan, 2007).

3 See Strauss's comment on Rousseau's explanation of this point, *Natural Right and History*, 273. On necessity and chance, cf. Diderot, *"The Interpretation of Nature," in Diderot's Selected Writings*, trans. and ed. Lester Crocker (New York: Macmillan, 1966).

4 Strauss articulates this view on page 271 of *Natural Right and History* but raises doubts about it on pages 280–1, where he argues that in articulating his view of moral freedom as self-legislation, Rousseau relies on a dualism of nature versus freedom.

5 Strauss, 'Three Waves of Modernity,' in *Political Philosophy: Six Essays by Leo Strauss*, ed. Hilail Gildin (Indianapolis: Pegasus/Bobbs-Merrill, 1975).

Cf. Ferry, *Political Philosophy I*. For a related but somewhat different view, see Asher Horowitz, '"Laws and Customs Throw Us Back into Infancy": Rousseau's Historical Anthropology,' *Review of Politics* 52, no. 2 (Spring 1990): 215–41. Horowitz notes that for Marxists, Rousseau is often not historicist enough.

6 Amédée Jacques, for example, asserted in the 1845 edition of the *Dictionnaire de sciences philosophiques* that faculties are latent but active causes and gave free will as the primary example of such a cause. See the entry '*Facultés de l'ame*' (Paris: Hachette, 1845), 558–71. The idea of the faculties also provided the basis of resistance to Lockean and Humean empiricism during the Scottish Enlightenment. Thomas Reid argued that we have an innate and natural moral faculty that issues in our concept of justice.

7 The quotes are from Strauss, *Natural Right and History*, 274 and 271 respectively. But the approach Strauss takes later in the chapter (at 280–1) is incompatible with this radical historicist reading.

8 It is rather odd to suggest that the fact that perfectibility emerges due to the work of natural causation indicates that it is not natural. But this puzzle can be explained by remembering that Marc Plattner defines a natural distinction as a teleological one. This is why he argues that although perfectibility may be considered the *species* distinction of man, it cannot be considered a *natural* distinction. Instead he thinks that perfectibility is a historical distinction: '*Nature* has placed no "specific distinction" between men and other living beings. In the decisive respects, man is by nature merely an animal like any other.' Plattner, *Rousseau's State of Nature: An Interpretation of the Discourse on Inequality* (DeKalb: Northern Illinois University Press, 1979), 129. Certain of Strauss's formulations pave the way for this reading, but it too quickly dismisses the possibility that the idea of a natural distinction can have a non-teleological but understandable sense.

9 Cf. his statement that 'the internal development of the faculties is the education of nature.' *Emile*, trans. Bloom, 38.

10 Plattner, in *Rousseau's State of Nature,* suggests that 'reason is not natural to man – not even "in potentiality"' (76). But Robert Derathé argues that reason is one of natural man's potential faculties. He quotes Rousseau's statement in his *Lettre à Franquières* that savage man 'has not yet made any use whatever of his own reason.' Derathé, *Le rationalisme de Jean-Jacques Rousseau* (Paris: Presses Universitaires de France, 1948), 13. Even as it emphasizes natural man's limitedness, this statement does imply that savage man has his own latent reason that will be used down the road; his possession of it predates his use of it. Cf. footnote 10(J), where Rousseau writes of

language that 'although the organ of speech is natural to man, speech itself is nonetheless not natural to him.' *OC* 3:210; Masters, 207.

11 I thank Joanna Mullard for this suggestion.

12 In *An Essay Concerning Human Understanding*, Bk II, ch. XXI, Locke argues that if by the term faculty one means an 'agent,' then the will cannot be called a faculty. It is there that he suggests that the will can only be understood to be a faculty in the sense that it is a 'power of operation.' See esp. sections 14–25.

In *Emile*, Rousseau assumes that animals have faculties for their self-preservation, and he even refers to instinct as a faculty. (See his note at *OC* 4:595; trans. Bloom, 286.) If instinct can be a faculty, it is unlikely that he uses the term rhetorically to advance the cause of anti-materialism. The notion of the faculties does not divide men from the animals, although the notion of necessary versus superfluous faculties may. See his poignant description of man's superfluous faculties in Book 2 of *Emile*. *OC* 4:304, trans. Bloom, 80. Cf. the third of the *Lettres morales*, where Rousseau writes as follows: '*Qui sait si ce qui distingue l'homme de la bête n'est point que l'ame de celle-ci n'a pas plus de facultés que son corps de sensations, au lieu que l'ame humaine comprimée dans un corps qui gêne la plus part de ses facultés veut à chaque instant forcer sa prison et joint une audace presque divin à la foiblesse de l'humanité?*' *OC* 4:1098.

David Owen suggests a distinction between the Scholastic conception of the faculties and the early modern conception. See ch. 1 of his *Hume's Reason* (Oxford: Oxford University Press, 1999).

13 David Cameron describes Rousseau's position this way: 'Man is not merely clay to be pressed into whatever shape the historical process makes possible; he possesses certain internal drives, and it is the conjunction of these drives with the exigencies of history which make him what he is at any particular time.' Cameron, *The Social Thought of Rousseau and Burke* (London: Weidenfeld and Nicolson, 1973), 92. Compare Judith Shklar, *Men and Citizens: A Study of Rousseau's Social Theory* (Cambridge: Cambridge University Press, 1969), 37–8.

14 Cf. Leo Strauss's argument that Rousseau saw that 'in accordance with the requirements of a "physical investigation," man's humanity must be understood as a product of accidental causation. This problem had hardly existed for Hobbes. But it arose necessarily on the basis of his premises … He had conceived man's leaving the state of nature and establishing civil society as a kind of revolt of man against nature. His notion of the whole required, however, as Spinoza had indicated, that the dualism of the state of nature and the state of civil society, or the dualism of the natural world

and the world of man, be reduced to the monism of the natural world or that man's transition from the state of nature to civil society, or man's revolt against nature, be understood as a natural process ... Rousseau was forced by his realization of the necessary implications of Hobbes's premises to conceive of that transition as consisting in, or at least decisively prepared by, a natural process: man's leaving the state of nature, his embarking on the venture of civilization, is due not to a good or bad use of his freedom or to essential necessity but to mechanical causation or to a series of natural accidents.' Strauss, *Natural Right and History*, 272; but cf. 280–1, where Strauss argues that Hobbes and Rousseau replaced 'the traditional dualism of body and soul, not with materialistic monism, but by the novel dualism of nature (or substance) and freedom.'

15 Jean Starobinski asks, 'How does one reconcile the assertion that "man is naturally good" with the assertion that "everything degenerates in the hands of man?"' Quoted in Joshua Cohen, 'The Natural Goodness of Humanity' in *Reclaiming the History of Ethics: Essays for John Rawls*, ed. Andrews Reath et al. (Cambridge: Cambridge University Press, 1997).

16 *OC* 3:1383. Victor Gourevitch states that 'Rousseau clearly thought of this *Letter* as an authoritative statement of his views. Although he did not publish it, he did make a clean copy of it, and a letter of Bonnet's in 1763 indicates that he had learned of the existence and of the tone, if not of the contents of Rousseau's reply.' See Rousseau, *The Discourses and Other Early Political Writings*, trans. Gourevitch (Cambridge: Cambridge University Press, 1997), 379n.

17 *OC* 4:939. For treatments of this question see Jacques-François Thomas, *Le pélagianisme de J.J. Rousseau* (Paris: Nizet, 1956); Melzer, *Natural Goodness*, 17–20; Lucio Colletti, 'Rousseau: Critic of Civil Society' in *From Rousseau to Lenin* (New York: Monthly Review Press, 1972); Paul Bénichou, '*Réflexions sur l'idée de nature chez Rousseau*' in *Pensée de Rousseau*, ed. Gerard Genette and Tzvetan Todorov (Paris: Seuil, 1984); and Alberg, *A Reinterpretation of Rousseau*. Augustine describes original sin in part 3 of *On the Freedom of the Will*, trans. Carroll Mason Sparrow (Richmond: University of Virginia Press, 1947).

18 It could be objected that Rousseau's account of the contingent development of the faculties and society is based on scientific research and observation and as such that it does not derive from his desire to situate himself with regard to the question of teleology in political philosophy. As Plattner points out, Rousseau criticizes Locke's view that the family is natural as follows: 'I shall observe first that moral proofs do not have great force in matters of physics, and that they serve rather to give a reason for existing

facts than to prove the real existence of those facts' (Footnote 12(L); quoted in Plattner, *Rousseau's State of Nature,* 102). So it might be held that the argument about contingent development derives from Rousseau's scientific observations and not from his desire to prove man's natural goodness. I accept this objection; therefore, in the main text I have been careful to phrase the argument so that I do not suggest that Rousseau's argument about natural goodness leads him to develop this position but only that it leads him to emphasize it. Note, too, however, that there may be a coincidence between the evidence for the accidental development of the faculties and society and the thesis about the natural goodness of man. See Melzer, *Natural Goodness,* part 2: 'Rousseau's Proof of the Principle of Natural Goodness.' The term 'teleology' was introduced into philosophy by Christian Wolff.

19 Rousseau stresses that natural man functions like any other beast, but he does not do so in order to show that history *rather than* nature accounts for man's distinctiveness. Instead, history distorts man's distinctiveness. History distorts man's proto-human potentialities even as it brings them to fruition.

20 *OC* 3:232. I have used the Bush, Kelly, and Masters translation except that in the last sentence I render *'les hommes sont les maitres'* literally as 'men are the masters' instead of 'men are in control of.' *Collected Writings of Jean-Jacques Rousseau.* trans. Judith R. Bush, Christopher Kelly, and Roger D. Masters, vol. 3 (Hanover: University Press of New England, 1993), 128–9.

21 His position on sociality in the *Letter to Philopolis* is close to that of the vicar, who contends that 'man is sociable by his nature or at least made to become so.' *OC* 4:600. Cf. *Du contrat social,* I.VI. Still, the position in the *Letter to Philopolis* contradicts his assertion in the *Discourse* that society need never have arisen. This may be one of the reasons why Rousseau neither published nor sent his letter.

22 I have been influenced here by Christopher Kelly and Roger D. Masters, 'Human Nature, Liberty, and Progress: Rousseau's Dialogue with the Critics of the *Discours sur l'inegalité*' in *Rousseau and Liberty,* ed. Robert Wokler (Manchester: Manchester University Press, 1995). See esp. 56, where the authors put the point as follows: 'The contention that the ills of human life are not intrinsic to human nature, but are the result of a combination of extrinsic accidental causes and wicked or foolish human decisions is one of the central theses of the *Discours* and, indeed of Rousseau's thought as a whole.' Cf. Susan Neiman, 'Metaphysics, Philosophy: Rousseau on the Problem of Evil' and Joshua Cohen, 'The Natural Goodness of Humanity,'

both in *Reclaiming the History of Ethics: Essays for John Rawls*, ed. Andrews Reath et al. (Cambridge: Cambridge University Press, 1997).

23 *Collected Writings of Jean-Jacques Rousseau*, vol. 3, 129. Civilized men pursue their interests and shape their societies with an often feverish activity. For example, in the *Discourse*, Rousseau refers to 'the petulant activity of our vanity.' There are plenty of examples of men's active self-destruction in the *Discourse* but plenty could also be found to indicate that they are passively moulded by circumstances and that they suffer the consequences of circumstances, which tend to spiral out of their control. At any rate, it is not clear what such arguments prove. It is true that in Rousseau's *La profession de foi du vicaire savoyard* the vicar stakes much of his case on the view that men are 'active in their judgments.' But this is separate from the idea that they are active in their behaviours and endeavours. Also, consider Hobbes's men: they are strikingly active in their interventions in the world but wholly determined.

24 Masters, 104. Rousseau's vindication of such a standard also reminds us of the quotation from Aristotle that he chose as the epigraph of the *Discourse*: 'Not in corrupt things, but in those which are well-ordered in accordance with nature, should one consider that which is natural.' (Masters, 229; Aristotle, *Politics* 1254a36–38.) Aristotle's statement occurs during his discussion of natural slavery. He argues that it is natural for the soul to rule the body. In depraved people, however, the body rules the soul. The condition of depraved people, he suggests, is not a reliable indication of the natural. Depraved people who cannot rule their own bodies may be fit for natural slavery. Compare Rousseau's discussion of Aristotle's view of slavery in *On the Social Contract*: *OC* 3:353. For Aristotle, nature made certain men suited to be slaves. For Rousseau, force worked against nature to turn some men into them. For Aristotle, natural depravity merits slavery; for Rousseau, slavery depraves nature. But it is important to note that despite their differences, for both thinkers depravity and corruption are unhealthy forms of nature; healthy nature is to be respected.

25 Rousseau's view that men both are moulded and mould themselves is particularly clear in the passage of the *Confessions* that we quoted in the introduction. There he described the method of the *Discourse On Inequality* as 'comparing man as he had made himself with man as he is by nature' to reveal 'in his pretended perfection the true source of his misery.' He added that men complain of nature but 'all your misfortunes arise from yourselves.' Trans. J.M. Cohen (London: Penguin, 1993), 362; *OC* 1:388–9.

26 This quotation is from a footnote to Arthur Melzer's *Natural Goodness*. Considering Rousseau's view that the legislator and the executive should

manipulate the people, Melzer suggests that Rousseau thinks free will is 'a more or less salutary illusion.' His explanation, which turns on an interpretation of natural goodness, puts the position succinctly: 'It seems that man has free will, Rousseau asserts, but since this is very unclear, he will only insist that man is free in a second sense, extreme malleability. But the second sense contradicts the first, showing men to be mere creatures of their environment. Man has fallen from his original goodness and become evil, the *Discourse* goes on to argue, *not* through the conscious abuse of free will (which was the biblical view) but due to accidental changes in the environment which mutilated man's malleable nature without his knowing it. Indeed, the whole point of the doctrine of natural goodness is that men are innocent victims of the contradiction of society. They are good precisely because they are not free. And therefore men can be saved only from the outside – by a legislator who, believing in human malleability, remakes men into virtuous citizens who believe in free will' (249n19). On this view of natural goodness, cf. Strauss, *Natural Right and History*, 271n19.

27 I have drawn in part on the translation of this passage in Melzer, *Natural Goodness*, 54.

28 See *OC* 4:936–7 and our discussion at the end of the next section. In the Folios, this passage asserting the dualism of *amour propre* originally followed upon the passage blaming the social order for man's evils. See *OC* 4:clxxii and the editor's remark: '*La brouillon de la Lettre nous montre donc le travail d'un esprit qui transforme un discours cohérent en discours efficace.*'

29 As he argues at the outset of *Emile*, man 'wants nothing as nature has made it, not even man. For him man must be trained like a school horse; man must be fashioned in keeping with his fancy like a tree in his garden.' *OC* 4:245; trans. Bloom, 37. Cf. his revealing draft in *Emile Favre: 'l'homme s'approprie tout mais ce qu'il lui importe le plus de s'approprier c'est l'homme même ... Cet homme n'est donc plus l'homme de la nature, c'est l'homme privé, l'homme domestique, l'homme que les hommes ont dressé pour eux.'* *OC* 4:56. Cf. Velkley, *Freedom and the End of Reason*, ch. 1.

30 Agency can be constrained and limited but allow a (restricted) area for the exercise of free will. Consider how Jean-Paul Sartre, as intransigent an advocate of free will as ever there was, conceived of how the agency of the proletariat becomes constrained and coerced. Sartre uses the idea of 'practico-inert reality' to explain how the material structures that men establish subsequently constrain their actions (at the same time that they make those actions possible). Practico-inert reality is practical in the sense that it is based on human conduct or praxis but inert in the sense that it has an inertia or sluggishness that makes it to a greater or lesser extent

resistant to human action. See *Critique of Dialectical Reason*, esp. 165 ff. and 765. According to *The Oxford Companion to Philosophy*, Sartre believes that alienation stems in part 'from the fact that the realization of human purposes creates material structures (houses, machines, etc. – the "practico-inert") that are inherently liable themselves to place further demands on people and, in some cases, to subvert the very purposes they were intended to promote. A central theme of Sartre's *Critique of Dialectical Reason* is, indeed, one of the attempt to overcome the constraints of the practico-inert through social institutions, and then of the failure of this attempt as social institutions themselves ossify and join the practico-inert. In the *Critique of Dialectical Reason*, as published, this theme is developed with particular reference to the French Revolution; in the projected second volume of the *Critique* (which was published posthumously) the same theme is discussed with reference to the Russian Revolution.' Ted Honderich, ed. (Oxford: Oxford University Press, 1995), 794. Cf. Iris Marion Young, 'Gender as Seriality,' in her *Intersecting Voices* (Princeton: Princeton University Press, 1997).

Obviously there are many differences between Rousseau and Sartre. Nonetheless, one might profitably undertake a comparison between Sartre's concept of agency and Rousseau's pioneering descriptions of how men are coerced and constrained by what he calls 'our institutions,' 'opinion' and the 'social system.' To take just one example, in his description of the Illumination of Vincennes in the second Letter to Malesherbes, he stresses the corrosiveness of institutions and the social system: '*O monsieur! si j'avais jamais pu écrire le quart de ce que j'ai vu et senti sous cet arbe, avec quelle clarté j'aurais fait voir toutes les contradictions du système social! avec quelle force j'aurais exposé tous les abus de nos institutions! avec quelles simplicité j'aurais démontré que l'homme est bon naturellement, et que c'est par ces institutions seules que les hommes deviennent méchant!*' In Christian Gauss, ed., *Selections from Rousseau* (Princeton: Princeton University Press, 1920), 196. See also Hannah Arendt's argument in *The Human Condition* (Garden City: Anchor-Doubleday, 1959), 35–8, that Rousseau discovers the concept of 'the social.'

31 In an unpublished paper, Tamara Vukov has argued that in contemporary North American political discourse there is a tendency to see agent and victim as mutually exclusive categories. She points out that one can be simultaneously a victim and an agent and gives the convincing example of gay activists for AIDS funding in organizations such as ACT-UP. She suggests that the gay men who organized and participated in these early confrontational protests were both clearly victims and indisputably active.

32 *OC* 4:1061. Here I have combined and modified translations by Roger Masters from his *The Political Philosophy of Rousseau* (Princeton: Princeton University Press, 1968), 68n22, and by Lester G. Crocker from his *The Age of Enlightenment* (New York: Harper & Row, 1969), 80.

See also Victor Gourevitch's comment on this passage: on pages 204–5 of his essay, 'The Religious Thought,' he writes that Rousseau 'closely links being free with being perfectible, being perfectible with speech, and speech with moral conduct or "progress in good as well as in evil." In short, the source of moral evil – and hence also of moral good – is "perfectibility," most particularly the distinctive capacity for artifice and convention that is set in motion "with the aid of circumstances," in other words by the workings of nature's necessary laws.'

33 Rousseau describes something of how this process works in his own case in the second of his four autobiographical letters to Malesherbes: '*Après avoir découvert, ou cru découvrir, dans les fausses opinions des hommes, la source de leurs misères et de leurs méchanceté, je sentis qu'il n' y avait que ces mêmes opinions qui m'eussent rendu malheureux moi-même, que mes maux et mes vices me venaient bien plus de ma situation que de moi même … je jugeai que si je voulais être conséquent, et secouer une fois de dessus mes épaules le pesant joug de l'opinion, je n'avais pas un moment à perdre. Je pris brusquement mon parti avec assez de courage, et je l' ai assez bien soutenu jusqu'ici avec une fermeté dont moi seul peux sentir le prix, parce qu'il n' y a que moi seul qui sache quels obstacles j'ai eus et j'ai encore tous les jours à combattre pour me maintenir sans cesse contre le courant.*' In Gauss, ed., *Selections from Rousseau*, 197–8. Rousseau is not deluded about the difficulty of resisting dominant opinion and achieving freedom of thought, even in his own case.

34 In the *Lettre à Voltaire* are a number of passages implying dualism. The passage about man's responsibility for moral evil quoted above continues as follows: 'and, as for physical evil [*mal physique*], if sensate and impassive matter is a contradiction, as it seems to me to be, they are inevitable in every system of which man is a part; and then the question is no longer why is man not perfectly happy, but why does he exist? In addition, I think I have shown that except for death, which is practically only an evil because of the preparations that are made for it, most of the physical evils are again our own work.' *OC* 4:1061. Later in the letter, Rousseau elaborates a dualism between a material, physical order and a moral order of intelligent, sensate beings. (See *OC* 4:1069–70 and Masters, *Political Philosophy*.) The terms of Rousseau's dualism here differ from those he uses in later formulations of dualism in *Emile* and the *Lettre à Franquières*. This may be in part because he is responding to the formulations in Voltaire's poem about

the Lisbon Earthquake. Voltaire had written in a note to the preface of his poem that a man could say 'I must be as dear to my master, me, a thinking and feeling [*pensant et sensant*] being, as the planets which probably do not feel.' See *OC* 4:1067, 1779n3. Rousseau replies that 'without a doubt this material universe is not dearer to its author than a sole thinking and feeling being': *OC* 4:1067. Note that he introduces dualism into the argument whereas Voltaire's reflection did not require it.

Rousseau sent a copy of this letter to Théodore Tronchin, asking him to decide whether to pass it on to Voltaire. He wrote to Tronchin as follows: *'Si je suis moins fondé que je n'ai cru l'être, ou que M. de Voltaire soit moins Philosophe que je ne le suppose, supprimez la lettre et renvoyez la moi sans la montrer. S'il peut supporter ma franchise, cachetez ma lettre et la lui donner en ajoûtant tout ce que vous croirez propre à lui bien persuader que jamais l'intention de l'offenser n'entra dans mon coeur.' Correspondance complètes,* ed. Ralph Leigh (Genève: Institut et Musée Voltaire, 1967), Letter 425, 18 aout 1756, IV:85. (In subsequent references, this edition will be abbreviated as *CC*.)

As to the question of whether Rousseau's references to will imply a free will, note that the Savoyard vicar suggests that the notion of will inherently implies a free will: 'There is no true will without freedom': trans. Bloom, 281. Descartes and Augustine agree with the vicar on this; see Hannah Arendt, *The Life of the Mind,* vol. 2: *Willing* (New York: Harcourt Brace Jovanovich, 1978), 26. Nietzsche and Hobbes take the opposite view.

35 Bertolt Brecht, *Threepenny Novel,* trans. Desmond I. Vesey (Harmondsworth: Penguin, 1965), 282. Quoted in Michael Kaufman, 'The Construction of Masculinity and the Triad of Male Violence' in *Beyond Patriarchy,* ed. Michael Kaufman (Toronto: Oxford University Press, 1987), 8.

36 Negotiating the divide between nature and history is a tricky affair. For example, Philopolis's reasoning leads him to assert that everything is natural: everything is simply part of God's natural plan. But this leaves no room for the understanding of artifice and, as Rousseau points out, leads one to condone all evil. On the other hand, Plattner suggests that for Rousseau, man is by nature an animal like all the rest; he denies there is anything natural that distinguishes man. Man is distinguished from the animals only by history. But how does history come about, on this understanding? Plattner states that the faculties develop because of the chance workings of mechanical causation. He is interested in stressing the historical origins of humanity. He does not plumb the question of whether these chance workings are natural – but they must be natural if they are provoked by natural causation. See Plattner, *Rousseau's State of Nature,* 50.

The task of declaring the moment when history and artifice emerge would be a particularly unenviable one. Perhaps this is one reason why Rousseau stresses the conjunction of several causes of civil society and the gradualness of the changes that led to it. Masters, 141, 148, and 178; *OC* 3:192. Cf. *Du contrat social* 1.1. 'How did this change occur? I do not know.'

37 Rousseau also says that considering man in the state of nature involves stripping him of the 'artificial faculties' he acquired over time. Masters, 105; *OC* 3:134. But cf. his description of the faculties as 'natural' in the Preface to the *Discourse*. Masters, 97, *OC* 3:127; and see also Plattner's discussion of this problem in *Rousseau's State of Nature*, 47 ff, as well as our own discussion below. Cf. Clifford Orwin and Nathan Tarcov: 'The fundamental polarity in Rousseau's thought, which seems to underlie all the others, is that between nature and society.' 'Introduction' in Orwin and Tarcov, eds., *The Legacy of Rousseau* (Chicago: University of Chicago Press, 1997), xi.

38 For a persuasive argument about the conjectural status of Rousseau's state of nature see Gourevitch, 'Rousseau's Pure State of Nature,' *Interpretation* 16 (1988): 23–59. Rousseau's account contains both scientific and conjectural elements. Scientific experiments might be devised based upon Rousseau's thought experiment conjecturing man's situation in the state of nature.

39 Of this passage, Rousseau wrote that he intended to respond to the following verse: *'La nature, croi-moi, n'est rien que l'habitude.'* The editors of the Pléiade suggest that Rousseau had in mind the following line from Voltaire's *Le Fanatisme ou Mahomet prophète*: *'La nature à mes yeux n'est rien que l'habitude'* (Act IV, scene 1). Note, too, the words Rousseau had originally written and then crossed out following the passage in *Emile* that we quoted in the main text: *'Enfin, si j'accorde que l'habitude peut quelquefois etouffer la nature, je conclurai de cela-même que l'une n'est pas l'autre.' OC* 4:1294–5nn(a),(b). But it appears to us that this in fact casts doubt on the sufficiency of the metaphor to ground, of itself, the society/nature distinction. Cf. the fragments of the *Second Discourse* in *Collected Writings*, III:96–101.

40 'Plutarch tells us of the supposed remark of Archimedes to the effect that "if there were another world, and he could go into it, he could move this one," a remark known in familiar form from Pappus of Alexandria (*Collectio*, Bk VIII, prop. 11): "Give me a place to stand on and I will move the earth."' *Dictionary of Scientific Biography* ed. Charles Coulston Gillispie (New York: Scribner, 1970), vol. 1. Cf. Arendt, *The Human Condition*, ch. 6, and Strauss, *Natural Right and History*, 172–4, 278–9.

I would like to thank Alan Patten for thoughtful conversations about the issues raised by Philopolis.

41 Rousseau's reference to the 'will of men' is adduced as proof that man's sociability is not immediately natural. Rousseau's assumption appears to be that the power of will has something unnatural about it, something, at any rate, independent of man's natural endowment.

42 Rousseau introduces the distinction in footnote 15 of the *Second Discourse*. *OC* 3:219–20. In the Masters edition, the reference is footnote O, 221–2. Cf. *Emile*, trans. Bloom, 93, 212–216, 243; and *Dialogues*, in *Collected Writings of Rousseau*, I:9–13. For other significant passages in which Rousseau discusses *amour propre* see Gourevitch's note, *The Discourses*, 377. Cf. Starobinski's *OC* 3:1376n1 on uses of the term *amour propre* prior to Rousseau.

43 In the first draft of *Emile*, the text of Bk I began with these words, an indication of their importance. In the earlier version, however, Rousseau used the phrase '*conscience de l'existence*' rather than '*sentiment de l'existence*.' See *OC* 4:61.

44 Cf. his statement in the same section that one should prepare the child for freedom 'by putting him in the condition always to be master of himself and in all things to do his will, as soon as he has one.' *OC* 4:282; trans. Bloom, 63.

45 Rousseau tries to distinguish the will simply from the irascible will to rebel or dominate by referring to the latter under the name '*fantasie*' or whim, 'a word by which I mean all desires which are not true needs and which can only be satisfied with another's help.' Trans. Bloom, 84, cf. 48. He contends that whim 'inasmuch as it does not come from nature, will not torment [children] if it has not been induced in them.' *OC* 4:290; trans. Bloom, 68. On Rousseau's discussion of the 'ill-will' of children in Bks I and II of *Emile*, cf. Joseph Cropsey, 'The Human Vision of Rousseau' in his *Political Philosophy and the Issues of Politics* (Chicago: University of Chicago Press, 1977), esp. 318–21. Gourevitch makes a facinating argument about idea that men resent depending on the will of another. He suggests it plays a key role in the debate between Rousseau and Voltaire about God and the origin of evil. See Gourevitch, 'The Religious Thought,' 203.

46 In the last section of this chapter, we return to the objection that Rousseau considers free will a salutary illusion. But here I would make two further points in response to the contention that in this passage Rousseau intends to show the careful reader the pitfalls of the illusion of free will. First, there is some textual evidence to contradict this reading. See, for example, Bk IV of *Emile* where Rousseau writes of 'those from whom one expects good or ill by their inner disposition, by their will – those we *see* acting freely for us

or against us' (emphasis mine). *OC* 4:492; trans. Bloom, 213. See also our discussion of this passage below. Cf. *OC* 4:556; trans. Bloom, 258. Second, if it is held that Rousseau pretends to believe in free will to support salutary politics and morality, is it not counterproductive to stress its problematic and pathological origins in this way?

47 Note that the Savoyard vicar sees the innateness of the sentiment of justice as an argument against comprehensive materialism: 'If to prefer oneself to everything is an inclination natural to man, and if nevertheless the first sentiment of justice is innate in the human heart, let him who regards man as a simple being overcome these contradictions, and I shall no longer acknowledge more than one substance.' Trans. Bloom, 279. Cf. Rousseau's suggestion that justice and goodness are 'only an ordered development of our primitive affections.' *Emile*, Bk IV, trans. Bloom, 235.

48 I have changed Bloom's translation of *'cri'* as 'scream' in the last line to 'cry' in order to give babies the benefit of the doubt.

49 A few paragraphs later Rousseau states his maxim that one should distinguish in the desires of children between 'what comes immediately from nature and what comes from opinion.' *OC* 4:290; trans. Bloom, 68. But what makes opinion unnatural?

50 *OC* 1:632. Cited and translated by Gourevitch, *The Discourses*, editorial note, 378–9.

51 But how can we be sure that Rousseau is talking about free will in this passage? There are solid reasons to believe that he is. He writes of 'those from whom one expects good or ill by their inner disposition, by their will – those we see acting freely for us or against us.' The least convoluted interpretation of this phrase is that he has in mind that we see that others freely will our own good or harm (that they act freely in our disfavour or favour on the basis of their free wills). He contrasts those we see willing in this way with 'insensible beings who merely follow the impulsion given them.' Note, too, the wording he uses: he refers to 'those we *see* acting freely for us or against us' on the basis of their wills – he does not refer to those whom we imagine or suppose to be acting freely. His wording implies that we are accurate in our perception that people act freely on the basis of the inner determination of their wills. Lastly, note that the entire context of the argument is Rousseau's effort to show there is an anti-natural dimension to our passions. Cf. his remark in Bk I that the capricious wills of children display 'moral effects whose immediate cause is not in nature.' Trans. Bloom, 66.

52 'To Rousseau, man is the only animal whose self-love can become altered or doubled in response to the recognition of others' existence.' Allan Bloom, *Love and Friendship* (New York: Simon & Schuster, 1993), 51.

53 Harry Frankfurt, 'Freedom of the Will and the Concept of a Person,' *Journal of Philosophy* 68, no. 1 (1971): 5–20. Cf. Rousseau's remark in Bk 1 of *Emile* that 'before the age of reason we do good and bad without knowing it, and there is no morality in our actions, although there sometimes is in the sentiment of other's actions which have a relation to us.' Trans. Bloom, 67.

54 Cf. *Discourse*, Masters, 149; and *Dialogues*, in *Collected Writings*, I:9.

55 Alexis Philonenko reports Leibniz's remark that if he ever 'saw a monkey *cheat* at cards, he would become a vegetarian' (emphasis in original). Philonenko, *Le traité du mal*, vol. I of *Jean Jacques Rousseau et la pensée du malheur* (Paris: Vrin, 1984), 167. Dostoyevsky's Underground Man claims we are at our freest when we are acting badly.

56 Philonenko, *Le traité du mal*, I:176.

57 Still, that something outside of the will triggers or launches it seems to indicate that it is in this sense not spontaneous but determined. But, again, when Rousseau presents the trigger as contingent, as something that might never have happened, he may actually be providing a condition of free will. Hannah Arendt points out in *The Life of the Mind* that Duns Scotus saw contingency as a condition of free will. She explains that the contingent 'corresponds to the experience of the willing ego,' which begins something new that it knows might never have been: 'After all, it was the Philosopher who had defined the contingent and the accidental (*to symbëbekos)* as that which "could as well not be" (*endechomenon më einai*), and what was the willing ego more aware of in every volition, than that it could also not will (*experitur enim qui vult se posse non velle*)?' Arendt, *Willing*, 136.

58 There is the same element of contingency in the process Rousseau describes in the *Letter to Philopolis*. There, too, society and corruption emerge not immediately from nature but through the intervention of circumstances 'many of which depend upon the will of men.' We contend he employs a both/and description of man's decline rather than an either/or explanation. For a discussion of the contingent character of Rousseau's discovery of the split between nature and convention, see Christopher Kelly, *Rousseau's Exemplary Life: The Confessions as Political Philosophy* (Ithaca: Cornell University Press, 1987), 243–6.

59 I have used elements of both the Masters (149) and Gourevitch (166) translations here.

60 I have retained the French terms but used Clifford Orwin's translation from 'Rousseau on the Sources of Ethics' in *Instilling Ethics*, ed. Norma Thompson (Lanham: Rowman & Littlefield, 2000); *OC* 3:219–20. Cf. Masters edition, 221–2nO.

61 Here I have followed the Masters translation with the following exceptions: I have retained the French *amour propre* instead of adopting 'vanity' in the first sentence; I have adopted Gourevitch's translation of '*ni s'apprecier ni se comparer*,' and his rendering of '*véritable état de nature*' as 'genuine state of nature.' I have also followed him in retaining the capitalization of Animals. Trans. Masters, 222; trans. Gourevitch, 218.

62 The difference between *Emile* and *Discourse* in this regard can be explained through the different purposes of the works. The *Second Discourse* draws more centrally on debates about natural science; it was meant to be acceptable to the scientific thinkers among Rousseau's readers, many of whom were likely to be materialist. It stands to reason that Rousseau would be more hesitant to affirm free will in such a context. He leaves it in the background rather than bringing it out to be assailed by his opponents.

63 Again, a major objection to this position is that what Rousseau actually implies is that people are mistaken to attribute free will to one another. But if this interpretation holds that Rousseau champions free will because it is salutary, it would have to account for his odd way of proceeding, by showing that it gets going along with resentment, rebellion, and violent revenges. As further evidence that Rousseau believes men are right to hold one another responsible for their actions, consider his remark in *Emile* that 'reason tells us that man can be punished only for mistakes of his will.' *OC* 4:556; trans. Bloom, 258.

64 In this and subsequent usages, I use the term 'consciousness of freedom' to denote the implication of consciousness of free will.

65 This is what Gourevitch suggests in 'Rousseau's Pure State of Nature,' and a rereading of the *Discourse* with this in mind confirmed his assertion. Gourevitch argues that the pure state of nature is a thought experiment that Rousseau uses to conjecture what men would be like without artifice or convention of any kind. Cf. John T. Scott, 'The Theodicy of the *Second Discourse:* The Pure State of Nature and Rousseau's Political Thought,' *American Political Science Review* 86, No. 3 (September 1992): 696–711. Scott suggests that the pure state of nature describes man's existence as a 'purely physical being,' shorn of all 'moral needs or passions, that is, needs or passions with particular, conscious regard for other humans.' This latter interpretation, if accepted, would fit neatly with our own, but some possible objections to it are presented in the text itself. For a recent treatment that emphasizes the importance of Rousseau's pure state of nature, see Ioannis D. Evrigenis, 'Freeing Man from Sin: Rousseau on the Natural Condition of Mankind,' in *Rousseau and Freedom*, ed. Christie McDonald and Stanley Hoffmann (Cambridge: Cambridge University Press, 2010).

66 In the first paragraph of the *Essay on the Origins of Languages*, Rousseau writes that 'since speech is the first social institution, it owes its form to natural causes alone.' He also notes that it 'antedates even morals.' Trans. Gourevitch, *The Discourses*, 248.

67 Gourevitch rightly emphasizes this point. A similar argument could be made about sociality, since the existence of families settled in huts predates the emergence of *amour propre* characterized by the consciousness of freedom in Rousseau's account. Note, too, that in *Emile*, this recognition of freedom predates language in the infant although it does not, of course, predate sociality. One would then have to consider whether all human sociality entails convention or whether it can be seen as an animal activity like herding, or like the grouping into troops of monkeys or packs of wolves.

68 As Kerah Gordon put it, 'Perfectibility only takes the development of artifice and convention so far.' I thank her for this formulation and for her comments on the argument as a whole.

69 The passage continues as follows: 'Finally the accord of those brute creatures is natural; but accord between men is based merely on agreement, i.e. is artificial; it is not therefore surprising that something more is needed if men are to live in peace.' Thomas Hobbes, *On the Citizen*, ed. Richard Tuck and Michael Silverthorne (Cambridge: Cambridge University Press, 1998), 72. The entire section is highly relevant to our argument. In the rest of the chapter Hobbes goes on to articulate his conception of political will. Compare Hobbes, *Leviathan*, Chapter 17, paragraph 11 and following.

70 Quoted in Leo Strauss, *The Political Philosophy of Hobbes* (Chicago: University of Chicago Press, 1952), 10. In *On the Citizen*, ch. 1, Hobbes writes that men have a 'mutual will of hurting.'

71 See Strauss, *Natural Right and History*. There Strauss argues that in order to leave room for the possibility of science in a materialist scheme, Hobbes had to 'discover or invent an island that would be exempt from the flux of mechanical causation.' Strauss suggests that Hobbes turns not to a natural island based on the corporeal mind but to the notion of an artificial island 'whose construction is in our own power or depends on our arbitrary will ... The world of our constructs is therefore the desired island that is exempt from the flux of blind and aimless causation.' 172–3. Later in the work, referring to Rousseau's desire to ground morality on 'a right or a freedom which is specifically human,' Strauss writes that 'Hobbes had implicitly admitted the existence of such a freedom. For he had implicitly admitted that if the traditional dualism of substances, of mind and body, is abandoned, science cannot be possible except if meaning, order, or truth

originates in man's creative action, or if man has the freedom of a creator. Hobbes was, in fact, compelled to replace the traditional dualism of body and mind, not by materialistic monism, but by the novel dualism of nature (or substance) and freedom. What Hobbes had, in fact, suggested in regard to science was applied by Rousseau to morality.' 280–1.

72 I suppose one could object that man has a natural endowment for a consciousness of free will. But once man is conscious of his free will he can make a choice about how to use it. Man 'realizes he is free to acquiesce or resist' and he is therefore at a further remove from the auspices of nature.

73 Locke defines will as a 'determination of the mind.' See his *Essay*, Bk II, ch. XXI (Of Power). The gaze of animals does not hold the same kind of fascination for us. Rousseau has said that before man attributes intentions to others and develops *amour propre*, he sees 'his fellow-men hardly otherwise than he would see other animals of another species.' Masters, 222n15(O). Kant's note to *Observations on the Feeling of the Beautiful and Sublime* is worth considering here: 'An animal is not yet a complete being, because it is not conscious of itself … it knows nothing of its own existence.' Quoted in Ernst Cassirer, *Rousseau–Kant–Goethe*, trans. J. Gutmann, P. Kristeller, and J. Randall, Jr (New York: Harper & Row, 1963), 17. Cf. Sartre, *Being and Nothingness*, part 3, ch. I, section IV.

74 Rousseau's interpreters have suggested various numbers of stages: from two (John T. Scott) to five (Lovejoy). Rousseau himself presents a three-stage account in the description of *amour propre* and natural goodness in the *Lettre à Beaumont* (a passage that we discuss later in this chapter). I follow this account. In focusing on anthropological or ethnographic stages, I have put aside the question of the 'pure state of nature.' In 'Rousseau's Pure State of Nature,' Gourevitch argues that Rousseau thinks of the pure state of nature as a conjectural thought experiment rather than a scientifically documented anthropological stage. I am partial to this view, given both the history of the concept as Gourevitch presents it and most of Rousseau's uses of the term in the text of the *Discourse*. In his critique of Locke on the family in footnote 12(L), however, his references to the 'pure state of nature' appear to give the term an anthropological or ethnographic meaning.

75 Interestingly, this passage leaves open the possibility that the development ought to have happened for the good of at least some individuals. Cf. Rousseau's important statement in his *Lettre à Beaumont*: '*Ces réflexions me conduisirent à de nouvelles recherches sur l'esprit humain considéré dans l'état civil, et je trouvai qu'alors le développement des lumieres et des vices se faisoit toujours en même raison, non dans les individus, mais dans les peuples; distinc-*

tion que j'ai toujours soigneusement faite, et qu'aucun de ceux qui m'ont attaqué n'a jamais pu concevoir.' OC 4:967.

76 On this point see Arthur Lovejoy's 'The Supposed Primitivism of Rousseau,' 32. This lucid and rigorous essay is contained in his *Essays in the History of Ideas* (Baltimore: Johns Hopkins University Press, 1948).

77 *OC* 4:936. I have used Plattner's fine translation of this passage in *Rousseau's State of Nature* (79–80) but I have changed this term. He provides the term *amour de soi* but I believe *amour propre* is correct. The problem originates with the Pléiade edition. It replaces *amour propre* with *amour de soi* and offers an explanatory note that reads as follows: *'L'édition originale porte amour propre, ce qui est manifestement faux. Nous rétablissons la leçon du brouillon: amour de soi.' OC* 4:1734. I disagree with this move: if *amour propre* was the wrong term it is hard to say why Rousseau, who was so meticulous about more minor typographical matters in his publications, would tolerate such a glaring mistake in editions published during his lifetime. (The editions of the *Lettre à Beaumont* from 1763, 1765, and 1766 in the McGill University Rare Book library all feature *'amour propre'* in this sentence.) I would surmise that in this sentence Rousseau refers to what he calls *amour propre* in the extended sense, that is he refers to both *amour de soi* and *amour propre*. As he puts it in *Emile*, 'The sole passion natural to man is *amour de soi* or *amour propre* taken in an extended sense.' *OC* 4:322; trans. Bloom, 92. On this point, see also Orwin, who argues that 'In *Emile*, Rousseau ... abandons the opposition between *amour-propre* and nature and thereby the claim that while *amour de soi-même* is natural to us *amour-propre* is factitious.' 'Rousseau's Ethics,' 24. Joshua Cohen deals neatly with the terminology problem posed by Rousseau's recuperation of *amour propre* by adopting the term 'healthy *amour propre*' when needed. For a useful discussion of Rousseau scholarship that refuses 'to cast *amour propre* in an intrinsically negative light,' see Christopher Brooke, 'Rousseau's *Second Discourse*: between Epicureanism and Stoicism,' in *Rousseau and Freedom*, ed. Christie McDonald and Stanley Hoffmann (Cambridge: Cambridge University Press, 2010). Cf. 'Natural Goodness.'

78 The *Lettre à Beaumont* is highly rhetorical, but it contains startling and – many religious believers would say – heretical statements. The motive of avoiding persecution did not hinder Rousseau from making these. Rousseau gives indications, however, of his motive to shore up healthy politics in the *Lettre*. It is, in a sense, Rousseau's *Apology*.

79 It is true that Rousseau's historical dualism, his historical interpretation of man's mixed nature, has not inspired many followers on the political Left. Historical materialism, presuming philosophical materialism and

determinism, has been by far the most popular vein. Cf. Alfred Schmidt's seminal discussion of Marx on philosophical and historical materialism in his *The Concept of Nature in Marx*, trans. Ben Fowkes (London: New Left Books, 1971) and Marx's own discussions in *The Holy Family*. Rousseau's historical discussion of man's dual soul has more kinship with Hegel than with Kant's idealism. But in his 'Speculative Idea of Human History,' Kant does take a historical approach to the idea of man as a physical species *and* a moral species.

I would suggest that the originality of Rousseau's account is in keeping with his bold independence of mind. For his own comments on the sceptical reactions of the philosophes to his anti-materialist views, see the *Lettre à Franquières*, *OC* 4:1142; and *The Reveries of the Solitary Walker*, Third Walk, *Oeuvres complètes*, ed. Bernard Gagnebin and Marcel Raymond et al. (Paris: Editions Gallimard, 1959), 1:1011–23; *The Reveries of the Solitary Walker*, trans. Charles Butterworth (New York: Harper Colophon, 1979), 27–42. In subsequent references, I will refer simply to this work as *Reveries*. As we mentioned in earlier, the *Lettre à Voltaire* contains a moral reading of man's freedom based on dualism, which is reaffirmed in his letter to Tronchin about Voltaire.

80 Gourevitch suggests that Rousseau's formulation '*il est bête*' implies not that natural man is a beast but merely that he is stupid. He adds that Heinrich Meier 'very correctly calls attention to the fact that Rousseau never refers to man as a beast.' See 'Rousseau's Pure State of Nature,' 41n28. Cf. Velkley, *Being after Rousseau*, ch. 2.

81 Compare Plattner, who contends that 'in the *Second Discourse* proper there is not a single mention of conscience' (80). Plattner does signal a reference to conscience in the Dedication. See *OC* 3:122.

82 That this would involve a sleight of hand that represses our consciousness of our free will to do evil is one of our main arguments in the rest of the chapter.

83 The most significant objection to this reading arises from the presentation of *amour propre* that Rousseau offers at the outset of *Rousseau Juge de Jean-Jacques: Dialogues*. His account of man's distraction from the goals of self-preservation and happiness there contains no reference to the attribution of freedom from instinct to other humans. Of course, there is a question to be raised about the authority of the *Dialogues*, given that it is such a distressing record of what has been called Rousseau's 'obsession with a conspiracy directed against him.' *Collected Writings*, ed. Bush, Masters and Kelly, I:xxv. Cf. Maurice Cranston's comment that from the day Rousseau read Voltaire's anonymous slander of him, '*Le Sentiment des citoyens*,' 'his

capacity for clear judgment faltered.' *The Solitary Self: Jean-Jacques Rousseau in Exile and Adversity* (Chicago: University of Chicago Press, 1997), 103. That day was 31 December 1765. Nonetheless, I do not think this presentation of *amour propre* can be simply dismissed, especially because Rousseau appears to have written it very carefully. It seems to me likely, however, that the *Dialogues* were written during one of his periods of 'doubts and faltering hopes' about matters metaphysical that Rousseau describes in the Third Reverie. Cf. chapter 4 below. But even in the discussion of *amour propre* that begins the *Dialogues*, Rousseau appeals to a conception of virtue as an activity that requires 'fighting and conquering nature.' See the *Collected Writings*, I:10–11. Cf. the discussion of freedom of will, morality, and the character of his intention on 140–1 of the same volume and his note to it.

84 Rousseau then describes the progressive smothering of conscience in this important passage interpreting natural goodness in the *Lettre à Beaumont*. Once men begin to perceive their relations with others and the relations of things and understand justice, order and moral beauty, their consciences come into play: 'Then they have virtues and if they also have vices, it is because their interests crisscross [*se croisent*] and their ambition awakens but as long as there is less opposition of interests than concurrence of enlightenment, men are essentially good. This is the second state.

'When, finally, all the agitated particular interests clash [*s'entre-choquent*], when *l'amour de soi* set in fermentation, becomes *amour propre*, when opinion, making the entire universe necessary to each man, makes them all born enemies of one another and works in such a way that none finds his good except in the misfortune [*mal*] of another, then conscience, weaker than the exalted passions, is smothered by them and it is no longer anything in men's mouths but a word used to deceive one another.' *OC* 4:936–7.

85 Quoted in Plattner, *Rousseau's State of Nature*, 47.

86 Nietzsche writes that it is precisely in the word 'will' that 'the popular prejudice lurks, which has defeated the always inadequate caution of the philosophers.' *Beyond Good and Evil*, trans. Walter Kaufmann (New York: Vintage, 1966), section 19. Cf. section 21. Tolstoy compares the view that the will is free to the pre-Copernican conviction that the earth was the centre of the universe. *War and Peace*, appendix, excerpted as 'The Difficulty of Defining the Forces That Move Nations' in *Theories of History*, ed. Patrick Gardiner (Glencoe, Illinois: Free Press, 1959). In the Eighth Walk of the *Reveries*, Rousseau himself attributes his reluctance to deny free will in himself to his *amour propre*. See our discussion in chapter 4. Advocates of free will make the opposite argument. C.A. Campbell, for example,

identifies two forces that may blind thinkers to the need for free will as the basis of moral responsibility: 'One is sympathy with the general tenets of Positivism. The other is the conviction ... that man does not in fact possess a contra-causal type of freedom; whence follows a strong presumption that no such freedom is necessary to moral responsibility.' Campbell, 'Is "Free-will" a Pseudo-problem?' in *Free Will and Determinism*, ed. Bernard Berofsky (New York: Harper & Row, 1966), 127. Isaiah Berlin asks: 'Could it not be maintained that determinism itself is a superstition generated by a false belief that science will be compromised unless it is accepted, and is therefore itself a case of "false consciousness" generated by a mistake about the nature of science?' Berlin, 'Introduction' in *Four Essays on Liberty* (Oxford: Oxford University Press, 1969), xxv. Cf. the Savoyard vicar's comparison of materialists to a deaf man, *OC* 4:585; and *Emile*, trans. Bloom, 279–280.

87 Bloom, *Love and Friendship*; Orwin, 'Rousseau's Ethics'; Peter Emberley, 'Rousseau versus the Savoyard Vicar,' *Interpretation* 14 (1986): 299–329 at 299–300; Melzer, *Natural Goodness*, 249n.

88 I have drawn in part on Patrick Riley's translation in *The General Will before Rousseau: The Transformation of the Divine into the Civic* (Princeton: Princeton University Press, 1986), 255.

89 Franquières's premise that the 'law of necessity alone ... rules the working of the world' is a key determinist premise. Rousseau responds with a critique of the moral implications this deterministic premise. Note, too, that Rousseau suggests that Franquières has been led away from the 'bosom of *truth* and virtue' through his reasoning (emphasis mine). We discuss Rousseau's critiques of the limits of comprehensive materialism in the letter to Franquières in the next chapter. Gourevitch notes that Ralph Leigh identified Rousseau's correspondent to be Laurent Aymon de Franquières. See Rousseau, *The Social Contract and Other Later Political Writings*, trans. Victor Gourevitch (Cambridge: Cambridge University Press, 1997), 320.

90 Here Rousseau does not argue simply that an empirical need for the morally edifying concept of free will indicates that it exists. Instead, he puts the argument in negative form: the fact that norms of moral conduct rest on free will casts doubt on determinism.

91 Earlier in the *Lettre à Franquières*, Rousseau seems to suggest that the conscience can be seen as authentic because of its very innerness. He tells his correspondent that we should not confound the 'secret inclinations of our heart that can mislead us, with the dictamen, more secret and even more internal, that declaims and murmurs against self-interested decisions, and brings us back, in spite of ourselves, to the path of truth.' *OC* 4:1138.

92 Hans Jonas, 'Philosophical Meditation on the Seventh Chapter of Paul's

Epistle to the Romans,' in *The Future of Our Religious Past: Essays in Honour of Rudolf Bultmann* ed. James M. Robinson (New York: Harper & Row, 1971), 338.

93 I have used the translation by Bloom, 280, except that I have changed 'wanted to do' to 'willed to do' (for *voulu faire*) in the sixth line. For other discussions of the vicar's argument here, see Matthew Simpson, *Rousseau's Theory of Freedom* (London: Continuum, 2006), esp. 99; and F.M. Barnard, 'Will and Political Rationality in Rousseau,' *Political Studies* 32 (1984): 369–84.

In a passage earlier in the *Profession of Faith*, the vicar also has recourse to his own interior feeling to prove that motions can be spontaneous: 'You will ask me again how I know that there are spontaneous motions. I shall tell you that I know it because I sense it. I want to move my arm, and I move it without this movement's having any other immediate cause than my will. It would be vain to try to use reason to destroy this sentiment in me. It is stronger than any evidence. One might just as well try to prove to me that I do not exist.' Trans. Bloom, 272.

94 The relation between the terms sentiment of freedom and consciousness of freedom remains unclear. But note that, later in the *Profession of Faith*, the vicar contends that 'the acts of conscience are not judgments but sentiments.' Trans. Bloom, 290. Cf. his definition of conscience at 289.

95 Regarding remorse, Bernard Berofsky writes that indeterminists contend that 'it is impossible to believe that such a deep seated feeling invariably gives rise to erroneous belief. Thus we must sometimes be right in thinking that we could have done otherwise.' See Berofsky, ed., 'Introduction' in *Free Will and Determinism*, 8–9. This topic is also addressed in Campbell's rigorous defence of free will in his 'Is "Freewill" a Pseudo-problem?' A useful summary of the debate is found in *A Dictionary of Philosophy*, ed. A.R. Lacey (London: Routledge, 1996), 115. Indeterminists, that book tells us, 'insist that determinists, of whatever complexion, can give no sense to the sentence "He could have done otherwise," where this means something more than simply "He might have done otherwise (had his nature or circumstances been different)." Soft determinists often hold that what justifies praise and blame is solely that they can influence action. This, say indeterminists, misses the point of these concepts, which are essentially backward-looking.' Isaiah Berlin makes the point this way: 'If (as happens to those who are capable of genuine self-criticism) the more we discover about ourselves the less we are inclined to forgive ourselves, why should we assume that the opposite is valid for others, that we alone are free,

while others are determined?' *Four Essays on Liberty*, xix. For a critique of remorse see Nietzsche, *The Genealogy of Morals*, trans. Walter Kaufmann (New York: Vintage, 1969).

96 Cf. Locke's definition of liberty as 'the power in any agent to do or forbear any particular action, according to the determination or thought of the mind,' in the *Essay Concerning Human Understanding*, Book II, chap. XXI (Of Power) Section 8, 167.

97 In effect, whereas at first the will is an arbiter whose independence consists in that it is free to acquiesce or resist in the senses, here the will is a partisan of resistance whose independence consists in the unmixed wish to resist them. This appears to correspond to the Kantian distinction between the *Willkür* (the corruptible capacity for choice) and the *Wille* (the moral will). See the entry for 'Will' in *A Kant Dictionary*, ed. Howard Caygill (Oxford: Blackwell, 1995). The editor notes that the two terms are frequently translated into English as 'will,' even at times in Norman Kemp Smith's translation of the *Critique of Pure Reason*.

98 The vicar also moves from an initial focus on the senses, to a focus on the passions, to a focus on the vices. This transition makes possible the mounting moralism of the passage. A few paragraphs before our passage, the vicar refers to man's subjection to 'the empire of the senses and to the passions which are their ministers.' *OC* 4:583; trans. Bloom, 278–9.

99 As Charles Taylor argues in 'What Is Human Agency?,' it is ignoble to be moved by spite. See Taylor, in *The Self*, ed. Theodore Mischel (Oxford: Blackwell, 1977), 104. From a very different perspective, Nietzsche seeks to defend a deterministic, aesthetic understanding of moral freedom. But note that one can engage in self-mastery in the name of heinous goals and cruel principles. As Nietzsche famously remarked, 'the categorical imperative smells of cruelty.' *Genealogy of Morals* 2.6, 65.

100 Recall his original example in the *Discourse* of the freedom of the dissolute men whose reason depraves their senses, who risk fever and death to pursue their misguided wills. Recall, too, that in the same work, men's attribution of free will to others causes 'violent revenges.'

101 Cf. the vicar's discussion of non-material freedom as wanting one's own good: 'it is in this precisely that my freedom consists – my being able to will only what is suitable to me, *or what I deem to be such*, without anything external determining me'; trans. Bloom, 280 (emphasis mine). Here the vicar implicitly admits that freedom of the will can involve erroneous or poor judgment – I may be mistaken about my good but I freely will it. These passages also show that, for the vicar, there is no need to identify

moral freedom with free will in order to respond to the determinists. On the contrary, if man has free will, he must be free to choose or reject the disposition toward virtue and the counsel of conscience.

102 According to the Pléiade, originally, these statements about man's responsibilty for choosing good or evil directly followed the vicar's description of his freedom through remorse. *OC* 4:1541n(a) to 586.

103 The vicar also argues that conscience 'is to the soul as instinct is to the body.' *OC* 4:595; trans. Bloom, 286.

104 There are a few small differences between the two passages. Here is the version from the *Lettres Morales: 'Conscience, conscience, instinct divin, voix immortelle et celeste, guide assuré d'un être ignorant et borné mais intelligent et libre, juge infaillible du bien et du mal, sublime émanation de la substance éternelle, qui rends l'homme semblable aux Dieux; c'est toi seule qui fais l'excellence de ma nature.*

'Sans toi je ne sens rien en moi qui m'eléve au dessus des bêtes, que le triste privilége de m'égarer d'erreurs en erreurs à l'aide d'un entendement sans régle et d'une raison sans principle'(*OC* 4: 1111).

How sure can we be that Rousseau speaks frankly in the *Lettres Morales*, written for Mme D'Houdetot? Rousseau had fallen in love with her and because she was both a married woman and the lover of an admired acquaintance, it is true that he had incentives to extol modesty and control of the passions in these writings; this he does frequently. But in the passage under consideration, Rousseau's first-person account of the burden of his own will does correspond to the accounts we have of his struggle with his feelings for Mme D'Houdetot. For a detailed account, see Maurice Cranston, *The Noble Savage: Jean-Jacques Rousseau 1754–1761* (Chicago: University of Chicago, 1991). Also, consider Rousseau's description of his intentions in the first of the *Lettres Morales*: *'En vous exposant mes sentiments sur l'usage de la vie, je preténds moins vous donner des leçons que vous faire ma profession de foi, à qui puis-je mieux confier mes principles qu' à celle qui connoit si bien tous mes sentimens.'* *OC* 4:1085.

105 Cf. *DCS* 1.8. The vicar's expressions of pride in man's free will are followed by reflections about human responsibility for 'evil on earth.' Trans. Bloom, 277–8 ff.; Cf. *Lettres Morales*, *OC* 4:1098.

106 As Christopher Kelly points out, the philosopher in Rousseau's so-called '*Fiction ou Morceau allégorique sur la révélation*' is torn between the view that the order of the physical universe is the result of a 'fortuitous arrangement' or the result of an 'ordering principle.' See Kelly, *Rousseau as Author: Consecrating One's Life to the Truth* (Chicago: University of Chicago, 2003), 156; cf. *OC* 4:1046.

Chapter 3

1 *Essai sur les Revolutions*, 1797, quoted in *Emile II extraits* (Paris: Classiques Larousse, 1938), 95. Mme de Stael's discussion of *Emile* in her *Lettres sur Jean Jacques Rousseau* (1788) begins as follows: '*Je vais maintenant parler de l'ouvrage qui a consacré la gloire de Rousseau; de celui que son nom d'abord nous rapelle, et qui confounde l'envie, après l'avoir l'excité*' (Genève: Slatkine Reprints, 1979), 47.

2 In the same passage Rousseau goes on to say that the second part of the Profession 'proposes doubts and difficulties about revelations in general' and that it thereby attempts to render each of us more tolerant of other religions (*OC* 3:996–7). In our discussion of civil religion in this chapter, we consider the significance of these aspects of the *Profession*.

Roger Masters's careful exegisis of the *Profession* in *The Political Philosophy of Jean-Jacques Rousseau* (Princeton: Princeton University Press, 1968) inspired me to undertake my own exegisis of the first part. On the *Profession*, see also Allan Bloom, *Love and Friendship* (New York: Simon & Schuster, 1993); Melzer, 'The Origin of the Counter-Enlightenment: Rousseau and the New Religion of Sincerity,' *American Political Science Review* 90, no. 2 (June 1996): 344–360; idem, 'Rousseau and the Modern Cult of Sincerity' in Clifford Orwin and Nathan Tarcov, eds., *The Legacy of Rousseau* (Chicago: University of Chicago Press, 1997); P.-M. Masson, *La Profession de foi du vicaire savoyard* (Paris: Hachette, 1914); idem, *'Rousseau Contre Helvétius,' Revue d'histoire litteraire de la France* 18 (1911): 103–24; Peter Jimack, *La genese et la redaction de L'Emile*, vol. 13: *Studies on Voltaire and the Eighteenth Century* (Geneva: Institut et Musée Voltaire, 1960); Yvon Belaval, *'La théorie du jugement dans L'Emile,'* in *Jean-Jacques Rousseau et son Oeuvre*, ed. Comité national pour la commémoration de J.-J. Rousseau (Paris: Kilncksieck, 1964); Martin Rang, *'Le dualisme anthroplogique dans L'Emile'* in the same volume as Belaval; Joseph Cropsey, 'The Human Vision of Rousseau,' in his *Political Philosophy and the Issues of Politics* (Chicago: University of Chicago Press, 1977); Peter Emberley, 'Rousseau Versus the Savoyard Vicar' *Interpretation*, 14 (1986): 299–329; Jeffrey Macy, '"God Helps Those Who Help themselves": New Light on the Theological-Political Teaching in Rousseau's Profession of Faith of the Savoyard Vicar,' *Polity* 24, no. 4 (1992): 615–32; Yves Vargas, *Introduction à L'Emile de Jean-Jacques Rousseau* (Paris: Presses Universitaires de France, 1995), 156–95; and Laurence Mall, *Emile, ou les figures de la fiction: Studies on Voltaire and the Eighteenth Century* (Oxford: Voltaire Foundation, 2002), ch. 9.

3 Emile must also be prepared for his increasing interactions with others and to control his emerging desires. Regarding the latter, see both Rousseau's remarks before the *Profession* (*OC* 4:557; trans. Bloom, 259) and after it (*OC* 4:635 ff; trans. Bloom, 313 ff).

4 In the *Confessions*, Rousseau reveals that the character of the vicar is in fact based on both Abbé Jean-Claude Gaime whom he met in Turin and Abbé Baptiste Gâtier whom he met in Annecy. See *OC* 1:1505–6n2.

5 In the same note on the margins of *De l'esprit*, Rousseau mentions that the anonymous author of the article 'Evidence' in the Encyclopedia maintains the same principle that human judgment is passive: 'If I am right,' Rousseau continues, 'and the principle of M. Helvétius and the above mentioned author is false, the reasoning of the following chapters [of *De l'esprit*], which are only the consequences, fall and it is not true that inequality of minds is only the effect of education, although it can influence them a lot.' *OC* 4:1129. Masson reports that M. de Montmollin, the Swiss pastor, wrote that Rousseau informed him that one of the purposes of the *Profession* was to refute Helvétius's assertion that judging and sensing are the same thing. According to Masson, Rousseau confirms this by adding '*ce qui est évidenment établir le matérialisme.*' (For Helvétius's argumentation that '*tout jugement n'est qu'une sensation,*' see especially his *De l'esprit* [Paris: Fayard, 1998], I.I.) Masson suggests that since refutations of Helvétius first appear in a late draft of the *Profession*, '*ce n'est point pour refuter Helvétius que Rousseau s'est mis à écrire la Profession du Vicaire. Les intentions de l'oeuvre sont plus profoundes, plus générales et moins conditionés par actualité immédiate.*' But Rousseau's remark to Montmollin indicates the primary importance this question took on for him. See Masson, '*Rousseau Contre Helvétius,*' 124. Rousseau's marginal notes on his copy of *De l'esprit* can be found in the Pléiade Edition: *OC* 4:1119–30. Cf. *Lettres écrites de la montagne*, I, *OC* 4:693n.

6 See Masson, '*Rousseau Contre Helvétius*'; Descartes, *The Meditations Concerning First Philosophy*, Fourth Meditation; Henri Gouhier, 'Ce que le Vicaire doit à Descartes,' *Annales Jean-Jacques Rousseau* 30 (1959–62): 139–54; and Jimack, *La genese et la redaction de L'Emile*. This study appeared as a volume of *Studies on Voltaire and the Eighteenth Century*, vol. 13 (Genève: Institut et Musée Voltaire, 1960). For an insightful discussion about the differences between Rousseau's method and that of Descartes, see Vargas, *Introduction à L'Emile*, 156 ff.

7 This passage begins as follows: 'You will ask me if the motions of animals are spontaneous. I shall tell you that I know nothing about it, but analogy

supports the affirmative.' Marc Plattner notes that this is a change from Rousseau's position in the *Discourse*. But it is not clear what we should make of this change, given that the vicar seems to concede more to the materialists on this point than does Rousseau himself. Compare Roger Masters's analysis of the vicar's remark that animals may have spontaneous motion: Masters, *The Political Philosophy*, 72. On the whole, it seems to us that the vicar is less concerned with the (perilous) task of drawing a precise line between men and the animals than he is with articulating his own view of human nature.

8 See Masters, *The Political Philosophy*, 64, for an able critique of the vicar's argumentation in support of this point. The vicar's argument may be following that of the author of the article 'Evidence' in the Diderot's *Encyclopaedia*; see Masson's critical edition of Rousseau, *La Profession de foi du vicaire savoyard* (Paris : Librairie Hachette, 1914), 95n1.

The principle of inertia holds that a body will continue at rest or continue to move in a straight line unless moved by another object. The vicar provides a response to modern thinking about inertia that allows for a first cause of movement. Non-organized matter cannot move itself. Rousseau considers the question of matter in motion both in his *Lettre à Voltaire* (*OC* 4:1059–78) and in his *Lettre à Franquières* (*OC* 4: 1133–47). For a fascinating account of the impact of the modern scientific teaching about inertia on modern political thought, see Thomas Spragens, 'The Politics of Inertia and Gravitation: The Functions of Exemplar Paradigms in Social Thought,' *Polity* 5, no. 3 (1973): 288–310. Spragens compares the role of the doctrine of inertia in Hobbes's political thought to the role of gravitation in the political thought of Enlightenment liberals. For an attempt to wrestle with the theological implications of inertia in the light of modern physics, see Wolfhart Pannenberg, *Toward a Theology of Nature: Essays on Science and Faith*, ed. Ted Peters (Louisville: Westminster John Knox Press, 1993), 19–20.

9 See *OC* 4:1527n2; see also, in the same text at page 875, Rousseau's draft fragment referring to Aristotle's *De caelo*. Graeme Garrard quotes the letter to Moultou of 14 February 1769 (CC XXXVII:57), where Rousseau writes that if 'you reject the First Cause and have everything done through matter and motion, you take all morality from human life.' Garrard, *Rousseau's Counter-Enlightenment: A Republican Critique of the Philosophes* (Albany: SUNY Press, 2003), 98.

It might be objected that the vicar's argument that his sentiment of his own free will grounds the idea that a will moves a universe is anthropomorphic, and this might lead one to question whether it reflects Rousseau's actual position. Rousseau criticizes anthropomorphism a few pages before the *Profession*, suggesting of Christians that 'we ourselves, with our terms *spirit, trinity, persons,* are for the most part veritable anthropomorphites. I admit that we are taught to say that God is everywhere, but we also believe that air is everywhere, at least in our atmosphere. And in its origin the word *spirit* itself signifies only breath and wind.' *OC* 4:552; trans. Bloom, 256. In fact, I suspect that this anthropomorphic connotation of the term 'spirit' is what leads Rousseau to abandon his earlier use of the term 'spiritual' to describe free will and to replace it with the term 'immaterial' in the *Profession*. In considering whether the vicar's argument is anthropomorphic, note that rather than attributing the physical properties of man to God, he makes a connection between what is non-material in man and the will of deity. Also, the entry 'Anthropomorphism, Anthropomorphites' in the *The Catholic Encyclopedia* suggests that an analogy between the human power of will and the will of God could be a pious and legitimate form of argumentation. That entry is worth quoting at length: 'Throughout the writings of the Fathers the spirituality of the Divine Nature, as well as the inadequacy of human thought to comprehend the greatness, goodness, and infinite perfection of God, is continually emphasized. At the same time, Catholic philosophy and theology set forth the idea of God by means of concepts derived chiefly from the knowledge of our own faculties, and our mental and moral characteristics. We reach our philosophic knowledge of God by inference from the nature of various forms of existence, our own included, that we perceive in the Universe. All created excellence, however, falls infinitely short of the Divine perfections, consequently our idea of God can never truly represent Him as He is, and, because He is infinite while our minds are finite, the resemblance between our thought and its infinite object must always be faint. Clearly, however, if we would do all that is in our power to make our idea, not perfect, but as worthy as it may be, we must form it by means of our conceptions of what is highest and best in the scale of existence that we know. Hence, as mind and personality are the noblest forms of reality, we think most worthily of God when we conceive Him under the attributes of mind, will, intelligence, personality. At the same time, when the theologian or philosopher employs these and similar terms with reference to God, he understands them to be predicated not in exactly the same sense that they bear when applied to man, but in a sense controlled and qualified by the principles laid down in the doctrine of analogy.' James Fox, 'Anthropomorphism, Anthropomorphites,' *The Catholic Encyclopedia*, vol. 1 (New York: Robert Appleton Company, 1907), http://www.newadvent.org/cathen/01558c.htm. The vicar also emphasizes that deity exceeds our comprehension.

10 As enthusiastic a materialist as Diderot himself suggested in 1746 that a butterfly's wings and the eye of a mite in themselves provide substantial proof of an intelligent organization of the world. See *Pensées philosophiques* XX in *Diderot's Selected Writings*, trans. Lester Crocker (New York: Macmillan, 1966), 4–5. For Descartes's possible influence on Rousseau's formulation here, see *OC* 4:1530n3. Cf. *Lettre à Voltaire* of 18 August 1756: *OC* 4:1065.

11 *OC* 4:1071; Rousseau, *Collected Writings*, trans. Judith R. Bush, Christopher Kelly, and Roger D. Masters (Hanover: University Press of New England, 1990–), III:117–18 (except that I retained the French for *pensée philosophique*). The remainder of this paragraph is also relevant to our case. Regarding it, cf. *OC* 4:1781n(b) and the discussion on page 1881. Cf. *Lettre à M. de Franquières*, *OC* 4:1139. Victor Gourevitch notes that versions of Diderot's argument appear in the work of Hume and Shaftesbury. See Gourevitch, 'The Religious Thought' in *The Cambridge Companion to Rousseau*, ed. Patrick Riley (Cambridge: Cambridge University Press, 2001), 239n62.

12 Rousseau, *Citizen of Geneva: Selections from the Letters of Jean-Jacques Rousseau*, ed. and trans. Charles William Hendel (New York: Oxford University Press, 1937), 147–8.

13 Cf. his argument that 'combination and chance will never result in anything but products of the same nature as the elements that are combined.' *OC* 4:579; trans. Bloom, 276.

14 This evidence of Rousseau's rejection of comprehensive materialism is interesting in part because of the mockery and irony in his tone. It raises the following question: If he meant to portray himself as an opponent of comprehensive materialism not because he was one but for the sake of salutary politics, why would he bother with the mockery and irony, especially in a private letter? On the other hand, his argument is plausible, but this too supports the opinion that it reflects his own true view.

Still, it might be argued that in the *Lettre à M. de Franquières* Rousseau adopts another kind of persona in order to avoid persecution and to support healthy politics. But since Rousseau's critiques of materialism are found not only in these letters but also in the *Lettre à Voltaire* of 18 August 1756, the letter to Jacob Vernes of 18 February 1758, and in the letters to Moultou of 23 December 1761 and 14 February 1769, proponents of the counter-case would have to argue that all of these statements are part of an elaborate pretence, extending, in the last cases, to his correspondence with an intimate friend.

Also, note that Rousseau requests that Franquières send the letter back to him without commentary once he has read it. It is plausible Rousseau thought this was a necessary precaution because the metaphysical positions he takes in the letter (e.g., regarding creation) are both unorthodox and frankly expressed.

15 The scholarly consensus is that the last sentence of the passage is addressed to Helvétius. See Masson, *'Rousseau Contre Helvétius,'* 117; and *OC* 4:1536n. Cf. *Lettres écrites de la montagne*, I, *OC* 4:693n. *De l'esprit* begins with a fascinating discussion of the distinction between men and the animals. Helvétius claims that the difference is to be found in the fact that in humans the faculties of memory and sensibility are accompanied by a *'certaine organisation extérieure.'* It is because animals lack this physical organization that their memory and sensibility remain, as he puts it, *'facultés steriles.'* He has the good grace and the good humour to finish his note on the question as follows: *'Il n'est pas nécessaire d'avoir recours au bon mot du P. Malebranche, qui, lorsqu'on lui soutenait que les animaux étaient sensibles à la douleur, répondait en plaisantant, qu' "apparemment ils avaient mangé du foin défendu."'* *De l'esprit*, I.I., ed. Guy Besse (Paris: Fayard, 1998), 72–3. On Helvétius himself, cf. David Wootton, 'Helvétius: From Radical Enlightenment to Revolution,' *Political Theory* 28, no. 3 (June 2000): 307–36.

16 The passage continues as follows: 'And for all that any philosopher who comes to tell me that trees sense and rocks think may entangle me in his subtle arguments, I can see in him only a sophist speaking in bad faith who prefers to attribute sentiment to rocks than to grant a soul to man.' In the footnote to this passage, Rousseau comments on the vicar's view as follows: 'It seems to me that far from saying that rocks think, modern philosophy had discovered, on the contrary, that men do not think. It no longer recognizes anything but sensitive beings in nature, and the whole difference it finds between a man and a stone is that man is a sensitive being with sensations while a stone is a sensitive being without them.' In this note Rousseau goes on to question whether modern philosophy can accept sentiment while rejecting thought. The orientation of the note is supportive of the vicar's position, even as it qualifies it. And once again, Rousseau seems to be replying to Helvétius. Regarding rocks that sense, see Helvétius, *De l'esprit*, I.4, 43. Cf. *OC* 4:1541n and Masson, 'Rousseau Contre Helvétius,' 114. Cf. Rousseau's letter to Vernes of 18 February 1758, quoted above. For Locke's argument, see John Locke, *An Essay Concerning Human Understanding*, Bk IV, ch. 3, esp. section 6.

17 This is an important change, for the argument about immaterial thought

underlies the dualism between two principles of human nature that the vicar explicates at *OC* 4:583. See especially the vicar's contention that 'a machine does not think; there is neither motion nor figure which produces reflection. Something in you seeks to break the bonds constraining it. Space is not your measure, the whole universe is not big enough for you. Your sentiments, your desires, your uneasiness, even your pride have another principle than this narrow body in which you sense yourself enchained.' *OC* 4:585; trans. Bloom, 280. This passage should be compared to Rousseau's statement in the third of the *Lettres morales* that *'l'ame humaine comprimée dans un corps qui géne la plus part de ses facultés veut à chaque instant forcer sa prison et joint une audace presque divine à la foiblesse de l'humanité.' OC* 4:1098. In the first draft of *Emile*, the *manuscrit Favre*, Rousseau made an inconclusive attempt to deduce the dualism of two substances from a dualism of two qualities. See *OC* 4:216–20. Cf. *OC* 4:553; trans. Bloom, 256.

18 I would like to thank Reuben Levy for his insistence on the importance of Rousseau's use of the term 'understanding' as opposed to 'reason' in the relevant passages of the *Discourse.*

19 For the view that in writing the treatment of free will in the *Discourse*, Rousseau was dependent on Diderot, see Maurice Cranston, *The Noble Savage: Jean-Jacques Rousseau 1754–1761* (Chicago: University of Chicago Press, 1991).

20 'What, then, is the cause which determines his will? It is his judgment. And what is the cause which determines his judgment? It is his intelligent faculty, it is his power of judging: the determining cause is in himself. Beyond this I understand nothing more.' Trans. Bloom, 280.

21 Some readers will continue to think that the *Second Discourse* should be given the most credence of all of Rousseau's works. But consider his remark to Beaumont that the *Profession of Faith* was the 'best and most important writing' in the eighteenth century (*OC* 4:960), as well as his repeated statements that he thought *Emile* was his best work. Also, I think the context of Rousseau's remark in the *Confessions* that the *Discourse* was the work in which his principles were expressed *'avec le plus de hardiesse pour ne pas dire d'audace'* needs to be carefully considered. The context does not imply that his intent is to send readers a special message about the unique truthfulness of the *Discourse.* At least, that is not at all how it reads to me. Instead, he is making the point that he has been unfairly attacked because of his person rather than because of the content of his writings. As proof, he expresses his surprise that the daring aspects of the *Second Discourse* and *Julie* did not provoke the attacks that those of the *Social Contract* and *Emile* did (*OC* 1: 406–7; trans. Cohen, 378–9).

22 The vicar addresses the question of the determination of his will by his own conception of his good or self-interest as follows: 'Doubtless I am not free not to want my own good. I am not free to want what is bad for me. But it is in this precisely that my freedom consists – my being able to will only what is suitable to me, or what I deem to be such, without anything external determining me' (trans. Bloom, 280). The editors of the Pléiade note that Rousseau added this paragraph after reading Helvétius. In his discussion of liberty in *De l'Esprit*, I.IV, Helvétius puts the opposing case very well. '*En effet*,' he writes, '*si le desir du plaisir est le principe de toutes nos pensées et de toutes nos actions, si tous les hommes tendent continuellement vers leur bonheur réel ou apparent, toutes nos volontés ne sont que l'effet de cette tendance*.' But for an argument that would support the plausibility of the vicar's position, see Isaiah Berlin's 'From Hope and Fear Set Free' in *Concepts and Categories*, ed. Henry Hardy (New York: Viking Press, 1978).

23 The vicar's formulations regarding the aspiration toward justice and the *beau morale* should be compared to Rousseau's description of how men acquire ideas of order and justice and 'begin to be sensitive to moral beauty [*le beau morale*]' in the *Lettre à Beaumont OC* 4:936–7. For an aesthetic understanding of morality, cf. the end of Book IV of *Emile*. Regarding seeing the good and doing the bad, see St Paul, Letter to the Romans, 7:19; and Ovid: 'I see the right and approve it, too / Condemn the wrong and yet the wrong pursue.' *Metamorphoses* VII:17, quoted in *The Shorter Bartlett's Familiar Quotations* (New York: Pocket Books, 1953).

24 This statement corresponds closely to his position in the *Lettre à Franquières*. The vicar also stops short of endorsing creation. See trans. Bloom, 285 and 277.

25 '*Mais supposer deux principles des choses, supposition que portant le Vicaire ne fait point, ce n'est pas pour cela supposer deux Dieux; à moins que, comme les Manichéens, on ne suppose aussi ces principes tous deux actifs; doctrine absolument contraire à celle du Vicaire, qui très-positivement, n'admet qu'une Intelligence premiere, qu'un seul principe actif, et par conséquent qu'un seul Dieu*.' *OC* 4:956.

26 Cf. *OC* 4:600–1; trans. Bloom, 290.

27 Cf. *Emile*, Bk IV, *OC* 4:522–3; trans. Bloom, 235. See also Rousseau's important footnote to this passage.

28 '*O Montaigne!*' exclaims the vicar, '*toi qui te piques de franchise et de vérité, sois sincére et vrai si un philosophe peut l'être, et di-moi s'il est quelque pays sur la terre où ce soit un crime de garder sa foi, d'être clément, bienfaisant, généreux? où l'homme de bien soit méprisable et le perfide honoré?*' *OC* 4:598–9. The passage appears in almost the same form in the *Lettres Morales*: *OC* 4:1108–9.

29 Later in the *Profession*, the vicar argues that we are corrupted but 'our vices come to us from ourselves,' that the weakness of the wicked is 'their own work,' and that 'their first depravity comes from their own will': *OC* 4:604; trans. Bloom, 293. This seems to conflict with teaching on compassion in Book IV of *Emile*, which suggests that society determines outcomes; but the vicar's position is consistent with *Lettre à Voltaire*.

An exchange between Malesherbes and Rousseau about a passage from *La Nouvelle Héloïse* is also of relevance here. St Preux, the male protagonist, maintains that his '*sentiment intérieur*' belies the reasoning of those who deny the '*liberté de l'homme*': '*Nous ne supposons point actifs et libres,*' St Preux asserts, '*nous sentons que nous le sommes. C'est à eux de prouver non seulement que ce sentiment pourroit nous tromper, mais qu'il nous trompe en effet.*' Part VI, letter VII, *OC* 2:683–4. When Malesherbes complained that St Preux's argument was unconvincing, Rousseau responded in a letter written in March 1761: '*elle me semble à moi très forte, même sans réplique; et j'y crois trouver la solution de toutes les difficultés manichéens … D'ailleurs, il faut bien qu'il défende la liberté de l'homme, puisqu'il fait ailleurs de l'abus de cette liberté la cause du mal moral: il faut absolument qu'il soit moliniste, pour ne pas être manichéen.*' *CC*, VIII:237, letter 1350. Regarding molinism and related issues, see Jacques-François Thomas, *Le pélagianisme de J.J. Rousseau* (Paris: Nizet, 1956).

Rousseau, however, also appended a note to St Preux's remarks about the interior sentiment of freedom: '*Ce n'est pas de tout cela qu'il s'agit. Il s'agit de savoir si la volonté se détermine sans cause, ou quelle est la cause qui determine la volonté?*': 684. The editors point out that this note is a late addition, '*en liason avec la rédaction définitive de la Profession de foi.*' *OC* 2:1780n(g).

30 *OC* 4:996.

31 Masters, *SC* 127. See Ronald Beiner, 'Machiavelli, Hobbes, and Rousseau on Civil Religion,' *Review of Politics* 55, no. 4 (1993): 617–38. Cf. Beiner's important book, *Civil Religion: A Dialogue in the History of Political Philosophy* (Cambridge: Cambridge University Press, 2011), ch. 1. Cf. Simon Critchley, *The Faith of the Faithless: Experiments in Political Theology* (London: Verso, 2012), ch. 2.

32 Cf. the *Geneva Manuscript*, where Rousseau writes that 'the Gospel is not a civil religion.' Masters, *SC* 198 (quoted by Beiner in 'Machiavelli, Hobbes, and Rousseau on Civil Religion,' 635). In the final version of the text, this sentence was modified to the more discreet: 'The Gospel does not establish a national religion.' Masters, *SC* 130.

33 *CC*, letter 2028, 24 July 1762. Note that this passage continues as follows: 'And indeed a lot of people up to this time have regarded the Republics

of Sparta and Rome as well-constituted, although these did not believe in J.C. Let us suppose nonetheless that in this the Author is mistaken; he would have made a political error because here it is a question of nothing else. I do not see where the heresy would be, still less the crime to punish.' This passage might be used to argue that Rousseau's new civil religion is not so much a variant of Christianity as a neo-paganist religion of nature. An objection to this reading is that it conflates religion and politics. Rousseau uses the distinction here and elsewhere in his own defence. See *OC* 4:706. Nonetheless, his civil religion blends the two. Cf. Jacques Maritain, *Three Reformers: Luther–Descartes–Rousseau* (Westport: Greenwood, 1950). Maritain writes that 'by nature,' Rousseau 'tends to … a devilish parody of Christianity': 160.

34 *Collected Writings of Rousseau,* trans. Terence Marshall (Hanover: University Press of New England, 1990–); III:114; *OC* 4:1073–4, emphasis mine. Rousseau refines his thinking about the proscription of beliefs that conflict with a civil profession in chapter 8 of Book 4 of *Du contrat social, OC* 3: 460–9.

35 Arthur M. Melzer points out that he makes this appeal to Voltaire 'although he here hints, and elsewhere states, that Voltaire himself is an atheist.' Melzer, 'The Origin of the Counter-Enlightenment,' 355.

36 In the *Lettre à Beaumont,* the two most dramatic passages follow this positive–negative pattern: in the first passage, Rousseau describes a hypothetical agreement on the positive principles of essential religion by sensible men of varied faiths; on the negative side, in the second passage a Parsis – which is to say, a Zoroastrian from Surate who has been condemned to die for his religion – makes a noble and dignified speech denouncing intolerance. See *OC* 4:975–8 and 4:981–3 respectively.

37 What does Rousseau mean by his reference to a 'purely civil' profession of faith? It is civil because its articles 'are for the sovereign to establish, not exactly as religious dogmas, but as sentiments of sociability without which it is impossible to be a good citizen or a faithful subject.' *OC* 1:468; Masters, *SC* 130–1. That is, even though its content is religious, the motivations for the civil profession of faith are civil, rather than religious, in the sense that they look to the conditions for a stable and secure life for citizens. According to Antoine Furetière's *Dictionnaire Universel* of 1690, the term '*civil*' pertains to the 'administration, public good and tranquility of the citizens,' as well as to 'laws that are established in favour of the society of men.' The French is as follows: '*ce qui regarde la police, le bien public, le repos des citoyens … civil, se dit aussi, des loix qui sont établies en faveur de la société des hommes*' (Geneva: Slatkine Reprints, 1970). The key teachings of the *Profession of Faith* are, we would argue, civil in this sense.

Beiner, in *Civil Religion,* defines civil religion as 'the empowerment of religion, not for the sake of religion but for the sake of enhanced citizenship': 2. Cf. his suggestion that 'generally speaking, *civil* is a liberal word and *civic* is a republican word': 83n. For a useful overview of various interpretations of Rousseau's civil religion, see Terence Ball, 'Rousseau's Civil Religion Reconsidered' in his *Reappraising Political Theory: Revisionist Studies in the History of Political Thought* (Oxford: Clarendon, 1995).

38 Neither does Rousseau mention the teaching about the legislator in this summary of the *Social Contract*. Such an omission would help dissimulate the extent of Rousseau's intention to legislate a new form of politics and morality through the teaching of *Emile.*

39 See Beiner, 'Machiavelli, Hobbes, and Rousseau,' 620–1 and 632–7. Beiner reiterates this argument in *Civil Religion,* where he adds that what Rousseau offers in the last five paragraphs of the *Social Contract* is 'a highly attenuated "phantom" religion, an Enlightenment-style "religion of tolerance," one might say, in which liberal or negative tenets prevail over tenets that might positively build republican citizenship. In embracing this rather watered down quasi-religion, it is as if Rousseau bids farewell to his republican ideal, with the hearty parochialism and potential illiberalism that it implies' (15).

40 Beiner suggests that Rousseau does not fully reconcile the 'unbridgeable tension between Christian universalism and pagan parochialism.' He comments that 'Rousseau's thought fluctuates between two opposed and contradictory standpoints, the standpoint of cosmopolitan brotherhood and the standpoint of national particularism and the idea of civil religion seems to get caught in the interstices of that tension … True politics is particularistic and true religion is universalistic and so "civil religion" does not name a genuine synthesis of religion and politics, but rather identifies the necessary contradiction.' Beiner, 'Machiavelli, Hobbes, and Rousseau,' 636–7. He makes this argument in *Civil Religion* at 82–3.

41 Note, too, that at the outset the speech is presented as a collective effort whereas Rousseau attributes it to a single individual at the end.

42 From Rousseau's perspective, the minimalist core of religious belief is not so much watered-down as distilled. Moreover, the parochial expression of religious belief might be hearty and robust (rather than anemic) as long as it is not intolerant. All this would depend upon how peoples who accept a basic profession of faith choose to express their beliefs. For a different view, see Beiner, *Civil Religion,* 214–16.

43 In the *Geneva Manuscript,* after describing the 'purely civil profession of faith,' Rousseau explains its potential advantages as follows: 'Beyond this,

one should allow the introduction of all opinions that are not contrary to the civil profession of faith and all the cults that are compatible with the public cult. And neither religious disputes nor holy wars should be feared. No one will think of refining the dogmas when there is so little interest in discussing them. No apostle or missionary will have the right to come and criticize the errors of *a religion that serves as the basis for all the religions in the world and condemns none of them* … Thus the advantages of the religion of man and the religion of the citizen will be combined.' Masters, *SC* 200 (emphasis mine). Perhaps Rousseau removed these words from the final draft out of prudence, for they would seem to reveal too obviously the vaulting ambitions of the work he predicted would one day 'cause a revolution among men.' *The Reveries of the Solitary Walker* (*OC* 1:1018); trans. Butterworth, 34. Regarding the logic of the vicar's solution, cf. *Emile, OC* 4:627; trans. Bloom, 308; and Beiner, *Civil Religion*, 213.

The interpretation that the vicar's *Profession of Faith* provides the basis for Rousseau's new civil religion cannot by its very nature be conclusively proven. Instead, it requires a leap of faith (no pun intended). That is, Rousseau intentionally leaves gaps regarding the nature and execution of his project – gaps that might protect him if he were persecuted. According to our reading, the gaps in the text are better explained by Rousseau's subtlety than by his incapacity.

44 See Roger D. Masters, 'Rousseau and the Rediscovery of Human Nature' in *The Legacy of Rousseau*, ed. Clifford Orwin and Nathan Tarcov (Chicago: University of Chicago Press, 1997).

45 There are also a number of contradictions within the *Profession of Faith* itself. Consider, too, his remark in the Second Preface to *Julie: 'Vous voulez qu'on soit toujours conséquent; je doute que cela soit possible à l'homme; mais ce qui lui est possible est d'être toujours vrai: voilà ce que je veux toujours taché d'être'* (*OC* 2:27).

46 See Mark Hulliung, *The Autocritique of Enlightenment: Rousseau and the Philosophes* (Cambridge, MA: Harvard University Press, 1994), 218 and 283n82. Melzer cites Hulliung to suggest that 'most of the philosophes doubted the seriousness of the Profession of Faith.' 'The Origin of the Counter-Enlightenment,' 355. But Hulliung's evidence appears inconclusive to me. In particular, Diderot's letters to Sophie Volland in the wake of Rousseau's troubles following the publication of *Emile* are too ambiguous to shed light on the question.

47 Peter Gay, *The Enlightenment: An Interpretation*, vol. 2: *The Science of Freedom* (London: Norton: 1969), 515.

48 *'"Juger," dit M. Rousseau, "n'est pas sentir." La preuve de son opinion "c'est*

qu'il est en nous une faculté ou force qui nous fait comparer les objects. Or, dit-il, cette force ne peut être l'effet de la sensibilité physique." Si M. Rousseau eût plus approfoundi cette question, il eût reconnu que cette force n'étoit autre chose que l'intérêt même que nous avons de comparer les objects entre eux, et que cet intéret prend sa source dans le sentiment de l'amour de soi, effet immédiat de la sensibilité physique.' Claude-Adrien Helvétius, *De l'homme*, tome I (Paris: Fayard, 1989), section 5n4, 514 (emphasis in original).

49 See Bloom's riveting posthumous work, *Love and Friendship* (New York: Simon and Schuster, 1993), 72.

50 See *Lettres écrites de la montagne* III: *OC* 3:727–54.

51 I owe this point to Arthur M. Melzer, who writes that Rousseau 'protested bitterly against those who simply equated the "editor" of the "Profession of Faith" with its "author" (*Montagne* 750, *Beaumont* 935, 1029).' Melzer, 'The Origin of the Counter-Enlightenment,' 355.

52 Rousseau à Isaac-Ami Marcet de Mézières, *CC*, lettre 2028, 24 July 1762.

53 For a fascinating illustration of how Rousseau anticipates that the character of the vicar will allow him to play both sides of the street, see *OC* 3:1028–30.

54 For Julie's Profession of Faith, see part 6, letter 11, *OC* 2:714–16.

55 *CC*, letter 1602. This letter was never sent, although it was dated and contains precise instructions to Moultou about the packet containing the *Profession*. Rousseau also requests that Moultou help arrange for his partner Thérèse's care after his death.

56 On the question of desiring religious belief, compare Rousseau's correspondence with the abbé de Carondelet in the Fall of 1764 (discussed in Beiner, *Civil Religion*, 209–10). The abbé, a young priest experiencing doubts about his faith, wrote to Rousseau asking his advice. Rousseau responded, and the abbé wrote back that Rousseau's response had contributed to a resurgence of his faith in God. However, the abbé continued to disagree with some Catholic teachings. As he explained it to Rousseau in his letter of 22 October 1764, '*Je respecte la profession de foi du Catholique, mais Ce n'est pas la mienne.*' He then asked Rousseau whether he should attend confession and admit these thoughts, risking public denunciation. In his letter of reply of 11 November 1764, Rousseau put himself in the abbé's place, imagining what he would do in the abbé's situation. Rousseau said he would choose a wise and sensible priest as a confessor and would say to him: '*je vois l'ocean de difficulties où nage l'esprit humain dans ces matiéres; le mien ne cherche point a S'y noyer; je cherche ce qui est vrai et bon; je le cherche Sincérement; je sens que la docilité qu'exige l'Eglise est un état desirable pour être en paix avec Soi; j'aime cet état, j'y veux vivre; mon esprit murmure il est*

vrai, mais mon cœur lui impose Silence; et mes Sentimens Sont tous contre mes raisons. Je ne crois pas, mais je veux croire, et je le veux de tout mon cœur. Soumis à la fois malgré mes lumiéres quel argument puis-je avoir à craindre? Je suis plus fidelle que Si j'étois convaincu.

'Si mon Confesseur n'est pas un Sot, que voulez-vous qu'il me dise? Voulez-vous qu'il éxige bêtement de moi l'impossible; qu'il m'ordonne de voir du rouge où je vois du bleu? Il me dira; Soumettez-vous. Je répondrai; c'est ce que je fais. Il priera pour moi et me donnera l'absolution Sans balancer; car il la doit à celui qui croit de toute Sa force et qui Suit la Loi de tout Son cœur.' The Abbé's letter is number 3593 in volume XXI of Ralph Leigh's edition of the *Correspondance complètes;* Rousseau's letter is number 3637 in volume XXII.

57 Introduction to *Emile,* 20. An example of this is the varying treatment given to the erotic needs and passions of the human body. In *Emile,* Rousseau critiques the view that the amorous needs of the body are base and sinful. While Rousseau defends the naturalness of the bodily passions and needs, the vicar appears to be an enemy of these passions and needs. He is rueful about his own erotic longings. He sees his inflamed desires as an obstacle and his body as a shackle.

58 See Bloom, *Love and Friendship*; and Arthur M. Melzer, *The Natural Goodness of Man: On the System of Rousseau's Thought* (Chicago: University of Chicago Press, 1990), 21. Clifford Orwin argues that Rousseau employs two contrary moral rhetorics: one involves the return to nature and the other the overcoming of nature. See Orwin, 'Rousseau's Ethics' in *Instilling Ethics,* ed. Norma Thompson (Lanham: Rowman & Littlefield, 2000).

59 See Larry Siedentop, 'Two Liberal Traditions' in *The Idea of Freedom: Essays in Honour of Isaiah Berlin,* ed. Alan Ryan (Toronto: Oxford University Press, 1979). Siedentop thinks that Rousseau helped uncover the weaknesses of empiricist epistemology for explaining human agency. He writes that 'early empiricist philosophy – or the sensationalist model of the mind – did not offer a satisfactory account of the nature of rule-governed action. It did not explain the role of social norms in shaping individual intentions and making action possible. It did not explore the dependence of the "self" on a social context. Rousseau was one of the first to discover this weakness, and struggled to remedy it, with mixed success': 155. Siedentop argues that the vulnerability of English liberalism to communitarian critiques stems from its dependence on empiricist epistemology. This neglected article was one of the most sensible and constructive contributions to the liberal–communitarian debate. Regarding Rousseau's relation to the sensualist tradition, see also Jimack, *La genese et la redaction de l'Emile;*

Simpson, *Rousseau's Theory of Freedom*, 62–4; and Garrard, *Rousseau's Counter-Enlightenment*. For an argument that Rousseau's 'account of human things is best understood as a form of Epicureanism,' see Gourevitch, 'The Religious Thought,' 213 ff.

60 See Leo Strauss, *Natural Right and History* (Chicago: University of Chicago Press, 1953), 265–6; Masters, *The Political Philosophy*, 66–74; and Daniel E. Cullen, *Freedom in Rousseau's Political Philosophy* (DeKalb: Northern Illinois University Press, 1993).

61 For Rousseau's description of the dualism of material body, and non-material soul' made in his own name, see *Emile*, trans. Bloom, 255–6; see also 235, 253, 442–9. Consider also Masters's comment in *The Political Philosophy*, 67n50.

Rousseau also often appears to juxtapose the moral and the physical. For discussions, see Robert Wokler, 'Rousseau's Two Concepts of Liberty' in *Lives, Liberties, and the Public Good: New Essays in Political Theory for Maurice Cranston*, ed. George Feaver and Frederick Rosen (London: Macmillan, 1987); and Frederick Neuhauser, 'Freedom, Dependence, and the General Will,' *Philosophical Review* 102, no. 3 (1993): 366n4.

62 See the *Profession*, trans. Bloom 290, 270 ff, 279. In 'Rousseau Contre Helvétius,' Masson points out that letter V of the *Lettres Morales* is the first draft of one section of the *Profession*.

63 While in both dualisms, the lower term refers to the body in a relatively straightforward way, the upper term of each dualism differs in ways that affect our inquiry.

64 Man's dualism does not follow from this indifference to good and evil but it does follow from a part of *amour de soi* (i.e., the capacity for 'loving order and justice' that he has described above).

65 As we saw earlier in the chapter, in the *Profession of Faith*, the vicar believes he discovers 'two distinct principles' in man's nature: 'one of which raised him to the study of eternal truths, to the love of justice and moral beauty [*le beau morale*], and to the regions of the intellectual world whose contemplation is the wise man's delight [*les délices du sage*]; while the other took him basely into himself, subjected him to the empire of the senses and to the passions which are their ministers, and by means of these hindered all that the sentiment of the former inspired in him.' *OC* 4:583, trans. Bloom, 278–9.

66 This passage is the same in the *Lettres Morales* version except that in that text Rousseau writes that the love of the good and hatred of the bad is as natural as 'our own existence' (rather than 'love of ourselves' as the vicar has it). Also, the sentence 'The acts of conscience are not judgments but

sentiments' occurs in the *Profession* but not in the *Lettres Morales*. See *OC* 4:1109.

67 Cf. *OC* 4:583; trans. Bloom, 278–9.

68 On Malebranche's influence on Rousseau, see Patrick Riley, *The General Will before Rousseau: The Transformation of the Divine into the Civic* (Princeton: Princeton University Press, 1986). It is because the reconciliation is partial that Rousseau's two-track strategy is necessary.

69 It could be objected that this exhortation to overcome nature conflicts with Rousseau's vindication of nature as a standard for conduct in other passages and works. But Rousseau's conception of nature is extremely complex. See Pierre Burgelin's apt comments about this: *OC* 4:lxxxix. Some interpreters have suggested that Rousseau has two concepts of nature. In the introduction to his edition of Rousseau's *Economie politique* (Paris: PUF, 1986), at 9–10, Yves Vargas suggests a division between *La Nature-Physique* and *La Nature-Essence*. Cf. Paul Benichou, '*Réflexions sur l'idée de nature chez Rousseau*' in *Pensée de Rousseau*, ed. Gerard Genette and Tzvetan Todorov (Paris: Seuil, 1984); Laurence D. Cooper, *Rousseau, Nature, and the Problem of the Good Life* (University Park: Pennsylvania State University Press, 1999); and Jacob L. Talmon, *The Origins of Totalitarian Democracy* (London: Secker and Warburg, 1952). I would suggest the following two senses of nature in Rousseau. One conception is that of physical nature. Nature according to this understanding would include the original endowment of human beings. But Rousseau also uses the term to describe a fully human nature. This seems to be his usage in the *Discourse on Inequality*, for example, when he refers to the 'present nature of man.' Note, too, that the vicar's dualism is called a 'natural religion.' Kant sheds light on this question in these remarks about Rousseau's work: 'In his *On the Influence of the Sciences and On the Inequality of Man* [Rousseau] shows quite correctly that there is an inevitable conflict between culture and the human species, considered as a natural species of which every member ought wholly to attain his natural end. But in his *Emile*, his *Social Contract* and other writings he tries to solve this much harder problem: how culture was to move forward, in order to bring about such a development of the dispositions of mankind, considered as a *moral* species, as to end the conflict between the natural and the moral species' (emphasis in original). Quoted in Asher Horowitz, *Rousseau, Nature, and History* (Toronto: University of Toronto Press, 1987), 212.

70 In 'A Prayer for My Daughter' Yeats writes that the soul that 'recovers radical innocence' learns at last that 'its own sweet will is Heaven's will.'

71 See esp. *Emile*, trans. Bloom, 255–7. For a different view, see Emberley, 'Rousseau Versus the Savoyard Vicar.' Many interpreters have noted the

degree of control and manipulation that Rousseau allows the tutor and have suggested that it sits oddly with the freedom he says he is trying to foster in Emile. Patrick Riley has explored this question carefully. He finds the key to reconciling the problem in Emile's response to the tutor: 'I have decided to become what you have made me.' Riley, 'Rousseau's General Will: Freedom of a Particular Kind' in *Rousseau and Liberty*, ed. Robert Wokler (Manchester: Manchester University Press, 1995), 10.

Chapter 4

1 I have relied upon, but slightly altered, Terence Marshall's translation here.
2 For another statement of this sort, see the letter to Jacob Vernes of 18 February 1758. After remarking on the inadequacy of philosophy to resolve religious matters, Rousseau comments: 'So I have abandoned reason to its fate, and consulted nature, that is to say, the internal sentiment which directs my beliefs independently of my reason.' Rousseau, *Citizen of Geneva: Selections from the Letters of Jean-Jacques Rousseau*, trans. Charles William Hendel (New York: Oxford University Press, 1937), letter 474, 147. Cf. *Lettres écrits de la montagne*, *OC* 3:695–7.
3 Rousseau, *Politics and the Arts: Letter to D'Alembert on the Theater*, trans. Allan Bloom (Ithaca: Cornell University Press, 1960), 12.
4 Rousseau, *Collected Writings*, trans. Judith R. Bush, Christopher Kelly, and Roger D. Masters (Hanover: University Press of New England, 1990–), vol. 1, 170; *OC* 1:879. But where the *Collected Writings* renders '*le sentiment*' in the last sentence as 'the feeling,' I have substituted 'the sentiment.'

   Note, too, that Rousseau writes that 'the obstacle of difficulties' is common to both the side of his direct conviction and that opposed to it. This recalls his formulation in the *Discourse* about the 'difficulties' surrounding the problem of free will.
5 *OC* 1:1016; Rousseau, *The Reveries of the Solitary Walker*, trans. Charles Butterworth (New York: Harper Colophon, 1979), 32. Subsequent references to this translation will be embodied parenthetically in the text.

   In an early fragment about freedom, written around 1750 or 1751, at a time when Rousseau was closely associated with Diderot, Rousseau did express doubt as to the existence of free will and as to the moral need for it. This unpublished early fragment begins as follows: '*Si les actes de ma volonté sont en ma propre puissance ou s'ils suivent une impulsion étrangére je n'en sais rien et je me soucie trés peu de le savoir, puisque cette connoissance ne sauroit influer sur ma conduit en cette vie et, s'il en est une autre, comme Je le crois, je suis convaincu que les mêmes moyens par lesquels je puis faire mon bon-*

heur actuel doivent encore m'acquérir l'immortelle félicité. Je ne veux donc point parler ici de cette Liberté metaphysique et morale.' *OC* 3:1894.

David Lay Williams makes a very persuasive case for the view that Rousseau wrote this fragment when he was undecided about the question of free will for a time, 'before deciding the matter' in favour of the view that humans have it. Williams rightly points out that this interpretation is supported by the fact that he did not publish the fragment and that 'everything written thereafter supports the existence of metaphysical freedom.' Importantly, Williams also argues that 'Rousseau's period of indecision corresponds to the time he spent in the salons and with Diderot. It is only after the publication of his *Second Discourse* that the break with the *philosophes* becomes permanent ... Indeed, strong evidence for this interpretation also exists in his "Preface to Narcissus," written in the winter of 1752–53, where he acknowledged that he had "not always the good fortune to think as I do now." Rather he had "long been seduced by the prejudices of my century."' See Williams, *Rousseau's Platonic Enlightenment* (University Park: Pennsylvania State University Press, 2007), 71. This is the view I take; cf. the relevant evidence in note 12 below.

6 See Arthur M. Melzer, 'The Origin of the Counter-Enlightenment: Rousseau and the New Religion of Sincerity,' *American Political Science Review* 90, no. 2 (June 1996): 344–603 at 355 and 358.

7 Rousseau describes his own metaphysical researches in almost the same terms in the *Letter to Franquières*. *OC* 4:1135–6.

8 Melzer, 'The Origin of the Counter-Enlightenment.'

9 Ibid., 358. Cf. Melzer's statement on the same page: 'Founded on the inner sentiment, the Profession of Faith makes contact with the innermost hope or faith of the civilized soul, brings this faith to the surface, and gives it a systematic elaboration.'

10 The passage continues as follows: 'In any other arrangement I would live without resource and die without hope. I would be the most unhappy of creatures. Let me hold then to this one, which alone suffices to render me happy in spite of fortune and men.' Trans. Butterworth, *Reveries*, 35.

11 Note that here the inner assent is distinguished from his heart. But how is the inner assent that reinforces his conviction different from the sentiment in favour of the anti-materialist side Rousseau starts out with? He never explicitly explains the distinction but unless it can be defended there is a problematic circularity in his defence of his method. The vicar says at the outset of the *Profession* that he will be guided by 'the inner light' (trans. Bloom, 269). In response to the vicar's speech, Rousseau says that he 'ought to be guided by the inner sentiment' in his own reflections (294).

And we have just quoted his statement in the Third Reverie that 'it is important to have one's own sentiment and to choose it with all the maturity of judgment one can put into it.' But unless the sentiment one has at the outset can be distinguished from the inner assent that gives its sanction at the end, the latter adds nothing to the former. Rousseau is aware of this difficulty as he writes the Third Reverie. Rather than simply basing his principles on the 'prejudices of childhood,' which he admits could distort his view, he begins with the 'sentiment best established by direct means and most believable in itself' – which we have argued is a sentiment based on a direct form of reason. If this initial sentiment based on direct proofs is wedded more closely to reason perhaps it can be distinguished from the final 'inner assent' described in this passage, which, since it involves approbation or approval, may be more closely wedded to conscience than to reason. But approbation requires judgment and therefore some level of reason. These distinctions are not fully articulated and perhaps they cannot be made fully convincing. Nonetheless, Rousseau's careful choice of terms shows an attention to detail that argues the earnestness of his endeavour, while it indicates the maturation of his thinking about his relation to his hopes. Cf. *OC* 4:1138–9. Cf. Arash Abizadeh, 'Banishing the Particular: Rousseau on Rhetoric, *patrie*, and the Passions,' *Political Theory* 29, no. 4 (2001): 556–82.

12 In the *Dialogues*, Rousseau refers to the 'brilliant authors' of his century who pretend to teach virtue but in fact believe that 'there is neither virtue nor vice in the heart of man because there is neither freedom in his will nor morality in his actions, that everything up to this will itself is the work of a blind necessity, that finally conscience and remorse are only prejudices and chimeras because one can neither applaud a good action one was forced to do, nor reproach oneself for a crime from which one did not have the power to abstain' (*OC* 1:841–2). Cf. Diderot's *Jacques le fataliste*, ed. Anne Chevalier (Paris: Bordas, 1993). In this context, consider, too, the work of Rousseau's admirer, Pierre Choderlos de Laclos, *Les Liaisons dangereuses*.

Rousseau again defended the idea of free will and the moral need for it in his letter to the abbé de Carondelet on 4 March 1764. He writes that in the latter's system the word virtue can have no sense: '*Car enfin, selon vous, tout est nécessaire: où tout est nécessaire, il n'y a point de liberté; sans liberté, point de moralité dans les actions; sans moralité des actions, où est la vertu? Pour moi, je ne le vois pas. En parlant du sentiment intérieur je devais mettre au premier rang celui du libre arbitre, mais il suffit de l'y renvoyer d'ici.*' This letter, along with another of his letters to the abbé, is reprinted in Ronald Grimsley's *Rousseau's Religious Writings* (Oxford: Clarendon Press, 1970) under the title, 'Letters to a Doubter,' 345–80. The quote cited is at 379–80.

13 In the 'Interpretive Essay' of his fine translation of the *Reveries* (New York: Harper Colophon, 1979), Butterworth suggests that the fact that Rousseau expresses doubts about his earlier metaphysical teachings shows that, although he thinks it is useful for the 'majority of mankind' to hold such beliefs, he does not believe them himself (179). But if this is the case, why would Rousseau use such passionate language to articulate these doubts? Why would he, for example, write that objections to his teachings 'torment' him and 'finish striking' him down when he is already discouraged?

Butterworth also notes that Rousseau makes little effort to defend the content of his metaphysical teaching in the Third Reverie; he suggests that this is a sign he does not believe it (172–81). But Rousseau does give his reasons (notably, the decline in his abilities) for not undertaking another articulation of his metaphysical ideas. As we argue in the text, he energetically defends the *method* that led to his conclusions, and the fact that his defence of his method becomes sounder and more precise suggests that he undertakes this concerted effort because he sincerely wants to defend the teaching obtained through it. It could, of course, be objected that he undertakes these efforts simply in order to convince the public that he believed his earlier teaching. But this runs counter to evidence in the First Walk, where he contends that he writes the *Reveries* 'only for myself.' (*OC* 1:1001; trans. Butterworth, 7.) Also, as Butterworth points out, Rousseau writes that he undertook the venture that culminated in the writing of the *Profession of Faith* because he needed a philosophy so as to 'have a set rule of conduct for the rest of my days.' *OC* 1:1016; trans. Butterworth, 32. As Butterworth also notes, there is a focus on method throughout the *Reveries*.

14 In the Eighth Reverie, written about December 1777, Rousseau takes a determinist position as regards his contemporaries. He writes that he saw 'a whole generation rush headlong' into the opinion that he was a detestable monster. Unable to get his accusers to explain themselves to him, he sought for just and reasonable men who refused to go along with the tide of opinion against him. He says that he found none, but that he was finally able to attain a kind of serenity because he was able 'to bear the yoke of necessity without a murmur.' *OC* 1:1077; trans. Butterworth, 113. He describes the results as follows: 'After long and vain research … I saw a frenetic generation completely cede to the blind fury of its leaders against an unfortunate man who never did, willed or rendered evil to anybody. After having sought ten years for a man in vain, I finally had to extinguish my lantern and cry out: "There are no more!" Then I began to see myself

alone on earth and I understood that in relation to me my contemporaries were nothing more than automatons [*êtres mécaniques*] who acted only on impulse and whose action I could calculate only from the laws of motion.' *OC* 1:1078; trans. Butterworth, 114. Rousseau then suggests that it was only his *amour propre* that made it difficult for him to accept this conclusion: 'I ought to regard all the details of my fate as so many acts of pure fatality to which I ought not ascribe direction, intention or moral cause.' *OC* 1:1079; trans. Butterworth, 115. Here I would make a few comments. Note that Rousseau describes this as a feature of his contemporaries 'in relation to' him rather than as a characteristic of all peoples at all times. Moreover, he presents this deterministic view of his contemporaries as a view that he should adopt: it is salutary for him to do so. Finally, he presents this as a change from his former views and one he came to very late. (At the earliest this would be ten years after the opinion that he was a monster was propagated. Cf. Rousseau's letter to the Marquise of Mesme of 14 August 1772. There he writes that for ten years '*J'ai cherché quelqu' un qui eût assez de droiture pour m 'éclairer sur ma situation ... j'ai porté partout ma lanterne inutilement, je n'a trouvé d'homme, ni d'âme humaine.*' Cited in *Les rêveries du promeneur solitaire*, ed. Henri Roddier [Paris: Garnier, 1997], 110.) At any rate, since he presents his acceptance of necessity in the Eighth Reverie as an alteration of his earlier opinions, this implies that he did not take a determinist position when he composed his major published works. Thus, the Eighth Reverie represents both a confirmation and limitation of my case. Regarding Rousseau's doubts about matters metaphysical, cf. Christopher Kelly, *Rousseau As Author: Consecrating One's Life to the Truth* (Chicago: University of Chicago Press, 2003), 168.

15 In his thought-provoking article, 'Banishing the Particular: Rousseau on Rhetoric, *patrie* and the Passions,' Arash Abizadeh writes that the rational articulation of Rousseau's speech stems from 'a sentimental, natural reason' and that he uses this category to navigate the long-standing debate between the partisans of rhetoric and those of philosophy.

16 The philosophy book Rousseau mentions has sometimes been thought to be Helvétius's *De l'esprit*, but Jean Starobinski presents very compelling evidence that it was instead Pufendorf's *Droit de la nature et des gens*. See Starobinski's 'The Motto *Vitam impendere vero* and the Question of Lying' in *The Cambridge Companion to Rousseau*, ed. Patrick Riley (Cambridge: Cambridge University Press, 2001), 383–4.

17 Plato, *Republic*, trans. Allan Bloom (New York: Basic Books, 1968) 331c.

18 See Butterworth's 'Interpretative Essay' in his translation of the *Reveries*. Cf. Leo Strauss, 'On the Intention of Rousseau,' *Social Research* 14 (1947):

455–87, esp. 271–2; Victor Gourevitch, 'Rousseau on Lying: A Provisional Reading of the Fourth Reverie,' *Berkshire Review* 15 (1980): 93–107; and Ruth W. Grant, *Hypocrisy and Integrity: Machiavelli, Rousseau, and the Ethics of Politics* (Chicago: University of Chicago Press, 1997), ch. 4. For a convincing argument that Rousseau saw himself as developing the practice of responsible authorship, see Kelly, *Rousseau as Author*.

19 Cf. Rousseau's statement at the outset of the *Social Contract* that he will try to ensure that 'justice and utility are not at variance [*ne se trouvent point divisées*],' 1.1, *OC* 3:351; trans. Masters, *Social Contract*, 46. See also Gourevitch, 'Rousseau on Lying,' 94 and 94n8.

20 In Book II of the *Republic*, while Socrates condemns a real lie in the soul about the most sovereign things, he suggests the usefulness of 'lies in speeches.' Regarding the lie in speeches, he asks: 'Isn't it useful against enemies, and, as a preventative, like a drug, for so-called friends when from madness or some folly they attempt to do something bad?': trans. Bloom, 382b-d, 60.

21 The first question focused our attention more on truths, while the second question focuses our attention more on lies. Having missed or avoided the opportunity to discuss harmful truths in treating the first question about owing truths, Rousseau does directly consider harmful lies in discussing the second question about innocent lies. But it could be argued that by focusing on harmful lies, he more effectively buries the question of dangerous truths.

22 The argument also has a flaw: if injustice is defined as bringing about bad consequences for someone else and the truth concerned is truly inconsequential, if this truth can have no consequences, it would be hard for our comportment with regard to something that has no consequences to bring about bad consequences.

23 *OC* 1:1028; trans. Butterworth, 47. Kant, of course, takes this very position. See his admirable argument in 'On a Supposed Right to Lie from Altruistic Motives' in *The Critique of Practical Reason and Other Writings in Moral Philosophy*, trans. Lewis White Beck (Chicago: University of Chicago Press, 1949), 346–50.

24 *OC* 1:1028; trans. Butterworth, 47-48. I have, however, translated the French '*dictamen*' as 'dictamen,' whereas Butterworth translates the word as 'dictates.' In the Fourth Walk, Rousseau consistently distinguishes his conscience from the rules he deduces.

25 I have slightly altered Butterworth's translation here.

26 Could Rousseau's legislator or even Emile's tutor boast such certainty? But in spite of appearances, there is some evidence that this could have been

Rousseau's standard for innocent lying. Rousseau's discussion of conspiracies in his letter to the Countess of Wartensleben of 1766 is germane here. He wrote to her that he would never become involved in even the 'most legitimate' conspiracy because these enterprises often lead to disorder and bloodshed 'and in my opinion the blood of a Single man has greater weight than the liberty of the whole human race. Those who sincerely love liberty do not need so many machinations in order to find it, and without causing revolutions or troubles, whoever wants to be free is so in fact.' *CC* XXX:5440. Even allowing for rhetorical effect here, a man who writes that participation in the most legitimate conspiracy is unacceptable if it sheds blood could well believe that the most beneficial lie is not innocent if it harms one individual.

This passage was quoted by Jean Starobinski in 'Rousseau in the Revolution,' *New York Review of Books*, 12 April 1990, 50. He notes that the passage was quoted by Mme de Staël in defence of Rousseau after the Revolution, but the Countess's name is given incorrectly as Wartenheim. I have used but altered David Bellos's translation.

27 And this in spite of his statements to Mme Wartensleben quoted in the previous note. Cf. Mably's explanation to Rousseau about why he criticized the *Lettres écrites de la montagne*: 'I pity you in your misfortunes, as I would pity Socrates, but allow me to say to you that Socrates did not seek as revenge against his judges to excite sedition in Athens.' Cited in Maurice Cranston, *The Noble Savage: Jean-Jacques Rousseau 1754–1761* (Chicago: University of Chicago Press, 1991), 103–4. To show the significance of this judgment, Cranston points out that Mably was a 'man of the Left' and an advocate of 'socialism and even communism.'

28 Spinoza, for example, presents determinism as a doctrine that engenders cheerfulness in the *Ethics*. See Proposition XXXII and Propositions XLVIII–XLIX in Benedict de Spinoza, *Ethics*, trans. James Gutmann (New York: Hafner, 1949), 67–8 and 119–6. Cf. the Eighth Reverie, *OC* 1:1078.

29 In the *Phenomenology of Spirit*, Hegel argues that the general will requires that individual wills seeks absolute fusion. But this, he maintains, means that, aside from passing laws, the individuals cannot act in any positive way (e.g., in classes or associations) and still embody the general will. Positive action in political life, Hegel suggests, is inherently pluralistic. Since the general will precludes these concrete positive forms of individual action, its expressions can only be negative and destructive; thus, the general will results in the destruction of individuals at the guillotine in acts of absolute terror. Georg W.F. Hegel, *Phenomenology of Spirit*, trans. A.V. Miller (Oxford: Oxford University Press, 1977), sections 582–95, 355–64. Cf. Fran-

cois Furet, 'Rousseau and the French Revolution,' in *The Legacy of Rousseau*, ed. Clifford Orwin and Nathan Tarcov (Chicago: University of Chicago Press, 1997), 170–1. Cf. Keith Michael Baker, *Inventing the French Revolution* (Cambridge: Cambridge University Press, 1990).

30 I would suggest this possible link between Rousseau's doctrine of freedom of the will and his doctrine of the general will: The vicar acknowledges that the individual's free will is inherently oriented towards the individual's interest. 'I am not free not to want my own good,' he writes. 'I am not free to want what is bad for me. But it is in this precisely that my freedom consists – my being able to will only what is suitable to me, or what I deem to be such, without anything external determining me.' Trans. Bloom, 280. I believe that this orientation towards well-being is a feature of individual free will that is transposed to the collective level in the concept of the general will. The general will is always right in the sense that it is well-intentioned, that it is always oriented towards the good of the people as a whole. In *Du contrat social*, Rousseau refers to the link between individual will and the general will when he describes in what sense the general will can be mistaken: 'One always wants one's good but one does not always see it': II.III. Rousseau's teaching about the general will in his *Discourse on Political Economy* differs from that of *Du contrat social*. But he first introduces the concept of the general will in the *Discourse on Political Economy*, and the terms he uses in his first mention of the idea are worth noting here: 'The body politic is, then, also a moral being that has a will; and this general will, which always tends to the preservation and well-being of the whole and of each part, and which is the source of the laws, is, for all the members of the state, in relation to one another and to it, the rule of what is just and what unjust.' *OC* 3:245; trans. Gourevitch, 6.

For a different argument linking free will to the general will, see Pierre Manent, *Naissances de la politique moderne* (Paris: Payot, 1977).

Conclusion

1 See 'De la nature de l'homme' in comte de Buffon, *Histoire naturelle de l'homme*, vol. 1 of *Oeuvres Complètes* (Bruxelles: Lejeune, 1829), 1–6. Cf. Otis Fellows, 'Buffon and Rousseau: Aspects of a Relationship,' *Publications of the Modern Language Association of America* 75, no. 3 (3 June 1960): 184–96.

2 *Du contrat social* 1.4, trans. Masters, *SC* 50; *OC* 3:356. In the same passage Rousseau argues that to renounce one's liberty is to renounce *'sa qualité d'homme, aux droits de l'humanité, même à ses devoirs.'*

3 Rousseau's critique of representative government and his defence of direct democracy may be motivated in part by his belief in freedom of the will. It may be because of this belief that he disagrees with Hobbes's assertion that sovereignty based on will can be transferred. 'Power can perfectly well be transferred,' he argues, 'but not will.' *Du contrat social*, II.I, *OC* 3:369; trans. Masters, 59. Consider, in this context, J.G.A. Pocock's explication of a critique of Locke by the English conservative Josiah Tucker: 'if – as Tucker believed – it was as a moral being that Locke supposed the individual to possess the right of consent, that premise made the latter incapable of choosing a representative to exercise his rights for him: a truth which the "honest, undissembling" – but unfortunately mad – Rousseau had been able to perceive and declare.' Pocock, *Virtue, Commerce, and History* (Cambridge: Cambridge University Press, 1985), 120. My thanks to Leah Bassel for drawing this reference to my attention.

4 Cf. note 35 of chapter 1 above. But see, too, Frederick Neuhouser, 'Freedom, Dependence, and the General Will,' *Philosophical Review* 102, no. 3 (July 1993): 363–95. See especially his discussions of Hegel's view that 'Rousseau is the first thinker to recognize "the free will" as the fundamental principle of political philosophy': 363 ff.

5 On freedom and dependence, cf. Neuhouser, 'Freedom, Dependence, and the General Will'; and F.M. Barnard, 'Will and Political Rationality in Rousseau,' *Political Studies* 32 (1984): 369–84.

Selected Bibliography

Abizadeh, Arash. 'Banishing the Particular: Rousseau on Rhetoric, *patrie,* and the Passions.' *Political Theory* 29, no. 4 (2001): 556–82.

Alberg, Jeremiah. *A Reinterpretation of Rousseau: A Religious System.* New York: Palgrave Macmillan, 2007.

Augustine, S. Aurelii. *On the Freedom of the Will.* Translated by Carroll Mason Sparrow. Richmond: University of Virginia Press, 1947.

Arendt, Hannah. 'What Is Freedom?' In *Between Past and Future: Eight Exercises in Political Thought*. New York: Viking, 1954.

– *The Human Condition*. Garden City: Anchor–Doubleday, 1959.

– *The Life of the Mind,* vol. 2: *Willing*. New York: Harcourt Brace Jovanovich, 1978.

Baker, Keith Michael. *Inventing the French Revolution*. Cambridge: Cambridge University Press, 1990.

Ball, Terence. 'Rousseau's Civil Religion Reconsidered.' In *Reappraising Political Theory: Revisionist Studies in the History of Political Thought.* Oxford: Clarendon, 1995.

Barnard, F.M. 'Will and Political Rationality in Rousseau.' *Political Studies* 32 (1984): 369–84.

Barth, Karl. *Protestant Thought: From Rousseau to Ritschl*. Translated by Brian Cozens. London: SCM, 1959.

Beiner, Ronald. 'Machiavelli, Hobbes, and Rousseau on Civil Religion.' *Review of Politics* 55, no. 4 (1993): 617–38.

– *Civil Religion: A Dialogue in the History of Political Philosophy*. Cambridge: Cambridge University Press, 2011.

Belaval, Yvon. *'La théorie du jugement dans L'Emile.'* In *Jean-Jacques Roussseau et son Œuvre*. Edited by Comité national pour la commémoration de J.-J. Rousseau. Paris: Klincksieck, 1964.

Berlin, Isaiah. *Four Essays on Liberty*. Oxford: Oxford University Press, 1969.
– 'From Hope and Fear Set Free.' In *Concepts and Categories*. Edited by Henry Hardy. New York: Viking Press, 1978.
Bénichou, Paul. *'Réflexions sur l'idée de nature chez Rousseau.'* In *Pensée de Rousseau*. Edited by Gerard Genette and Tzvetan Todorov. Paris: Seuil, 1984.
Berofsky, Bernard, ed. *Free Will and Determinism*. New York: Harper & Row, 1966.
Bertram, Christopher. *Rousseau and the Social Contract*. London: Routledge, 2003.
Bloom, Allan. Introduction to *Emile, or On Education*. New York: Basic Books, 1979.
– 'Rousseau.' In *History of Political Philosophy*. Edited by Leo Strauss and Joseph Cropsey. Chicago: University of Chicago Press, 1987.
– *Love And Friendship*. New York: Simon & Schuster, 1993.
Brooke, Christopher. 'Rousseau's *Second Discourse*: between Epicureanism and Stoicism.' In *Rousseau and Freedom*. Edited by Christie McDonald and Stanley Hoffmann. Cambridge: Cambridge University Press, 2010.
Buffon, Comte de. *Histoire naturelle de l'homme*. In *Oeuvres Complètes*. Bruxelles: Lejeune, 1826.
– *Oeuvres Philosophiques de Buffon*. Edited by Jean Piveteau. Paris: PUF, 1954.
Burgelin, Pierre. *La philosophie de l'existence de Jean-Jacques Rousseau*. Paris: Presses Universitaire de France, 1952.
Butterworth, Charles. 'Intrepretive Essay.' In *The Reveries of the Solitary Walker*. New York: Harper Colophon, 1979.
Cameron, David. *The Social Thought of Rousseau and Burke*. London: Weidenfeld and Nicolson, 1973.
Cassirer, Ernst. *The Question of Jean-Jacques Rousseau*. Translated by Peter Gay. New York: Columbia University Press, 1954.
– *Rousseau–Kant–Goethe*. Translated by J. Gutmann, P. Kristeller, and J. Randall, Jr. New York: Harper & Row, 1963.
Charvet, John. *The Social Problem in the Philosophy of Rousseau*. Cambridge: Cambridge University Press, 1974.
Cobban, A. *Rousseau and the Modern State*. London: Allen & Unwin, 1934.
Cohen, Joshua. 'The Natural Goodness of Humanity.' In *Reclaiming the History of Ethics: Essays for John Rawls*. Edited by Andrews Reath et al. Cambridge: Cambridge University Press, 1997.
Cohler, Anne. *Rousseau and Nationalism*. New York: Basic Books, 1970.
Colletti, Lucio. 'Rousseau: Critic of Civil Society.' In *From Rousseau to Lenin*. New York: Monthly Review Press, 1972.

Condillac, Etienne Bonnot de. *Condillac's Treatise on the Sensations*. Translated by Geraldine Carr. London: Favil Press, 1930.

– *Oeuvres Philosophiques*. Edited by Georges Le Roy. Paris: Presses Universitaire de France, 1947.

Cooper, Laurence D. *Rousseau, Nature, and the Problem of the Good Life*. University Park: Pennsylvania State University Press, 1999.

– 'Between Eros and Will to Power: Rousseau and "The Desire to Extend Our Being."' *American Political Science Review* 98, no. 1 (2004): 105–19.

Cranston, Maurice. *Freedom: A New Analysis*. London: Longman's, Green and Company, 1954.

– *Jean-Jacques: The Early Life and Work of Jean-Jacques Rousseau 1712–1754*. London: Allen Lane, 1983.

– *The Noble Savage: Jean-Jacques Rousseau 1754–1761*. Chicago: University of Chicago Press, 1991.

– *The Solitary Self: Jean-Jacques Rousseau in Exile and Adversity*. Chicago: University of Chicago Press, 1997.

Critchley, Simon. *The Faith of the Faithless: Experiments in Political Theology*. London: Verso, 2012.

Crocker, Lester G., ed. *The Age of Enlightenment*. New York: Harper & Row, 1969.

Cropsey, Joseph. 'The Human Vision of Rousseau.' In *Political Philosophy and the Issues of Politics*. Chicago: University of Chicago Press, 1977.

Cullen, Daniel E. *Freedom in Rousseau's Political Philosophy*. DeKalb: Northern Illinois University Press, 1993.

Descartes, René. *Philosophical Essays*. Translated by Laurence J. Lafleur. New York: Macmillan, 1964.

de Man, Paul. *Allegories of Reading: Figural Language in Rousseau, Nietzsche, Rilke, and Proust*. New Haven: Yale University Press, 1979.

Derathé, Robert. *Le rationalisme de Jean-Jacques Rousseau*. Paris: Presses Universitaires de France, 1948.

– *Jean-Jacques Rousseau et la science politique de son temps*. Paris: Vrin, 1950.

Derrida, Jacques. *De la grammatology*. Paris: Les Edition de Minuit, 1967.

Diderot, Denis. *Diderot's Selected Writings*. Translated and edited by Lester Crocker. New York: Macmillan, 1966.

– *Jacques le fataliste*. Edited by Anne Chevalier. Paris: Bordas, 1993.

Dostoevsky, Fyodor. *Notes from Underground*. Translated by Michael R. Katz. New York: Norton, 2001.

Ellenburg, Stephen. *Rousseau's Political Philosophy: An Interpretation from Within*. Ithaca: Cornell University Press, 1976.

Emberley, Peter. 'Rousseau versus the Savoyard Vicar.' *Interpretation* 14 (1986): 299–329.

Evrigenis, Ioannis D. 'Freeing Man from Sin: Rousseau on the Natural Condition of Mankind.' In *Rousseau and Freedom*. Edited by Christie McDonald and Stanley Hoffmann. Cambridge: Cambridge University Press, 2010.

Fellows, Otis. 'Buffon and Rousseau: Aspects of a Relationship.' *Publications of the Modern Langauge Association of America* 75, no. 3 (3 June 1960): 184–96.

Fetsher, I. 'Rousseau's Concepts of Freedom.' In *Nomos: Liberty*. Edited by Carl T. Friedrich. New York: Atherton, 1966.

Ferry, Luc. *Political Philosophy I*. Translated by Franklin Philip. Chicago: University of Chicago Press, 1990.

Flathman, R.E. *The Philosophy and Politics of Freedom*. Chicago: University of Chicago Press, 1978.

Frankfurt, Harry. 'Freedom of the Will and the Concept of a Person.' *Journal of Philosophy* 68, no. 1 (1971): 5–20.

Furet, François. 'Rousseau and the French Revolution.' In *The Legacy of Rousseau*. Edited by Clifford Orwin and Nathan Tarcov. Chicago: University of Chicago Press, 1997.

Gardiner, Patrick. 'Rousseau's Concept of Liberty.' In *Conceptions of Liberty in Political Philosophy*. Edited by Z.A. Pelczynski and J. Gray. New York: St Martin's, 1984.

Garrard, Graeme. *Rousseau's Counter-Enlightenment: A Republican Critique of the Philosophes*. Albany: SUNY Press, 2003.

Gay, Peter. *The Enlightenment: An Interpretation*, vol. 2: *The Science of Freedom*, London: Norton, 1969.

Gildin, Hilail. *Rousseau's Social Contract: The Design of the Argument*. Chicago: University of Chicago Press, 1987.

Gillispie, Charles Coulston, ed. *Dictionary of Scientific Biography*. New York: Scribner, 1970.

Goldschmidt, Victor. *Anthropologie et politique*. Paris: Vrin, 1974.

Gough, J.W. *The Social Contract: A Critical Study of its Development*. Oxford: Clarendon, 1957.

Gouhier, Henri. 'Ce que le Vicaire doit à Descartes.' *Annales Jean-Jacques Rousseau* 35 (1959–62): 139–54.

– *Les Méditations métaphysiques de Jean-Jacques Rousseau*. Paris: Vrin, 1970.

Gourevitch, Victor. 'Rousseau on Lying: A Provisional Reading of the Fourth Reverie.' *Berkshire Review* 15 (1980): 93–107.

– 'Rousseau's Pure State of Nature.' *Interpretation* 16 (1988): 23–59.

– 'The Religious Thought.' In *The Cambridge Companion to Rousseau*. Edited by Patrick Riley. Cambridge: Cambridge University Press, 2001.

Grant, Ruth W. *Hypocrisy and Integrity: Machiavelli, Rousseau, and the Ethics of Politics*. Chicago: University of Chicago Press, 1997.

Gray, John. 'Greek Ideas of Freedom.' In *Conceptions of Liberty in Political Philosophy*. Edited by Z. Pelczynski and J. Gray. New York: St Martin's, 1984.

Gray, Tim. *Freedom*. London: Macmillan Education, 1991.

Grimsley, Ronald. *Rousseau and the Religious Quest*. Oxford: Clarendon, 1968.

Groethuysen, Bernard. 'La Liberté selon Rousseau.' *La NEF* 33 (August 1947): 3–17.

Grotius, Hugo. *Of the Law of Nature and Nations*. Translated by Basil Kennett. London: R. Sare, 1717.

Hegel, Georg W.F. *Phenomenology of Spirit*. Translated by A.V. Miller. Oxford: Oxford University Press, 1977.

Helvétius, Claude-Adrien. *De l'homme*, tome 1. Paris: Fayard, 1989.

– *De l'esprit*. Paris: Fayard, 1998.

Hobbes, Thomas. *Leviathan*. Edited by C.B. Macpherson. Harmondsworth: Penguin, 1982.

– *On the Citizen*. Edited and translated by Richard Tuck and Michael Silverthorne. Cambridge: Cambridge University Press, 1998.

Horowitz, Asher. *Rousseau, Nature, and History*. Toronto: University of Toronto Press, 1987.

– '"Laws and Customs Thrust Us Back into Infancy": Rousseau's Historical Anthropology.' *Review of Politics* 52, no. 2 (Spring 1990): 215–41.

Hulliung, Mark. *The Autocritique of Enlightenment: Rousseau and the Philosophes*. Cambridge, MA: Harvard University Press, 1994.

Jimack, Peter. *La genese et la redaction de L'Emile*, vol. 13: *Studies on Voltaire and the Eighteenth Century*. Geneva: Institut et Musée Voltaire, 1960.

Jonas, Hans. 'Philosophical Meditation on the Seventh Chapter of Paul's Epistle to the Romans.' In *The Future of Our Religious Past: Essays in Honour of Rudolf Bultmann*. Edited by James M. Robinson. New York: Harper & Row, 1971.

Kane, Robert. *A Contemporary Introduction to Free Will*. Oxford: Oxford University Press, 2005.

Kant, Immanuel. *Critique of Pure Reason*. Translated by Norman Kemp Smith. London: Macmillan, 1986.

– *The Critique of Practical Reason and Other Writings in Moral Philosophy*. Translated by Lewis White Beck. Chicago: University of Chicago Press, 1949.

– *Perpetual Peace, and Other Essays on Politics, History, and Morals.* Translated by Ted Humphrey. Indianapolis: Hackett, 1983.

Kelly, Christopher, and Roger D. Masters, 'Human Nature, Liberty, and Progress: Rousseau's Dialogue with the Critics of the *Discours sur l'inegalité.*' In *Rousseau and Liberty*. Edited by Robert Wokler. Manchester: Manchester University Press, 1995.

Kelly, Christopher. *Rousseau's Exemplary Life: The Confessions as Political Philosophy.* Ithaca: Cornell University Press, 1987.

– *Rousseau As Author: Consecrating One's Life to the Truth.* Chicago: University of Chicago Press, 2003.

Kryger, Edna. *La notion de liberté chez Rousseau et ses répercussions sur Kant.* Paris: Nizet, 1979.

Locke, John. *An Essay Concerning Human Understanding.* London: Ward, Lock and Company, n.d.

– *Second Treatise of Government.* Edited by Richard Cox. Arlington Heights: Harlan Davidson, 1982.

Lovejoy, Arthur. 'The Supposed Primitivism of Rousseau.' In *Essays in the History of Ideas.* Baltimore: Johns Hopkins University Press, 1948.

Macy, Jeffrey. '"God Helps Those Who Help Themselves": New Light on the Theological-Political Teaching in Rousseau's Profession of Faith of the Savoyard Vicar.' *Polity* 24, no. 4 (Summer 1992): 615–32.

Mall, Laurence. *Emile ou les figures de la fiction: Studies on Voltaire and the Eighteenth Century.* Oxford: Voltaire Foundation, 2002.

Manent, Pierre. *Naissances de la politique moderne.* Paris: Payot, 1977.

Marini, John. 'Progressivism, Modern Political Science, and the Transformation of American Constitutionalism.' In *The Progressive Revolution in Politics and Political Science: Transforming the American Regime.* Edited by John Marini and Ken Masugi. Lanham: Rowman & Littlefield, 2005.

Maritain, Jacques. *Three Reformers: Luther–Descartes–Rousseau.* Westport: Greenwood, 1950.

Marks, Jonathan. *Perfection and Disharmony in the Thought of Jean-Jacques Rousseau.* Cambridge: Cambridge University Press, 2005.

Masson, Pierre-Maurice. *'Rousseau Contre Helvétius.' Revue d'histoire litteraire de la France* 18 (1911): 103–24.

– *La Religion de J.-J. Rousseau.* 3 vols. Paris: Librairie Hachette, 1916.

Masters, Roger D. *The Political Philosophy of Rousseau.* Princeton: Princeton University Press, 1968.

McDonald, Christie, and Stanley Hoffmann. *Rousseau and Freedom.* Cambridge: Cambridge University Press, 2010.

Meier, Heinrich. 'The Discourse on the Origin and Foundations of Inequality among Men: On the Intention of Rousseau's Most Philosophical Work.' *Interpretation* 16, no. 2 (Winter 1988–9): 211–28.

Melzer, Arthur M. *The Natural Goodness of Man: On the System of Rousseau's Thought.* Chicago: University of Chicago Press, 1990.

– 'The Origin of the Counter-Enlightenment: Rousseau and the New Religion of Sincerity.' *Amercian Political Science Review* 90, no. 2 (June 1996): 344–60.

Montaigne, Michel de. *The Complete Essays of Montaigne*. Translated by Donald M. Frame. Stanford: Stanford University Press, 1958.

Morel, Jean. '*Recherches sur les sources du Discours de l'Inégalité*.' *Annales de la Société Jean-Jacques Rousseau* 5 (1909): 119–98.

Neiman, Susan. 'Metaphysics, Philosophy: Rousseau on the Problem of Evil.' In *Reclaiming the History of Ethics: Essays for John Rawls*. Edited by Andrews Reath et al. Cambridge: Cambridge University Press, 1997.

Neuhouser, Frederick. 'Freedom, Dependence, and the General Will.' *Philosophical Review* 102, no. 3 (July 1993): 363–95.

Okin, Susan Moller. *Justice, Gender, and the Family*. Chicago: Basic Books, 1989.

Orwin, Clifford. 'Rousseau and the Discovery of Political Compassion.' In *The Legacy of Rousseau*. Edited by Clifford Orwin and Nathan Tarcov. Chicago: University of Chicago Press, 1997.

– 'Rousseau on the Sources of Ethics.' In *Instilling Ethics*. Edited by Norma Thompson. Lanham: Rowman & Littlefield, 2000.

Orwin, Clifford, and Nathan Tarcov, eds. *The Legacy of Rousseau*. Chicago: University of Chicago Press, 1997.

Owen, David. *Hume's Reason*. New York: Oxford University Press, 1999.

Pannenberg, Wolfhart. *Toward a Theology of Nature: Essays on Science and Faith*. Edited by Ted Peters. Louisville: Westminster John Knox Press, 1993.

Pennock, J. Roland. 'Hobbes's Confusing "Clarity" – The Case of "Liberty."' In *Hobbes Studies*. Edited by Keith C. Brown. Oxford: Blackwell, 1965.

Philonenko, Alexis. *Jean Jacques Rousseau et la pensée du malheur*. 3 vols. Paris: Vrin, 1984.

Pink, Thomas. *Free Will: A Very Short Introduction*. Oxford: Oxford University Press, 2004.

Plamenatz, John. '*Ce qui ne signifie autre chose sinon qu'on le forcera d'être libre*.' In *Rousseau et la Philosophie Politique*. Edited by P. Arnaud et al. Paris: PUF, 1965.

Plattner, Marc. *Rousseau's State of Nature: An Interpretation of the Discourse on Inequality*. DeKalb: Northern Illinois University Press, 1979.

Pocock, J.G.A. *Virtue, Commerce, and History*. Cambridge: Cambridge University Press, 1985.

Pufendorf, Baron Samuel de. *The Rights of War and Peace*. Translated by A.C. Campbell. Washington: M. Walter Dunne, 1901.

Rang, Martin. '*Le dualisme anthroplogique dans L'Emile*.' In *Jean-Jacques Rousseau et son Œuvre*. Edited by Comité national pour la commémoration de J.-J. Rousseau. Paris: Klincksieck, 1964.

Riley, Patrick. *The General Will before Rousseau: The Transformation of the Divine into the Civic*. Princeton: Princeton University Press, 1986.

– 'Rousseau's General Will: Freedom of a Particular Kind.' In *Rousseau and Liberty.* Edited by Robert Wokler. Manchester: Manchester University Press, 1995.

– ed. *The Cambridge Companion to Rousseau.* Cambridge: Cambridge University Press, 2001.

Roosevelt, Grace. *Reading Rousseau in the Nuclear Age.* Philadelphia: Temple University Press, 1990.

Rousseau, Jean-Jacques. *Citizen of Geneva: Selections from the Letters of Jean-Jacques Rousseau.* Translated by Charles William Hendel. New York: Oxford University Press, 1937.

– *Collected Writings of Jean-Jacques Rousseau.* 13 vols. Translated by Judith R. Bush, Christopher Kelly, and Roger D. Masters. Hanover: University Press of New England, 1990–.

– *The Confessions.* Translated by J.M. Cohen. London: Penguin, 1953.

– *Correspondance complètes.* 50 vols. Edited by Ralph Leigh. Geneva: Institut et Musée Voltaire, 1965–99.

– *The Discourses and Other Early Political Writings.* Translated by Victor Gourevitch. Cambridge: Cambridge University Press, 1997.

– *Economie Politique.* Edited by Yves Vargas. Paris: PUF, 1986.

– *Emile, or On Education.* Translated by Allan Bloom. New York: Basic Books, 1979.

– *The First and Second Discourses.* Edited by Roger D. Masters. Translated by Roger D. Masters and Judith R. Masters. New York: St Martin's, 1964.

– *Oeuvres complètes.* 5 vols. Edited by Bernard Gagnebin and Marcel Raymond et al. Paris: Editions Gallimard, 1959–95.

– *On the Social Contract with Geneva Manuscript and Political Economy.* Edited by Roger D. Masters. Translated by Judith R. Masters. New York: St Martin's, 1978.

– *Politics and the Arts: Letter to D'Alembert on the Theatre.* Translated and edited by Allan Bloom. Ithaca: Cornell University Press, 1960.

– *La profession de foi du vicaire savoyard.* Edited by Pierre-Maurice Masson. Paris: Librairie Hachette, 1914.

– *Les rêveries du promeneur solitaire.* Edited by Henri Roddier. Paris: Garnier, 1997.

– *The Reveries of the Solitary Walker.* Translated by Charles Butterworth. New York: Harper Colophon, 1979.

– *Rousseau: Religious Writings.* Edited by Ronald Grimsley. Oxford: Oxford University Press, 1970.

– *Selections from Rousseau.* Edited by Christian Gauss. Princeton: Princeton University Press, 1920.

– *The Social Contract and Other Later Political Writings*. Translated by Victor Gourevitch. Cambridge: Cambridge University Press, 1997.

Ryan, Alan, ed. *The Idea of Freedom: Essays in Honour of Isaiah Berlin*. Toronto: Oxford University Press, 1979.

Schmidt, Alfred. *The Concept of Nature in Marx*. Translated by Ben Fowkes. London: New Left Books, 1971.

Scott, John T. 'The Theodicy of the *Second Discourse*: The Pure State of Nature and Rousseau's Political Thought.' *American Political Science Review* 86, no. 3 (September 1992): 696–711.

Shklar, Judith. *Men and Citizens: A Study of Rousseau's Social Theory*. Cambridge: Cambridge University Press, 1969.

– 'General Will.' In *Dictionary of the History of Ideas*. Edited by Philip P. Weiner. New York: Charles Scribner's Sons, 1973. II:275–81.

Siedentop, Larry. 'Two Liberal Traditions.' In *The Idea of Freedom: Essays in Honour of Isaiah Berlin*. Edited by A. Ryan. Oxford: Oxford University Press, 1979.

Simpson, Matthew. *Rousseau's Theory of Freedom*. London: Continuum, 2006.

Smith, Adam. *Edinburgh Review* no. 1 (January–July 1755).

Spinoza, Benedict de. *Ethics*. Translated by James Gutmann. New York: Hafner, 1949.

Spragens, Thomas. 'The Politics of Inertia and Gravitation: The Functions of Exemplar Paradigms in Social Thought.' *Polity* 5, no. 3 (Spring 1973): 288–310.

Starobinski, Jean. *Jean-Jacques Rousseau: La transparence et l'obstacle*. Paris: Presses Universitaire de France, 1957.

– 'Rousseau et Buffon.' In *Jean-Jacques Rousseau et son oeuvre*. Edited by Comité national pour la commémoration de Jean-Jacques Rousseau. Paris: Klincksieck, 1964. 135–47.

– 'Rousseau in the Revolution.' *New York Review of Books*, 12 April 1990: 47–50.

– 'The Motto *Vitam impendere vero* and the Question of Lying.' In *The Cambridge Companion to Rousseau*. Edited by Patrick Riley. Cambridge: Cambridge University Press, 2001.

Strauss, Leo. 'On the Intention of Rousseau.' *Social Research* 14 (1947): 455–87.

– *The Political Philosophy of Hobbes*. Chicago: University of Chicago Press, 1952.

– *Natural Right and History*. Chicago: University of Chicago Press, 1953.

– 'The Spirit of Hobbes's Political Philosophy.' In *Hobbes Studies*. Edited by Keith C. Brown. Oxford: Blackwell, 1965.

– *Political Philosophy: Six Essays by Leo Strauss*. Edited by Hilail Gildin. Indianapolis: Pegasus/Bobbs-Merrill, 1975.

Strong, Tracy. *Jean-Jacques Rousseau: The Politics of the Ordinary*. Thousand Oaks: Sage, 1994.

Taylor, Charles. 'What Is Human Agency?' In *The Self*. Edited by Theodore Mischel. Oxford: Blackwell, 1977.

– 'What's Wrong with Negative Liberty?' In *The Idea of Freedom*. Edited by Alan Ryan. Toronto: Oxford University Press, 1979.

– 'Kant's Theory of Freedom.' In *Conceptions of Liberty in Political Philosophy*. Edited by Z.A. Pelczynski and John Gray. New York: St Martins's, 1984.

Taine, Hippolyte. *Les origines de la France contemporaire*, vol. II: *L'Ancien Regime*. Paris: Librairie Hachette, 1926.

Talmon, J.L. *The Origins of Totalitarian Democracy*. London: Secker and Warburg, 1952.

Thomas, Jacques-François. *Le pélagianisme de J.J. Rousseau*. Paris: Nizet, 1956.

Tolstoy, Leo. 'The Difficulty of Defining the Forces That Move Nations.' In *Theories of History*. Edited by Patrick Gardiner. Glencoe: Free Press, 1959.

Vargas, Yves. *Introduction à L'Emile de Jean-Jacques Rousseau*. Paris: Presses Universitaires de France, 1995.

Vartanian, Aram. 'Necessity or Freedom? The Politics of an Eighteenth Century Metaphysical Debate.' In *Studies in Eighteenth Century Culture*. Edited by Roseann Runte, vol. 7. Madison: University of Wisconsin Press, 1978. 157–74.

Vaughan, C.E. *The Political Writings of Jean-Jacques Rousseau*. Cambridge: Cambridge University Press, 1915.

Velkley, Richard. *Freedom and the End of Reason*. Chicago: University of Chicago Press, 1989.

– *Being after Rousseau*. Chicago: University of Chicago Press, 2002.

Voltaire. '*Le Poeme sur le Désastre de Lisbonne en 1755*.' In *Selections from Voltaire*. Edited by George R. Havens. New York: Century Company, 1925.

– *Philosophical Dictionary*. Translated by Theodore Besterman. Harmondsworth: Penguin, 1971.

Williams, David Lay. *Rousseau's Platonic Enlightenment*. University Park: Pennsylvania State University Press, 2007.

Wernham, A.G. 'Liberty and Obligation in Hobbes.' In *Hobbes Studies*. Edited by Keith C. Brown. Oxford: Blackwell, 1965.

Wokler, Robert. 'Perfectible Apes in Decadent Cultures: Rousseau's Anthropology Revisited.' *Daedalus* 107, no. 3 (1978): 107–34.

– 'Rousseau's Perfectibilian Libertarianism.' In *The Idea of Freedom: Essays in Honour of Isaiah Berlin*. Edited by Alan Ryan. Oxford: Oxford University Press, 1979.

– 'Rousseau's Two Concepts of Liberty.' In *Lives, Liberties, and the Public Good:*

New Essays in Political Theory for Maurice Cranston. Edited by George Feaver and Frederick Rosen. London: Macmillan, 1987.

– *Rousseau.* Oxford: Oxford University Press, 1995.

Wootton, David. 'Helvétius: From Radical Enlightenment to Revolution.' *Political Theory* 28, no. 3 (2000): 307–36.

Index

www.ingramcontent.com/pod-product-compliance
Lightning Source LLC
LaVergne TN
LVHW090157080826
844660LV00013B/843/J

* 9 7 8 1 4 4 2 6 4 4 9 5 3 *